Battle for the BIA

Battle for the BIA

G. E. E. Lindquist and the
Missionary Crusade against John Collier

DAVID W. DAILY

The University of Arizona Press
Tucson

The University of Arizona Press
© 2004 The Arizona Board of Regents
All rights reserved
∞This book is printed on acid-free, archival-quality paper.
Manufactured in the United States of America

09 08 07 06 05 04   6 5 4 3 2 1

Library of Congress Cataloging-in-Publication Data
Daily, David W., 1965–
Battle for the BIA : G. E. E. Lindquist and the missionary crusade against John Collier /
David W. Daily.
p. cm.
Includes bibliographical references and index.
ISBN 0-8165-2437-8 (cloth : alk. paper)
1. Indians of North America—Government relations—1934– 2. Indians of North America—
Government policy. 3. Indians, Treatment of—North America. 4. Lindquist, G. E. E. (Gustavus
Elmer Emanuel), b. 1886. 5. Collier, John, 1884–1968. 6. Home Missions Council of North
America—History. 7. United States. Bureau of Indian Affairs. 8. United States. Indian
Reorganization Act. 9. United States—Race relations. 10. United States—Politics and
government. I. Title.
E93.D22 2004
323.1197'09'04—dc22

2004008496

Publication of this book is made possible in part by the proceeds of a permanent endowment
created with the assistance of a Challenge Grant from the National Endowment for the Humanities, a federal agency.

Dedicated to my wife,

Teresa Wooten Daily,

and in loving memory to my twin brother,

Steven Wayne Daily

(1965–1999)

Contents

Illustrations

Acknowledgments

This book has occasioned numerous debts and obligations. I wish to thank those who guided this work early on—Peter Wood, Laurie Maffly-Kipp, Jackson Carroll, Russ Richey, and especially my adviser, Grant Wacker. I am grateful to other scholars who have responded to portions of the manuscript: Joel Martin, Clyde Ellis, Valerie Ziegler, Dan Bays, Phil Goff, Larry Snyder, and the members of the Duke–UNC Religion Colloquium. The Pew Program in Religion and American History funded a significant portion of my work, and I thank directors Jon Butler and Harry Stout for their friendly encouragement. A Dial Grant from the University of the Ozarks funded the research in its later stages. Friends at Yale, Duke, and Ozarks helped to make all of this worthwhile.

Among the librarians and archivists who lent a hand were Roger Lloyd and Roberta Schaafsma at Duke University; Bobbie Rahder at Haskell Indian Nations University; Daryl Morrison at the Holt-Atherton Department of Special Collections, University of the Pacific; the staff at the Presbyterian Historical Society in Philadelphia; Seth Kasten at Burke Library, Union Theological Seminary in New York; Richard Fusick and Mary Frances Morrow at the National Archives in Washington, D.C.; Barbara Larsen at the National Archives–Central Plains Region in Kansas City; and Stuart Stelzer at the University of the Ozarks.

Helen Lindquist Bonny deserves special mention for allowing me to stay at her home and rummage through her private collection of papers and memorabilia regarding her father. Her help has been invaluable.

Most important, I would like to indicate in some small way the loving support of my family, who encouraged me in countless ways, especially my parents, Herb and Betty Daily; my parents-in-law, Ernie and Ginny Wooten; and my brother's family, Lynda, Nicholas, and Austin Daily. I also credit my children, Emma and Wilson, for giving me something more important to do than write this book; their unmannerly intrusions saved me from missing the most rewarding moments of the past several years.

With a poignant mixture of joy and sorrow, I dedicate this work to my wife, Teri, and in loving memory to my twin brother, Steve. As I draw the writing of this book to a close, I think of Steve, my friend and soul mate since before we were born. He taught me how to find meaning in simple things, like riding a bicycle or tending a vegetable garden. Dedicating this book to him is one small way to say I still remember.

And finally, to Teri I owe a debt that this dedication cannot begin to repay. Although trained as a physician to care for the body, she has a heart that brings life and healing to the soul. Her patient love and her faith in me, more than anything else, made this book possible.

Battle for the BIA

Introduction

This book is about one of the great untold battles in the history of Indian affairs—G. E. E. Lindquist's missionary crusade against John Collier. Like any epic struggle, this one bristled with personal animosity, political calculation, and religious zeal. From the missionary point of view, it was Collier, the Indian Commissioner under Franklin D. Roosevelt, who played the spoiler, the marauding turk. Beginning in the 1920s, he was part of a rising group of activists who celebrated Indian cultures and challenged the assimilation policies that Protestant reformers and missionaries had long advocated. When he became commissioner in 1933, he attempted to revolutionize the work of the Bureau of Indian Affairs (BIA). He dropped the individualizing and Christianizing goals of assimilation and passed legislation to preserve the tribal basis for Indians' religious, political, and economic lives. Altogether, Collier's twelve-year administration created a crisis for Protestant leaders and their sense of custodial authority in Indian affairs.

Into that crisis stepped Collier's lesser known but formidable missionary antagonist, the sturdily named Gustavus Elmer Emanuel Lindquist (1886–1967). Often addressed more breezily as Elmer or "GEE" by his friends, he served as an itinerant representative of the ecumenical Home Missions Council of the Federal Council of Churches, and he was uniquely positioned to make his presence known all over the map, both literally and figuratively. He worked the East Coast lobbying prominent reformers, wealthy philanthropists, and high-ranking government officials. But as a resident of Lawrence, Kansas, and a traveling field agent, he made contacts among missionaries and Indian leaders in practically every Indian community across the country. Within himself he embodied the ideas and ambitions of the larger part of mainline Protestants in his time. And he brought every ounce of his influence to bear in a full-fledged assault on Collier's reforms.

Their rivalry might seem confined to a culture war between Collier, the unorthodox patron of indigenous cultures, and Lindquist, the Christian proponent of Western civilization. But it turned out to be much more than that. For the conflict that raged between them ultimately transformed the long, symbiotic relationship between the federal government and Protestant missionaries to the Indians. And as a result, it altered Protestant beliefs about how best to achieve their assimilation goals.

The Argument

The argument of the book runs something like this: By the early twentieth century, the relationship between missionaries and the BIA had evolved into a complex and multifaceted partnership in the push to assimilate the Indians. On one side of the partnership, the BIA helped missionaries gain easy access to the Indians by allowing them to operate religious education programs in federal boarding schools and by granting them tribal lands on which to build churches. The assistance of the BIA became so important to Indian missions that by 1932, George Hinman of the American Missionary Association confessed, "The work of present-day missionaries among Indians can never be wholly free from dependence on the Indian Service."[1]

In return for this federal assistance, missionaries supported the BIA's expanding programs by promoting the doctrine of Indian wardship. According to this doctrine, Indians were wards of the state who were not yet capable of supporting themselves in a cutthroat capitalist economy. So they required, according to Protestant leaders, the paternal hand of the BIA to help them assimilate gradually and minimize the loss of Indian properties. In their support for gradualism, missionaries like Lindquist provided strong backing for the BIA against those who wanted a more rapid, sink-or-swim approach to assimilation. Often called radical assimilationists, or "abolitionists" because of their desire to abolish the BIA, these more aggressive reformers believed the BIA intentionally thwarted the Indians' assimilation out of narrow institutional self-interests. Missionaries, though, defended the BIA, arguing that Native tribes needed a special federal agency to maintain trust protections over Indian lands and to administer health, education, and welfare services while the Indians made the slow and arduous journey into self-supporting citizenship.

But after John Collier became Indian Commissioner in 1933 and challenged the BIA–missionary partnership, Lindquist led Protestant missionaries toward a strategic change in how they approached assimilation. He appropriated the arguments of the radical assimilationists whom he had long opposed, and, inflecting those arguments with the language of the rising civil rights movement for African Americans, he called for the dismantling of the BIA and all the forms of race-based treatment that he believed were associated with it. That meant, in his mind, freeing the Indians from the federal guardianship of the BIA—which he now interpreted as a form of domination—and granting them full political equality with non-Indians. As long as Lindquist and his missionary peers saw the BIA as a cooperating partner in Indian uplift, they supported the federal government's unique guardian obligations to the Indians. But after Collier broke the tradition of church-state collaboration, they withdrew their support for the BIA and its fiduciary functions. In fostering this change during the 1940s, Lindquist helped to place Protestant organizations like the Home Missions Council at the forefront of the termination movement of the 1950s.

This story of Lindquist, Collier, and the larger relationship between missionaries and the BIA is a crucial part of Native American history for several reasons. The first has to do with the role Christian Indian leaders played in both fostering and resisting the changes Lindquist advocated. While Collier was in power, Lindquist formed new organizations to tap into Christian Indian hostility toward Collier's reforms. Without losing their sense of identity as tribe members, many Indians had invested themselves in adaptive strategies such as Western education, church membership, the holding of private property, and American citizenship. For them, Collier's programs threatened to erode the gains they had made. Lindquist, then, hoped to turn Collier's self-professed sympathy for "the Indian point of view" against itself by highlighting the strength of Indian support for assimilation goals.

But placing Christian Indians at the forefront of efforts to influence Indian policy brought some unintended outcomes. While Native Christian leaders readily espoused civil rights and political equality, they nevertheless refused, for the most part, to forsake treaty rights and federal protections founded upon aboriginal claims. That is, they laid claim to both the liberties of civil rights and the promise of tribal self-determination embedded within federal Indian treaties. This refusal to follow Lindquist's vision to its conclusion helps to sketch the limits of Christian Indians' commitment to assimilation. And it also indicates that the activist movement for tribal nationalism in the 1960s and 1970s can trace at least one of its sources to this dissenting posture of Christian Indians in the 1940s.[2]

Second, this study is significant because it shows how Protestant leaders were able to maintain a considerable measure of authority in Indian affairs in spite of Collier's effort to disestablish their religious prerogatives. To some degree, missionaries might have lost the ear of the commissioner when Collier took over, but they still had a lot of other places where they could build goodwill. In boarding schools, for example, missionaries continued to inject themselves in day-to-day activities through volunteer service, thereby obligating school administrators to cooperate with them in patterns of reciprocity and exchange. By giving much-needed support to the operations of the school, missionaries were able to preserve their access to Indian children. Official policies might change, but powerful interests resist and adapt before they capitulate. Protestant missionary influence in Indian affairs was no exception.[3]

Finally, a look at Lindquist's career raises important issues regarding tribal rights and the place of Native peoples in American society. Indians have long represented an anomaly in American legal and political history, for they are citizens of both the United States and their own tribal nations. And as this book shows, that anomaly has been central to Protestant engagement with federal Indian policy. Scholars today are still debating whether (or how) the group-differentiated rights of national minorities like American Indians and Native Hawaiians can be made a part of the broader project of liberalism, given its traditional preoccupation with individual rights.[4] This book shows how leading Protestant figures in the first half of this century wrestled with similar questions, often with conflicting results, but without for a moment losing what they considered to be the moral high ground.

The Adversaries

To gain a better sense of the principal characters of the story, it may be helpful to sketch portraits of the lives and conflicting passions of Lindquist and Collier.

In terms of his appearance, Lindquist stood a full six feet in height, and he remained trim and fit throughout his working life. His children remember him smelling of cigars when he returned from long trips in the smoke-filled railcars, even though, as a matter of conviction, he himself never smoked. With his dark hair and olive complexion, he did not look like the typical Swede, giving rise to his lighthearted claim to be "the last Swedish Indian in captivity." He always swept his thick hair back off his forehead because of a cowlick that persisted even as his hair turned completely gray. The flat-lipped smile apparent in photographs could easily mask his lively sense of humor and gregarious disposition. He enjoyed making new acquaintances and had the reputation of never forgetting the names and faces of the multitudes of people he encountered on his journeys.

Lindquist was born in 1886 in the small community of Swedish immigrants who settled around Lindsborg, Kansas. He grew up in a quaint two-story, four-room home that his parents built out of his father's income as a house painter. His religious convictions developed within the Evangelical Mission Church, a small sect that rejected the staid liturgies and predestinarian doctrines of Swedish Lutheranism. By the time Lindquist left Lindsborg in 1909 he had completed his college education at nearby Bethany College and found acclaim for his public speaking abilities in both Swedish and English.

Lindquist's sense of call to Indian missions grew out of a chance meeting with Walter and Mary Roe, two Reformed Church missionaries among the tribes of southwest Oklahoma. They convinced him to forsake the possibility of more glamorous overseas missions to work among America's indigenous peoples. So after teaching high school for a year, he left Kansas to study theology at Oberlin in Ohio. There he met Ethel Geer, his future wife, who was an accomplished piano student in the Conservatory of Music. Unlike Lindquist, she came from a wealthy Presbyterian family; her father had made his fortune as a real estate investor in Illinois and later Palm Beach, Florida. Ethel and Elmer would have married upon his graduation in 1912, but their divergent backgrounds created significant problems. Ethel's mother objected to her daughter's marriage to a Swede and acted quickly to send Ethel on a lengthy trip to Europe, followed immediately by a teaching appointment in Hawai'i. Only after Mrs. Geer's untimely death were the hapless couple married in 1915.

During those years, Lindquist's career in Indian missions began to take shape. While in seminary, he spent his summers among the Mescalero Apaches in southern New Mexico. And between 1912 and 1915, he served in his first full-time job as the secretary of the YMCA program at Haskell Indian Institute, a federal boarding school in Lawrence, Kansas. For two years he worked with the Winnebago Presbyterian Henry Roe Cloud to found an interdenominational college preparatory school for Indians in Wichita, Kansas. But when funding failed to keep up with ambitions, he had to return to employment with the YMCA, this time as national coordinator for its work with Indian soldiers during World War I. Then, with financial backing from J. D. Rockefeller's Institute for Social and Religious Research, he directed a monumental American Indian survey that culminated in the publication of *Red Man in the United States*. That book catapulted him into national prominence in Indian affairs, and its pronouncements on the secret dances of the Pueblos landed Lindquist squarely in the middle of the Indian dance controversy of 1923. With the survey complete and few other options available, he went back to Haskell to administer the Protestant religious education program there and oversee similar programs in other federal boarding schools. He also took on the title of field secretary for the Indian work of the Protestant Home Missions Council, a title he held until his retirement in 1953.

Ethel and Elmer's family grew over the years to include four children: Clara (1916), Harvey (1919), Helen (1921), and Elmer (1925). Lindquist's family life, though, was overshadowed by prolonged absences for his work. In a typical year, he lived at home for only twelve to fourteen weeks. That forced Ethel to give up whatever ambitions she might have had for a career of her own in piano performance. And it left her with the lion's share of responsibility for the children—a responsibility she dispatched, by all accounts, with much tenderness and skill. At times, the family afforded domestic help from Haskell students, who attended school just down the street from the Lindquist home in Lawrence. During the brief periods when Lindquist was at home, his children remember him as warm and engaged, though susceptible to flashes of temper from time to time.[5]

By the mid-1920s, Lindquist became dissatisfied with the limited scope of his work at Haskell and began to explore larger opportunities. At the same time, he and Ethel were struggling emotionally with the death of their seven-year-old child Harvey from pneumonia. So in 1927, Lindquist assumed a new position as missionary-at-large for the Society for the Propagation of the Gospel Among the Indians and Others in North America (SPG).[6] Founded by New England Congregationalists in 1787, the SPG was the oldest missionary-sending agency in the nation, and it drew support from many of Boston's most venerable families. This new appointment, along with supplementary income from the Home Missions Council, finally guaranteed Lindquist the freedom and flexibility to pursue a national agenda in Indian affairs. Over the next twenty-seven years he logged almost a million miles traveling for the SPG, organizing conferences, giving speeches, and making an annual round of meetings with missionaries and Native leaders around the country. This flexibility also allowed him to accept a presidential appointment to the Board of Indian Commissioners in 1930. And it gave him the resources and personal contacts he needed to serve as a key spokesperson for the grassroots campaign to obstruct Collier's programs. In 1935, he founded the National Fellowship of Indian Workers and built it up to include more than fifteen hundred members—all in an effort to strengthen the lobby of field missionaries

In 1908, Lindquist had just completed his
studies at Bethany College in Lindsborg,
Kansas, and was poised to begin a career that
would take him on travels throughout North
America and Europe. Photograph courtesy
Helen Lindquist Bonny.

John Collier sits at his Washington office desk, where he was rumored to
have sheltered a family of mice for a bit of relief from administrative
responsibilities. Photograph courtesy National Archives.

Lindquist experienced his first taste of missions as a seminary intern among the
Mescalero Apaches in southern New Mexico. This photograph dates from the early
1910s. Lindquist is kneeling on the right. Photograph courtesy
Helen Lindquist Bonny.

Lindquist was born in a sod house on the Kansas plains, and this quaint, four-room
home with picket fence served as his boyhood home in the Swedish-American
enclave of Lindsborg, Kansas. Lindquist, approximately eleven years old, is standing
on the porch (right) with his grandmother Lindquist and older brother, Robert.
Photograph courtesy Helen Lindquist Bonny.

Elmer Lindquist met his wife, Ethel, while they were both in
school at Oberlin, Elmer as a seminary student and Ethel as a
music student in the renowned conservatory. Photograph
courtesy Helen Lindquist Bonny.

This elegant family portrait was taken in 1923, the year that Lindquist published his groundbreaking survey, *Red Man in the United States*. Daughter Clara (age 7) is standing on the left. Son Harvey (age 4), who died tragically two years later, is standing in the center. And daughter Helen (age 2) is seated on her father's lap. Photograph courtesy Helen Lindquist Bonny.

This portrait of Lindquist was taken in 1932, on the eve of Collier's appointment as commissioner of Indian Affairs—an event that shaped Lindquist's life almost as much as it did Collier's. Photograph courtesy Helen Lindquist Bonny.

Henry Roe Cloud, the Winnebago missionary and educator, was one of Lindquist's closest friends at the beginning of their careers. They cofounded the Roe Indian Institute and collaborated on Lindquist's book *Red Man in the United States.* When Roe Cloud became the most prominent Native advocate for the Wheeler-Howard Act, Lindquist found himself fighting against his former companion. Photograph courtesy Helen Lindquist Bonny.

In 1953, Elmer and Ethel Lindquist retired to Palm Beach, Florida, to be close to her family. Here they are pictured at the home of their son Gus and his family in Portland, Oregon. Photograph courtesy Helen Lindquist Bonny.

and Christian Indians against Collier's reforms. Indeed, no other figure in Indian affairs combined Lindquist's zeal, energy, and resources for fighting John Collier.

The wide scope of Lindquist's writings provides another indication of his importance. Lindquist authored or compiled seven major books, dozens of articles, hundreds of speeches, and perhaps thousands of reports and detailed memoranda, occupying some thirty archival boxes of personal papers. His Indian survey, *Red Man in the United States* (1923), was the first comprehensive survey of socioeconomic conditions in Native communities. In the field of religious education, Lindquist published *The Jesus Road and the Red Man* (1929), a series of lessons for missionaries working with Indian boys in federal boarding schools. And in 1932 and 1951, he published professional manuals for mainline Protestant missionaries. These handbooks included everything from a chronology of the government's relations with the Indians to advice on surveying a new mission field, creating a good working relationship with BIA agents, and establishing medical, educational, and industrial programs.[7] One of his most widely read books was *The Indian in American Life* (1944), which sold more than sixty-five thousand copies as the text for a national Home Missions Council educational program. Lesser known, but of great import nonetheless, were two works he wrote in 1943—*Handbook on the Study of Indian Wardship* and "Indian Treaty Making." In these documents, Lindquist repudiated his earlier commitment to the wardship doctrine and helped to lay the groundwork for the termination policies of the 1950s. Thus, during much of the twentieth century, Lindquist's books played a significant role in the training and professional development of hundreds of Protestant missionaries to the Indians. When missionaries had questions about mission strategy or Indian policy, they knew that they could consult Lindquist. And when mainline Protestants wanted to know what their churches and the federal government were doing in the lives of Native Americans, Lindquist's writings would have been closest at hand.

Finally, after more than forty-four years of writing, speaking, and traveling, Lindquist retired to live near his wife's family in Palm Beach, Florida, in 1953. Aside from an interview with a local paper, an occasional speaking engagement, and a few letters, there is little evidence that Lindquist engaged in Indian affairs after his retirement. Heart problems began to take their toll in 1955, and, following a series of debilitating strokes, Lindquist died in 1967. His children went on to successful careers in education and private business. Helen Lindquist Bonny, for example, obtained a Ph.D. from the University of Maryland and, through a combination of her mother's musical talents and her father's organizational skills, she created an international foundation for music-centered therapies.

In contrast to Lindquist's vigorous and polished appearance, John Collier sported an unkempt head of blond hair, with a slight body that observers often mistook as frail and sickly. He was too preoccupied to care about how he looked, and he reportedly spent much of his down time "sucking on his corncob pipe, lost in time and space." Unlike Lindquist, who wore a suit like a second skin, Collier preferred old sweaters and dressed up only on the most special of occasions. According to John Jr., his father knew how to work a crowd for donations and support, but he nurtured a love of solitude that often distanced him from his family even during those limited periods when he was at home.[8]

Collier was born into a distinguished southern family in 1884, where he watched his father, Charles, become an influential architect of the new South as mayor of Atlanta in the late nineteenth century. Susie Rawson Collier, John's mother, claimed New England family roots and was known as an avid student of plants, animals, and literature. But when Collier's father became entangled in financial problems, his mother's difficulties coping with the embarrassment led to her death from a drug addiction in 1897. Within three years his father died in a shooting that John believed to have been a suicide. John's own grief as an orphan created a profound bitterness toward the drive for success that led to his father's downfall. Not only did Collier abandon his family's Methodist beliefs, but he also repudiated the bulk of Protestant Christianity for its apparent acquiescence to the acquisitive values of entrepreneurial capitalism.[9]

At first, an adolescent Collier found solace in the remote grandeur of the southern Appalachian wilderness, where he would hike and write poetry for months at a time. Although he never pursued a degree, he later attended Columbia University in New York and continued his studies in Europe, where in 1906 he met his wife, Lucy Wood, a native of Philadelphia. A gifted person in her own right, Lucy helped to found the Child Health Organization in 1916, and she continued to be active in public health issues while raising three children—Charles (1909), Donald (1911), and John Jr. (1913).[10] Like the Lindquists, the Collier family depended on domestic help. The Colliers' helper was an African American woman named Alice, who reportedly won the lifelong affection of the entire family, even though she occasionally expressed fear for the souls of the heterodox Collier clan she lived with.[11]

Between 1909 and 1919, Collier served as the civic secretary for the People's Institute on Manhattan's Lower East Side, where he designed social programs to help immigrant communities cope with the dehumanizing forces of modern industrial society. During that time, he was able to make his way into the elite, free-thinking circles of some of New York's most fashionable salons. He and Lucy also bought a historic Dutch home in Sparkhill, New York, where they lived with their boys on the weekends. During the week, while John and Lucy worked in the city, Charles, Donald, and John Jr. stayed in Sparkhill with nine other children as part of an experimental school based on the educational theories of Columbia professor John Dewey.[12] After World War I, Collier's plans to expand his community-based programs fell through, so the family moved to California for him to work as director of the state adult education program. But that job lasted only until 1919, when Collier's leftist sympathies made him a target of the red scare.

Collier's passion for reform in Indian affairs was ignited the next year when, jobless and disillusioned, he and his family followed friend and New York arts patron Mabel Dodge Luhan to Taos, New Mexico. While observing Pueblo ceremonies, Collier claimed to have "experienced the Indian religion to the center of my being and as a shaper of my life."[13] For Collier, Indian tribes—and the tenacious Pueblos in particular—offered an alternative model for American society, a model based on communal reciprocity and mutual aid, the transcendence of spiritual over material values, and reverence for the land and the natural environment. Collier's vision was grand in scope and evangelistic in tenor, for he was committed to protecting Indian cultures not simply for their own sake, but for the sake of regenerating a broader American culture held captive to the degenerative values of racism, individualism, and materialism.[14]

In the years following his experience at Taos, Collier founded and directed the American Indian Defense Association, which served as a platform for his vitriolic attacks against the BIA. Among other things, he criticized the Indian bureau for its effort to crack down on allegedly immoral dances and ceremonies. He also accused government officials of conspiring with Western land interests to rob the Indians of tribal property and the powers of self-government. And he attacked BIA administrators for forcing Indian school children to perform menial labor under the pretext of vocational training, while feeding them grossly inadequate diets of wormy bread and watered-down soup. A brilliant publicist, he was the gadfly who gave the BIA no rest. But then, by a remarkable turn of events in 1933, newly elected President Franklin D. Roosevelt shocked observers by appointing Collier as head of the very organization that he had long vilified.[15]

As commissioner, he guided the BIA through the most sweeping changes in its 180-year existence. He issued new regulations that rescinded the BIA's prohibitions on Indian dances and other traditions, and he changed policies in federal boarding schools so that Native traditionalists, and not just Christian missionaries, could conduct programs of religious education. His most important achievement was the passage of the Wheeler-Howard Act in 1934. The bill allowed tribes to set up their own councils to assume control over social services and land management programs. It also expanded tribal trust properties and reversed the fifty-year policy of individualizing tribal lands. But with the advent of World War II and subsequent cuts in budget and staffing, Collier became increasingly stifled in his efforts. His work took a more personal toll as well, evident in his 1943 divorce from Lucy Wood Collier and his remarriage to anthropologist Laura Thompson, who was twenty-four years younger than he. Finally, in 1945 he resigned, but not until after his twelve-year tenure made him by far the longest-serving commissioner in the history of the BIA.

Unlike Lindquist, who largely withdrew from Indian affairs when he retired, Collier remained active in the field long after retirement age. After leaving the BIA, he founded the Institute of Ethnic Affairs to pursue policy initiatives among indigenous peoples of both North and South America. He later taught sociology and anthropology at City College, New York, until he was forced to retire in 1954 at age seventy. The following year, his second wife divorced him, so he left New York to teach for a year at Knox College in Illinois. He then settled for the last time in Taos, where his commitment to Indian affairs had begun. He married his personal secretary, Grace Volk, and spent the last twelve years of his life writing his memoirs and other books before his death in 1968. According to his youngest son, his return to Taos was not so much a chance to gloat over his accomplishments as it was an opportunity to brood over his lingering sense of personal failure. John Collier Jr. wrote of his father's last years, "Most of the time I left him alone, respecting his withdrawal. Though our adobe houses were a hundred and fifty feet apart, we were simply not in his focus."[16]

By historical accident and the very nature of the passions that moved them, Collier and Lindquist were well matched. Chronologically speaking, their careers overlapped almost exactly, as their lives both began and ended within two years of each other. What is more profound, they were both missionaries in the broader sense of the word, peddling their visions for the Indians out of larger, though sharply different, spiritual frameworks. This factor lends their conflict a deeper resonance than one might otherwise find in most political dogfights. Collier's devotion to Indian reform grew out of a form of piety that would most aptly be called a "cosmic mysticism."[17] He sought a kind of harmony that results when the individual, the community, and the natural world are all aligned with the rhythms of the larger cosmos. As a child, he claimed to have had "a tremendous feeling of the oneness of the group with the natural surroundings." But after his parents died, when he was departing the family's home, he "had a visual hallucination of all the trees bowing and waving and crying a hopeless farewell. It was the break-up of the world, one of the experiences most stamped into my memory, the farewell of the neighborhood to me and to us. . . . Very early the terror of the world was the realization that the world I knew, the community, was being displaced."[18]

Collier passed through his grief and into what he termed a "planetary ecstasy," when, with the poetry of Wordsworth fresh in his mind, he lingered as a teenager on a mountain in the southern Appalachians. He wrote, "I saw the whole forest below shaking with the glory and joy which was of the universe." Within the next year he claimed to have received a "cosmic call" to be a "co-maker of a victory unimaginable."[19] Collier's experience of a paradisaical fall and mystical restoration inspired him to go into settlement work and then Indian affairs, with the hope that America's Native peoples would never have to know the painful dislocations he himself suffered as a child. This sense of vocation and self-transcendence undoubtedly empowered him to endure the dreadful tedium of Indian administration as he did for twelve years. For, even in the midst of things like land disputes, funding battles, and personnel problems, he never lost sight of his larger goal: to help those whom he called "the simple people of the world" to remain free to live within their own cosmic harmonies.[20]

While many of Collier's writings were saturated with his mystical reflections, Lindquist's own spirituality was more subdued and, unquestionably, more conventional. He told his daughter Helen that he experienced only two moments of mystical awareness in his life: one as a child standing on a rock near his home in Kansas, and the other at a YMCA camp in the Colorado mountains in 1908, when he devoted himself to Indian missions.[21] Curiously, both of these incidents occurred—like Collier's call experience—in a natural setting. But the parallels between the two end there. For when it came to the quest for self-fulfillment, Lindquist spoke mostly in the language of the Protestant work ethic. Hard work, he believed, made life meaningful for both himself and the Indians he evangelized.

In this regard, Lindquist drank deeply from the well of his Swedish upbringing in Lindsborg—a town so committed to individual industriousness that in the late twentieth century, its tourist brochure still touted Lindsborg as having "a history of a solid work ethic."[22] These attitudes were reinforced in his studies with Edward Bosworth, dean of Oberlin School of Theology. Bosworth invited students like Lindquist to look for what he called the "normal mysticism" found in the everyday sense of achievement from a job well done. So when Lindquist read the Bible, he was quick to find an image of Jesus that cohered with these values. In his outline for one sermon, his first point was "what a busy life [Jesus] led." And in another sermon he quoted the aphorism: "A man should not be measured by the shack he's born in but by the house he builds."[23]

As a result, whereas Collier rebelled against his own parents' drive for worldly success and prestige, Lindquist saw individual prosperity as a probable marker of personal character and integrity. When Lindquist looked at a Native community, he saw an opportunity to foster self-transcendence through material progress. But Collier saw the opportunity to redeem his own unhappy childhood by preserving the sense of wholeness found in Native kinship systems and nature mysticism. Given their conflicting points of view, it is no wonder that they were at such odds with one another.

While well matched at the level of contrasting ideals and rhetoric, Lindquist and Collier also pair up well for their willingness to fight down and dirty, tooth and claw. This is the case in spite of the fact that only twice, as far as I can tell, did they meet face to face, and then only as part of much larger gatherings.[24] They did not need personal contact in order to share an intense visceral hatred for one another. Collier accused Lindquist, a theological liberal with a progressive record on civil rights, of belonging to "the Mussolini Silver Shirts and stirring up the Indians in favor of Fascism."[25] He warned field agents not to cooperate with Lindquist, once dismissing him with a descriptive "negative-minus."[26] And although he could never touch Lindquist directly, Collier brought an abrupt halt to two missionaries' careers as a result of their participation in Lindquist's political intrigues. Similarly, Lindquist judged Collier on deeply personal terms. He sought to publicize rumors of Collier's family difficulties, including possible marital infidelities and problems with one of his sons.[27] Lindquist's vitriol even oozed out into his home life, where he subjected his wife and children to rants about Collier at the family dinner table.[28]

The high stakes and sheer passions involved make for an enticing story. The narrative of Lindquist's opposition to Collier is full of ironic turns, broken friendships, shifting alliances, and vengeful overreactions. There are FBI investigations, criminal arrests, and a steady run of scandals and allegations. Exploitation, alienation, and rank self-interest fall over the landscape of federal Indian policy like a heavy acid mist—with Lindquist and Collier both in the thick of it all.

Yet I do not want to be misleading here. There is a certain imbalance involved in matching Lindquist up against Collier. Collier despised Lindquist, to be sure, and Lindquist was his most persistent and resourceful national foe. But Collier did not live each day plotting how to deal with Lindquist. Lindquist, on the other hand, obsessed about Collier. By the time Collier became commissioner,

Lindquist could scarcely compose a letter, write up an administrative report, or give a public speech that did not take a stab at Collier or his views. This agonistic relationship suffused Lindquist's professional and personal identity. Collier did not live each day in Lindquist's shadow, but Lindquist always lived in his.

This imbalance alone, though, fails to explain why scholars have only occasionally mentioned Lindquist, and why, when they did, they typically made basic errors about his name, denominational affiliation, and place of residence.[29] The neglect of Lindquist is only one part of a larger problem of inattention to twentieth-century Christian missions as a whole. It is as if historians have finally managed to rid themselves of the myth of the Indians as a vanishing race, only to persist in the myth of a "vanishing mission" instead. Collier's own memoir, *From Every Zenith*, contains the same omission: he speaks of missionaries only rarely, and even then mostly as an anonymous block of opponents to his reforms.

Even so, it remains imperative to understand Lindquist and the ideas and passions he represented. For his apparent obscurity does not properly convey his true impact on Indian affairs. As an institution builder, field agent, religious educator, and author, he influenced hundreds of careers, and he refashioned assimilationist objectives to make them a viable and dynamic part of political discourse for yet another generation of decision makers. His thinking may sometimes strike us as outdated and backward looking, but it was compelling in his day, and it still finds echoes in the debates of our own day as well. Tribal sovereignty, federal paternalism, and freedom for indigenous religions—these issues all swirled in the tight vortex of hostility between Lindquist and Collier, and they continue to occupy the attention of Indian communities across North America. Then, as now, they beg our understanding.

1 The Making of an Ardent Assimilationist

On the eve of his retirement in 1953, reflecting on his forty-three years of labor as a missionary to the Indians, G. E. E. Lindquist recalled his very first evangelistic encounter with a Native American audience. He had ridden several hours on horseback to reach a small gathering of Mescalero Apache Indians in southern New Mexico. As a seminary student on summer break, Lindquist lacked even the slightest acquaintance with the tribal language, and no member of his audience understood English either. But by some providential dispensation, he found an Anglo-American rancher and an Apache youth who shared a smattering of Spanish. With Lindquist and his two translators in place, the young missionary's sermon managed to proceed, he recalled, "on an English-to-Spanish-to-Apache marathon."[1]

Concealed within this humorous reminiscence, however, was yet another process of linguistic and cultural translation—Lindquist's own pilgrimage from the obscurity of a rural ethnic community into the limelight of national prominence in Indian affairs. For the first twenty-two years of his life Lindquist had hardly ventured from the small Swedish enclave of Lindsborg, Kansas. English was for him a second language learned in public school but not typically spoken in the home of his immigrant parents or in the small, sectarian church of his childhood. But as an adult, Lindquist's speech bore little trace of a Swedish accent, and his formal church affiliation belonged to the mainstream and influential

Congregational Christian Church—the denominational descendant of New England Puritanism. He spoke on familiar terms with BIA commissioners, social scientists, philanthropists, and church figures in the ecumenical and missionary movements. He had become an assimilated Swedish-American.

This chapter outlines the formative experiences in Lindquist's life that propelled him into national politics and formed him into an ardent advocate of Indian assimilation. Most important among these influences were the rewarding experience of assimilation in his own life; his chance encounter with his missionary mentors, Walter and Mary Roe; and his participation in the significant but short-lived Society of American Indians (SAI). I argue that Lindquist was able to navigate his way from his ethnic home into the dominant society without facing harsh choices that might force him to repudiate his Swedish past. On the contrary, Lindquist reveled in his Swedish identity and used it to good advantage as he moved up the ladder of influence. As Lindquist understood it, assimilation was fully compatible with a generous respect for the diversity of human cultures, so that Americans from a variety of backgrounds could participate in the national life without forsaking their ethnic loyalties.

When Walter and Mary Roe took Lindquist under their wings, they helped to reinforce Lindquist's approach to assimilation as it applied to the Indians. By the turn of the century, they had come to regard previous approaches to assimilation as too hostile to Native cultures, so they advocated a more gradual approach that allowed Indians to maintain their racial pride as they adapted themselves to Euro-American society. With the Roes' guidance, and the strength of their connections in government and philanthropy, Lindquist rose rapidly in the circles of Indian reform. He ran YMCA programs at federal boarding schools, and he helped to found the Roe Indian Institute, a college preparatory school where his devotion to a liberal form of assimilation faced one of its first tests. Then, as an associate member of the Society of American Indians, Lindquist encountered in full force the radical assimilation ideas that he would spend the first half of his career fighting against. Each of these experiences taught him, in one way or another, to redefine assimilation for the Indians in more charitable and pluralistic terms. After Collier appeared on the scene in the 1920s and outflanked Protestant leaders in their respect for Indian cultures, Lindquist's views would begin to be labeled as obsolete, even reactionary. But at the beginning of his career he could comfortably identify himself with what many regarded as the most progressive and constructive approaches to "the Indian problem."

Swedish Formations

Born in a sod house near Lindsborg, Kansas, in 1886, Lindquist was the young-est of six children. His father, Andrew Lindquist, a professional glazier and painter, had immigrated from Gothenburg in 1872, while his mother, born Emily Carlson, came to America with her parents and siblings from Kyleberg sometime around 1869. The two met in Chicago, married in 1875, and moved to the Lindsborg area in 1879. In the year that Lindquist was born, they bought land in the town of Lindsborg and built the small two-story home where Lindquist, his parents, five siblings, and Grandmother Lindquist all lived.[2]

To understand Lindquist's attitudes toward assimilation, it is important to recognize that he grew up during "the heyday of Swedish America," when trends in America's Swedish communities kept ethnic pride in full flower. One important factor in promoting Swedish identity was the high migration levels, which re-mained steady from the early 1870s to the 1910s.[3] As Swedish migrants poured into the Midwest and plains, they energized communal interest in Old World customs and a lively Swedish-language press in Chicago and other cities. Swed-ish-American colleges like Bethany College in Lindsborg, where Lindquist earned his degree in 1908, boosted Swedish culture as well.[4] Bethany required profi-ciency in English, but it also actively promoted the study of Swedish literature and allowed degree candidates to write their theses in either English or Swed-ish.[5] Likewise, churches in the Lindsborg area conducted services in Swedish well into the 1930s.[6]

Carl A. Swensson, who founded Bethany College in 1881, epitomized the effort to blend Swedish nationalism with loyalty to the immigrants' new home. The hybrid identity he helped to create was ultimately neither Anglo-American nor Swedish, but uniquely Swedish-American. He explicitly rejected the creation of a "little, new Sweden" in America. "That would be as childish as it would be wrong," he wrote, "but on the other hand, we do not wish to become American-ized at the turn of a hand."[7] According to historian H. Arnold Barton, "If the Swedish part of the evolving Swedish-American identity was essentially cultural, the American part was primarily civic and political."[8] That position was borne out in one of Swensson's political speeches when, in a gush of patriotism and partisanship, he proclaimed, "A Swede is the best thing in Europe, an American is the best thing in the United States, and a Swedish American Republican is the best thing in the world."[9] Lindquist grew up, then, in a world where assimilation did not force a choice between ethnic and national loyalties. The two were com-patible and mutually reinforcing.[10]

The unique ecclesial history of Lindsborg, Kansas, also sheds some light on Lindquist's attitudes toward assimilation and the relative ease with which he moved into broader spheres of influence after college. Lindquist grew up attending the Evangelical Mission Church in Lindsborg—not the larger, more prominent Bethany Lutheran Church. To outsiders, the distinction hardly mattered, but the Evangelical Mission Church was a "come-outer" sect that separated from the more confessional Lutheran Church.[11] True to its sectarian character, Lindquist's church practiced closed communion and maintained strict evidentiary requirements for its experiential piety. But Lindquist's home church also harbored notable liberal elements as well. It adopted an ecumenical stance toward other denominations and rejected Lutheran versions of human depravity and predestination. In the Evangelical Mission Church of Lindsborg, Lindquist found himself on the cutting edge of Swedish support for middle-class values such as free will, intellectual innovation, and, in Lindquist's own words, "the right of individual thinking."[12]

So when Lindquist left Kansas in 1909, he took with him a rich heritage of conversations about how best to love, in the idiom of one Lindsborg resident, their mother Sweden and their young bride America.[13] But it did not take long for him to encounter the social prejudice that threatened assimilation ideals. As a student at Oberlin School of Theology in Ohio, Lindquist met Ethel Geer, a piano student in the music conservatory and the daughter of a wealthy real estate developer from Rockford, Illinois. Lindquist had hoped to marry Ethel upon graduation in 1912, but her mother's bias against the Swedish immigrant community in Rockford set Mrs. Geer against the proposed union. Meanwhile, Lindquist risked losing his first full-time position as YMCA director at Haskell Indian Institute in Lawrence, Kansas, because he delayed his departure from Ohio in hopes of winning Ethel's hand. Finally in 1915, the two were married, but only after Mrs. Geer's death, and not until Mrs. Geer had sent Ethel on a voyage to Europe and then a job assignment teaching music in Hawai'i, trying to keep the two apart. Through overcoming this painful experience of rejection, assimilation became for Lindquist a very personal project to fight social bias and prove—in himself and in his work among the Indians—the universal human capacity for advancement and self-improvement.[14]

However far he advanced in the elite circles of social, religious, and political power, Lindquist never burned the bridges of his Swedish past. He passed down to his children cherished customs for Christmas celebrations, and for more than forty years he playfully referred to himself as the nation's "only original Swede Indian in captivity."[15] But the most telling evidence of Lindquist's persistent Swedish identity appeared in his trip to the 1925 World Conference of Churches at Stockholm, Sweden. Only thirty-eight years old, he was one of the youngest church leaders in attendance, and he must have been awestruck by the prestige of the rest of the American delegation, which included such figures as University of Chicago theologian Shailer Matthews. While there, Lindquist looked up distant relatives, lectured in churches and YMCAs, and secured a respected publisher for his Swedish-language book on the American Indians. The entire journey renewed his awareness of the multiple and interlaced layers of loyalty he felt toward church, Sweden, and America.[16]

Lindquist described his experiences in a series of six installments published by *The Covenant Companion,* the denominational journal of his home church in Lindsborg. He extolled the geographical beauty and cultural excellencies of his native Sweden, giving the Vikings and their descendants credit for winning the pivotal Thirty Years War, discovering America, and revolutionizing modern botany, navigation, and warfare. Meanwhile, Lindquist could not resist chiding American and British delegations for the limitations of their "English-only" skills. And in a jab against the narrow outlook of British imperialism, he accused his "English friends" of being "weak on the subject of geography." For proof he recounted an anecdote from a recent international exposition at Wembley, where a Swede asked an Englishman in charge whether Sweden had its own display. "'No,' said the Englishman, 'that's the only one of our colonies that isn't represented.'" The joke played well for Lindquist's audience back home, but it also indicated something of the spirit of Lindquist's involvement in the Stockholm Conference, where he celebrated simultaneously his ethnic pride and his devotion to the internationalism of the burgeoning ecumenical movement.[17]

Clearly Lindquist's transformation into an assimilated Swedish-American was no simple, straightforward affair. Lindquist's negotiation of cultural identities held together a complex set of emotions and obligations. On the plains of Kansas he came to appreciate the advantages of speaking two languages and the richness of maintaining a twofold cultural identity. He learned the assimilative value of an ethnic identity, where ethnicity operated as a gateway rather than an obstacle to broader national loyalties. He proved to himself that the divide between ethnic community and dominant culture could be mediated in creative and salutary ways. And through the Swedish free-church tradition, he came to regard religion as a force for enlightenment and the kind of educational and social progress that assimilation promised as well.

To be sure, as a victim of ethnic prejudice from his wife's own mother, Lindquist could chart the distance between America's egalitarian ideals and the social realities of exclusion and discrimination. But in spite of these shortcomings, the opportunities of the "New World" convinced Lindquist of America's unique promise as a land of many peoples. The work of assimilation was for him something like a national specialty, a central part of America's calling that would help it surpass the descent-governed nations of the Old World. Today, the idea of assimilation typically connotes victimizing processes of alienation and conformity. But to Lindquist, assimilation offered both himself and America's Indians the tools to define themselves through self-discipline, moral rectitude, and increased prosperity.

Early Lessons in Indian Assimilation

But Lindquist's experience of assimilation could have given him only partial insight into what the process might have meant for Native Americans. As a Protestant of European descent, Lindquist endured nothing of the obstacles to middle-class prosperity faced by Native Americans. If immigrants chose to become aliens in a new land, indigenous peoples reluctantly became aliens in their own land. They had to be impelled into participation in the new national life through a deliberate federal policy and the expansion of a peculiar set of institutions under the Bureau of Indian Affairs. Complicating matters further, Indians held vast acres of land, enjoyed treaty rights, and cherished a long heritage of political sovereignty over their internal affairs. Their assimilation—in both its cultural and civic dimensions—could not be like Lindquist's assimilation. The Indians' assimilation had to be indigenized, in a sense, or adapted to the unique circumstances of Indians as a whole and numerous tribes in particular. To learn how to do that, Lindquist would have to move far beyond his family home in Lindsborg. He would have to find his way into a national network of missionaries and reformers who could guide him within the contested world of Indian affairs.

Lindquist's introduction to Indian missions began with a chance encounter during the summer of 1908. On a train to a student YMCA conference near Colorado Springs, a handsome, well-dressed couple sat down beside young Elmer and immediately began to captivate him with stories of their adventures among the Indians. Lindquist's letter to his mother described nothing short of a seduction whereby Walter and Mary Roe, Reformed Church missionaries from Oklahoma, recruited an ambitious young college graduate into their field of work. The icebreaker was Elmer's appearance. The winsome Mary Roe, "a dandy woman" in Lindquist's words, informed him that "from the very first she had taken an interest in me because I looked like a young man . . . they knew who went out among the Indians and offered up his life for them." The bait proved hard to resist. Once they arrived at the conference grounds, the three were almost inseparable. Open schedules in the afternoon allowed for long walks together along mountain trails. Gifts were given, smiles exchanged: Lindquist's initiation in Indian missions had just begun.[18]

To be sure, Lindquist could hardly have met a couple with more to offer an apprentice in Indian missions.[19] As missionaries with money and extensive connections in commerce, education, and politics, the Roes were rare birds in the field at the time. Lindquist tried to deny that these things meant anything to him in deciding how to channel his sense of call to ministry. "It isn't how much money I can make," he told his mother, "but of what good I can be." But with the Roes' support, Lindquist could reasonably expect to find a fast track to public leadership, rather than labor in the isolation and obscurity that often plagued the field. And yet, Lindquist still hesitated. He concluded his letter to his mother with a request that she pray for him, "that I may make a wise decision for the future."[20]

Lindquist had good reason to deliberate the momentous decision, for outside the spell of the Roes, most missionary candidates found little to attract them to the Indian field. "When I was in . . . seminary," he later told a colleague, "I was almost viewed with suspicion not to speak of pity, for choosing the Indian missionary field as a life task."[21] In American churches and seminaries, the poor image of Indian missions was not due to a lack of support for missions per se. In fact, colonial missionaries to the Indians, such as John Eliot and David Brainerd, continued to be revered as early founders of the Protestant missionary movement, although their life stories had the ironic consequence of inspiring far more men and women to go to foreign fields than to America's enduring Indian tribes.[22] Many of the missionaries who ended up among Native North Americans had originally set their sights for somewhere else.[23] And missionary boards were often accused of sending their least competent personnel to American Indians.[24]

No doubt, the enduring myth of the "vanishing Indian" dampened any enthusiasm for missions to Indians, but there were other factors that made it the neglected elder brother of the prodigal missionary story. First, the costs involved in reaching Native Americans were enormous. Unlike China and Burma—two of the more popular missionary destinations—Native American tribes were relatively low in population density, and while linguistic diversity was a problem in every field, missionaries elsewhere would probably never confront so many language groups of such small size. Mastering a Chinese dialect meant an open door to millions of people, but translating the Bible into a Native American language meant access to barely a few hundred or thousand in any single tribe. The poor cost-benefit ratio for American Indian missions made missions to the Indians of the Eastern Hemisphere significantly cheaper, so by the 1860s, many sending agencies admitted partial failure and devoted a larger proportion of their resources to more popular overseas stations.[25]

Second, the federal government's colonial relationship with indigenous populations cast a spell of failure and guilt over the entire endeavor.[26] Failure, because throughout the nineteenth century, mission stations would barely become established before military conflicts and forced removals pushed tribes westward to less desirable lands. And guilt, because unlike most foreign missionary settings, missionaries to the Indians could not avoid identification with an overwhelming imperial power. Comparing themselves to British or German missionaries, American foreign missionaries in the early twentieth century often boasted of freedom from entanglements with their own colonial governments overseas. Even if America's foreign missionaries were a bit deluded about their political purity, missionaries to Native Americans could hardly manage such self-deception. They were often quite frank about the bloodguilt of their government's dealings with Native Americans, but that admission, rather than inspiring more devotion to Indian missions, probably drove many off to foreign fields where they might work with clearer consciences.[27] The remedial, ameliorative task of making up for past sins placed Indian missions profoundly out of step with the ebullient spirit of the foreign missionary movement at the turn of the century.

Finally, it was the intractability of Indian impoverishment and cultural decline that ultimately pushed Indian missions to the margins of the Protestant missionary movement. By the time Lindquist committed himself to the field around 1909, Protestant missions to Indians were long past the romanticized glory days of the wilderness encounter between intrepid missionary and pristine, noble red man. Lindquist lived instead in an era when missions were tainted with generations of America's bad-faith dealings with the Indians, but when several hundred missionary stalwarts still nursed the hope that church cooperation with a repentant federal government might right the wrongs of forced removal, racism, and segregation.

Among those idealists, of course, were Walter and Mary Roe. Against the odds, they won Lindquist's commitment to the Indian field and proceeded to introduce him to the one bright spot for Indian missions: the powerful network of eastern reform organizations interested in Indian affairs. Those organizations provided the link at the national level between field missionaries and the federal government's public support for Christian missions. The Roes in particular were involved in the famous annual Mohonk Conference of the "Friends of the Indian," which brought together politicians, Indian commissioners, eastern clergy and reformers, and, when they could afford it, field missionaries. Through their contacts with New York pastor Lyman Abbott and the Smiley brothers, who owned the upstate resort where the group met, the Roes quickly initiated Lindquist into the small but well-organized Protestant institutions that had dominated federal Indian policy in the last two decades of the nineteenth century.[28]

Moreover, as a protégé of the Roes, Lindquist stood at the center of a critical shift in assimilation policy that took place around the turn of the century. Walter Roe lobbied for the change in 1901 when he wrote:

> Years of intimate association with these people have grounded in us the idea that the underlying mistake of our National policy toward the Indian has been the attempt to crush the Indian out of him. We found a lofty type of the savage, and have succeeded in transforming it into a wretched type of civilized man. Had we . . . treated the Indian more sympathetically as to his ideas, customs, arts, and even his dress and prejudices, larger results would have been secured.[29]

The Roes tried to implement their approach through the Mohonk Lodge at Colony, Oklahoma, which they founded in 1898 with the financial support of the Mohonk Conference. The lodge employed Indian women and older men—those who presumably would not be engaged in agriculture—by marketing their Native arts and crafts. The Roes believed that Indians could draw on their cultural heritage to support themselves, rather than doing laundry and other menial tasks for surrounding whites. Their endorsement of Indian cultures was tempered, though, by Roe's interest in subordinating native skills to the broader goal of instilling a Protestant work ethic in Indian laborers. Above all else, the Mohonk Lodge was intended to teach Christian Indians the skills of economic self-sufficiency amidst a new cash economy; certain aspects of the old life could be carried over, but only when they met that goal. It was not so much a license for pluralism as the introduction of a pluralistic element into an assimilationist framework. But even if Roe's endorsement of Indian customs was unstable and equivocal, it nevertheless attempted to offer the Indians the freedom to cultivate some of their traditional practices.

Roe's antagonists in Indian affairs—the more radical reformers like Richard Pratt and Alice Fletcher, who initially formulated assimilation policy in the 1880s—had not been so charitable about Indian cultures. While they opposed any hint of racism, believing the Indians to be every bit the intellectual equal of Euro-Americans, they held ethnocentric assumptions about the superiority of Western society. So assimilation for them meant merging the Indians into what they conceived as a homogeneous, Anglo-Saxon society. And because they believed racial differences were merely the product of environmental factors, they set out to transform the next generation of Indians into citizens fully capable of participating as equals in American society. In social terms, they proposed a process of rapid immersion in the dominant society—a sink-or-swim approach that involved removing Indian children from their homes and educating them in distant boarding schools where they were forbidden to use Native languages. Economically, radical assimilation entailed breaking up tribal landholdings in reservations and allotting the lands to individual Indians. In theory, land allotments—the mere possession of valuable private property—would instill a healthy self-interest in individual Indians, prompting them toward industrious habits and respect for the laws that protected their own property as well as that of others.[30]

But in missionary circles, the radical assimilation position rarely gained unqualified support outside of the mission board administrators who lived on the eastern seaboard. Missionaries in the field usually supported the eventual allotment of Indian lands, but they feared it would further disperse Indian populations in the short term, making them even less accessible to evangelistic efforts. And if lands were allotted prematurely, while Indians were still vulnerable to corrupt Indian agents and unscrupulous white neighbors, they risked the loss of the land base necessary for eventually supporting their own church institutions. Years of experience with cultural change taught most missionaries to see assimilation as a gradual process involving slow progress toward the ultimate goal. They found greater success when they taught their subjects to read their own tribal language first and when they sought to build upon existing cultural values.[31] Figures like the Roes, then, played a central role in bridging the gap between policy makers' dreams and reservation realities. With their missionary service in Oklahoma and their strong political ties in the East, the Roes formed part of a renewed dialogue between missionaries, who had always been a bit wary about rapid assimilation, and reformers, who altered their agenda to meet the realities in the field.

But for Richard Pratt, the most outspoken defender of rapid assimilation goals, this missionary influence clearly ran against national priorities. In a landmark speech delivered dozens of times around the turn of the century, Pratt strongly criticized missionaries for "encouraging the Indians to remain separate peoples" in order to evangelize them more effectively.[32] Missionary policies, he argued, "are always along the lines of their colonies and church interests, never toward citizenship." Moreover, he suggested that the missionaries' gradualism fed into racist beliefs that the Indians were simply incapable of assimilation in the first place. Missionaries might pay lip service to the goal of assimilation, Pratt believed, but their ends would ultimately be shaped by their separatist means.[33] Pratt's fears were realized in 1904, when, with hardly a word of protest from missionary and reform organizations, the BIA removed him as principal of Carlisle Indian school. Then Francis Leupp, commissioner of Indian affairs under Theodore Roosevelt (1905–1909), made gradualism the official policy of the BIA, and the Roes' support for Native crafts found tacit endorsement from government authorities.[34]

There remains some debate, however, about how to interpret the changes that Roe advocated. Most scholars recognize those changes as the very beginnings of a thirty-year retrenchment on assimilation—a retrenchment that reached its culmination in John Collier. But according to Frederick E. Hoxie and David W. Adams, the initial shift was a "fainthearted gesture on behalf of Indian culture," signaling a lack of confidence in Indians' mental capacities. For these scholars, the gradualists had been profoundly influenced by the rising dominance of scientific racism and its rigid racial determinism at the turn of the century. As a result, according to Hoxie and others, gradualists did not merely slow the assimilation process down, but they forsook assimilation policy's egalitarian underpinnings, gave up on assimilating Indians into a homogeneous American society, and settled instead for integrating them as a permanently peripheral, working-class minority.[35]

To be sure, one need not look far in missionary literature to find evidence of mixed motives behind the growing advocacy of a gradual assimilation. The increased tolerance for Indian cultures that Protestant leaders espoused carried with it little sense of obligation to Indian cultures qua cultures. They were more concerned about the harsh dislocations involved in the transition to white society, and the preservation of certain aspects of Indian culture would, they hoped, provide a useful compass for self-respect and morality during the brutal process. Moreover, a growing science of racial hierarchies did make its mark in missionary and reform circles. Thomas C. Moffett, secretary of Indian missions for the Presbyterian Church (U.S.A.), was a gradual assimilationist whose widely read *American Indian on the New Trail* (1914) made frequent references to the Indians' racial characteristics, from their "childlikeness" to their "cubical brain capacity." For Moffett, Native Americans' placement just below Caucasians on the racial ladder made them excellent candidates for civilization, so long as church and state approached them with patience and offered them protection from white exploitation in the transition.[36] For the Roes, however, the impact of scientific racism was less visible, even though it could well have been part of their conceptual framework for gradualism. More prominent in their arguments were the importance of maintaining the Indians' self-respect and a pragmatic sensibility—reinforced by Progressive concerns for efficiency—that sought to infuse particular cultural practices with Western individualism and self-reliance.[37]

Distinct echoes of the Roes' opposition to radical assimilation policies may be detected in some of Lindquist's earliest published work, based on his experience as YMCA director at Haskell Indian Institute, in Lawrence, Kansas. He moved there after graduating from seminary in 1912, having obtained the position through the strength of the Roes' connections with Hervey B. Peairs, the devout Methodist who served as superintendent of the school.[38] In a piece composed for a YMCA publication, Lindquist spoke with compassion about the difficulties young Indian boys faced making the transition from their rural, tribal homes to the disciplined, clock-bound life of the boarding school. For years, he noted, Indian education had been based on the radical assimiliationist model of Pratt's Carlisle Indian School. Publicity for those schools consisted of the notorious before-and-after pictures, which used haircuts and dress to measure the child's rapid progress, in Lindquist's words, "from forest and plain" to "imitation white man." For Lindquist, this measure of achievement was superficial and derogatory. He wrote:

> There seemed to be an impression current that the Indian as a race had no contribution of his own to make; that our Anglo-Saxon civilization should be rammed down his throat without regard for his own power of discrimination and standard of values. . . . Today the Indian student fully realizes that he must work out his destiny in the white man's civilization—'on the white man's road,' as some prefer to call it. He believes, however, that he can best do this by conserving the vital racial characteristics of his people's past.

Among those characteristics Lindquist listed were self-respect and race pride, bravery and physical endurance, calm and self-possession, loyalty and hospitality, and a profound spiritual sense of the "mystery around about him."[39] Like Walter Roe, Lindquist assumed that the tide of civilization would inevitably erode the tribal structures of Indian life (a loss neither of them ever thought to grieve), but with patient guidance, Indian boys might at least forego cheap imitation of white ways and adapt their own racial genius to a new setting.[40]

The work of YMCA director lent itself rather well to Lindquist's goals. The keynote of his initial years at Haskell was Indian leadership, and the Y work followed lines that gave students responsibility for planning their own activities and governing their own affairs. For Lindquist, the YMCA was like a garden in the wilderness: in the midst of the boarding school's military-style discipline,

Y work gave students an opportunity for "initiative" and "self-expression."[41] In light of the strict regimen of chores, studies, and still more chores, Lindquist wrote, "It is not surprising to find lack of initiative on the part of the pupils. The respect for the individual or reverence for personality on the part of the officials and employee staff is at the low water mark."[42] Only through the Christian Associations, he believed, would students develop the initiative that would help them preserve the lessons of their education when they returned to the reservations. It seemed to worry Lindquist very little that their exercises in self-expression would turn inevitably to Indian cultures for their inspiration. The important thing was how those resources were used to promote much-needed organizational skills in Western-style institutions. The Y sought to do for boarding school students what the Mohonk Lodge would do for Indian women and older men on the reservation: use existing interests to incorporate Indians into Western economic and social structures. Haskell's YMCA cabinet might have been planning an Indian pageant or a dance demonstration, for example, but they were doing so according to Robert's Rules of Order.

At one point, in fact, Lindquist's strategic support for Indian cultures got him into a spot of trouble. As regional supervisor of Indian YMCAs in 1915, he arranged to have the band from Chilocco Indian School play at a YMCA convention in Tulsa. To finance the trip, he scheduled the school band to play at several Oklahoma theaters en route. While the band performed an "Indian selection" called *Cante Masica,* one of the YMCA boys would appear in Indian costume and dance for the audience's amusement. But when the BIA superintendent at Chilocco got wind of the plan, he sent word that no such exhibition would take place, as "it would lower the tone of the band."[43] Faced with a disappointed audience, Lindquist attempted to put the theater "in the right light" by explaining why the administration would use its discretion in this case to "restrain the spectacular in dress and costumes." But one local paper reported the incident as a new, repressive ban on all Indian dances coming straight from the commissioner's office, and suddenly, Lindquist felt the heat from Washington for the paper's misrepresentation.[44]

Lindquist's embarrassment over the dancing incident likely did not last long, for as important as Lindquist's work at Haskell had been, it was for him an interim position—a temporary expedient while more grandiose plans took shape. All the while, he had been laying the groundwork with the Roes to build a more enduring legacy for assimilation and racial self-help: a nondenominational academy for advanced Indian students, modeled after the high-profile Yale-in-China project for Chinese Christians. According to their designs, the school would fill a gap in the government's educational program. Federal schools for the Indians carried students only to the sixth or eighth grade, so the planned Indian institute would offer courses specifically designed to prepare students for college matriculation. In time, the Roes hoped, graduates would form a core leadership in Indian churches and schools and make white oversight obsolete.[45]

For the present, though, the Roes were grooming Lindquist and their name-sake, Henry Roe Cloud, as the leading partners in the venture. Roe Cloud (born Wonah'ilayhunka, 1884–1950) was a young Winnebago from Nebraska who would become one of the most important figures in recent Native American history. By force of will and the help of missionary educational institutions, he had skirted the failings in government Indian schools to gain admission to Yale University in 1906.[46] There he met the Roes in his freshman year, accepted their name and patronage, and joined them in soliciting funds to establish a special high school for American Indians. With the Roes' knack for publicity, Roe Cloud soon became one of the darlings of the Protestant mission to the Indians. For missionaries in the field, he controverted prevailing racial hierarchies through his proverbial rise from a wigwam to the ivory towers of educational achievement within a single generation.

Part of Roe Cloud's popularity, too, resulted from his facility with the idiom of assimilation. He credited his achievements in part to his experiences on a farm, where "I learned to pay for what I got, and, by actual struggle, came to know the value of a dollar, the meaning of toil, and something of the worth of time."[47] But like the Roes and Lindquist, he interpreted assimilation in ways that allowed for continuities with his Indian heritage. In an essay for *Missionary Review of the World,* Roe Cloud extolled Indian contributions to the arts as "a pride to any nation" and called for "conserving what is distinctive in aboriginal American life." His proposed method for that conservation effort, however, was a "thorough-going character-building educational program." Only through education, an otherwise assimilating process, could Indians overcome the disintegrating impact of "a foreign civilization" without losing "pride and self-respect."[48] For Roe Cloud, then, assimilation and race-pride were not two opposing extremes, but rather race-pride was a necessary part of the assimilation process.

With the Roes' orchestrations in the background, Roe Cloud joined Lindquist in the fall of 1910 for ministerial training at the Oberlin School of Theology. Oberlin was a significant choice for several reasons. First, the school enjoyed a long and admirable record on race relations, from its antislavery agitation in the antebellum period to the multiracial campus Lindquist and Roe Cloud shared in 1910. Second, Oberlin carried them directly into the moderate liberalism of the

Protestant mainstream. Guest speakers at Oberlin during the early twentieth century included social gospel advocates Walter Rauschenbusch, Charles M. Sheldon, and Shailer Matthews. Also, two professors, Albert B. Wolfe and Herbert A. Miller, pressed the role that science should play in grounding progressive reforms upon objective social data—a lesson learned well, considering the major field surveys Roe Cloud and Lindquist conducted in the course of their careers.[49]

Judging from later writings, the professor who made the biggest impression on Lindquist in particular was dean and New Testament professor Edward Increase Bosworth—a man said to be "tolerant of old ideas" as well as new ones.[50] His books celebrated precisely the values that shaped Lindquist's commitment to Indian assimilation, such as an emphatic insistence on judging people by their individual character rather than their race or social status, and a profound respect for the spiritual growth potential in hard work and modern business endeavors.[51] In a manual for evangelism, Bosworth encouraged Christians to "count on the normal mysticism" in non-Christians' lives. People, he said, "need to be led to recognize the feel of God in certain familiar commonplace experiences," such as "the satisfaction produced by having done honest successful work."[52] For Lindquist and Roe Cloud, Oberlin reinforced their faith in hard work and right living, not only as ends in themselves, but also as tools for overcoming social prejudice.

Through their year together at Oberlin, plans for the proposed Christian Indian institute consumed their every thought. Lindquist saw in Roe Cloud the entire future of the Indian race and a model for the kind of students they would graduate from their school: intelligent, educated, and upright, with a potent mix of businesslike tact and exotic charm. The two partners were so committed to their call that they spent most of their spare time field-testing their theology of hard work by raising funds for the future school. Rather than visit their families during Christmas break, they traveled to Chicago and New York, knocking on the doors of America's best-known philanthropists.[53]

Oberlin ultimately proved too far from the northeast for them to raise money efficiently, so after only one year at Oberlin, Roe Cloud transferred to Auburn Seminary in New York, where he graduated in 1913 and was ordained a Presbyterian minister.[54] Soon thereafter, Roe Cloud gathered enough money to purchase land in Wichita, Kansas, and in 1915, Lindquist and his new bride reunited with Roe Cloud to welcome an inaugural class of eight students. The new school was named the Roe Indian Institute in memory of Walter Roe, who had died just months before seeing his vision realized. With his name and the legacy of his social connections, the school opened to the hearty endorsement of the Home Missions Council of the Federal Council of Churches.[55]

Powerful endorsements, however, were not enough. Educational tasks somehow lost priority when Lindquist got bogged down in discipline problems and when Roe Cloud was forced to devote most of his time to shoring up the institute's weak financial footing.[56] Many philanthropists offered only token support, wondering why the school did not receive funding from the oil-rich Indians so prominent in the Oklahoma papers. This problem alone almost led to a breach between Roe Cloud and Mrs. Roe when she told him that Indians "ought to do something gratuitously for their own people."[57] Roe Cloud felt his hands were tied: most progressive Indians were too poor to support a charity, and those who were still under federal guardianship had their properties under the control of Indian agents, whom Roe Cloud sometimes found to be "non-Christian" and "unscrupulous."[58]

Other difficulties revolved around obtaining qualified Indian students. Years of planning and forethought did not prepare the two educators for the scarcity of Indian students ready to enter a college preparatory high school. And much to their dismay, missionaries, who had been expected to identify most of the school's prospective students, were lukewarm toward the enterprise. Unlike Lindquist and Roe Cloud, some missionaries showed "a pronounced lack of faith" in Indians' ability to compete at the college level. For Roe Cloud, this lack of faith was self-serving, for it kept young Indians at home where the missionaries could use them as low-paid interpreters and "helpers in personal work around the missions."[59] On the other hand, the institute faced opposition from radical assimilationists like Richard Pratt, who believed in Indians' intellectual capacities but cared nothing for preserving a distinct Indian consciousness. He faulted the school for retarding the process of assimilation, suggesting that Indians would be better off attending integrated high schools where assimilation could move more swiftly.[60] Caught between advocates of cultural annihilation and a cynical acquiescence to a permanent Indian under-class, Lindquist and Roe Cloud struggled to promote a third and better way.

The Abolitionist Debate in the Society of American Indians

While the two young men fought to maintain support for their Indian academy, their engagement with federal Indian policy during the 1910s offered them a surer path to prominence in Indian affairs, although that path too was mixed with hopefulness and frustration. The best-documented site for charting their early involvement in the world of federal policy is in the rocky relationship between

Protestant reformers and the short-lived Society of American Indians.[61] The debates Lindquist witnessed there provide a clear indication of both the extent to which the agenda of radical assimilationists was dominating the scene at the time and the vigorous measures Protestant leaders had to take to maintain public support for the guardian role of the BIA.

At its founding in 1912, the Native-led SAI looked like it would become a valuable part of the Protestant establishment in Indian affairs. With the Episcopal priest Sherman Coolidge (Arapaho) as president and Roe Cloud as chairman of the advisory board, annual meetings sounded at times more like missionary gatherings than political deliberations. In one presidential address Coolidge exhorted society members to "moor the anchor of your politics to the Rock of Righteousness," and an informational pamphlet designated each member a "'Missionary of Life,' who gives hope and encouragement to men and women of a race all but crushed by despair."[62] Moreover, the cautious, consensus-building leadership style Coolidge and Roe Cloud exercised gave missionaries and reformers further confidence that the SAI's public image would find favor across a wide spectrum of political interests. And finally, its goals, such as to "promote good citizenship among the Indians" and to "preserve and emphasize" the "race characteristics and virtues" of the American Indian, harmonized well with those of the ecumenical organizations that supported it.[63]

Within just a few years, though, controversies divided the SAI and deflated Protestant hopes for the organization. The most damaging controversy hit especially close to home for Protestant leadership, for it called into question the very purity of their motives in Indian affairs. At the third annual meeting in 1915, in one of the most important speeches in twentieth-century Indian affairs, Carlos Montezuma (Yavapai) sharply criticized the SAI and the various friends of the Indian for their gradualist approach to assimilation and their measured, cooperative relationship with government authorities. He charged that their moderate approach to assimilation grew from their vested interest in keeping the Indian in bureaucratic and ecclesiastical chains. Echoing the views of his mentor, General Pratt, he said the Indians had become a growth industry that employed thousands of government officials, missionaries, anthropologists, and philanthropists in permanent vocations. And according to Montezuma, the strengthened emphasis on gradualism in Indian assimilation provided even more justification for the industry's growth while ultimately segregating the Indian still further. In a characteristically colorful analogy, Montezuma compared the gradualist approach to "the good Saint's method of shortening his dog's long tail"—one small piece at a time "so as not to hurt the dear dog too much."[64]

Montezuma therefore urged the society to prove its autonomy and ignite its activist spirit by publicly demanding the immediate abolition of the Bureau of Indian Affairs. The use of the language of "abolition" in this case was deliberate. For Montezuma, the BIA enslaved the Indians no less than the southern aristocracy had enslaved the Africans. As long as there was an Indian bureau, he argued, the Indian would be singled out, given a special legal status, and subjected to prejudiced treatment from the American public. For him, the failures of Indian boarding schools were due not to bureaucratic inefficiency or lack of congressional appropriations, but rather to the bureau's effort to dominate the Indians and justify its continued existence through their resulting impoverishment and ignorance. The guardian relationship that was meant to protect Indians from the loss of individually allotted lands was, for Montezuma, not a temporary expedient on the road to autonomy but a self-perpetuating prison that isolated Indians from the redemptive influences of white civilization. It would be easy to dismiss his position as an internalization of Pratt's radical assimilation attitudes. But it also grew out of the proud Indian heritage of tribal sovereignty and independence, only now transposed into an individualistic key. In its acerbic, provocative style, Montezuma's speech parted ways with the handshaking courtesies of the Protestant churchmen at the society's helm. In its content, though, Montezuma set the agenda for the most radical Indian critics of the BIA for years to come.[65]

More immediately at stake in this debate was the ongoing and critical financial support of the SAI's numerous associate (non-Indian) members, most of whom preferred to cooperate with the BIA rather than abolish it. After Montezuma presented another powerful speech at the 1916 conference, Thomas Moffett, the Presbyterian missionary executive who chaired the ecumenical Joint Indian Committee, combined threats with consensus building to call the society to its highest goals. He trivialized Montezuma's views and papered over the SAI's problems with a blast of boosterism, deeming the society a "success in this country" with a future guaranteed of "greater success." Meanwhile, Moffett reminded Montezuma of the importance of associate members like himself, warning, "the Society will receive its death blow when it forgets its friends and turns them into enemies."[66]

At the annual conference in 1918, Montezuma's hostility toward self-styled friends of the Indian resurfaced during discussion of a citizenship bill advocated by the Indian Rights Association (IRA). According to the bill's provisions, all Indians with one-half white ancestry would be granted immediate citizenship under the assumption that with one white parent, they would be sufficiently prepared to assume their full civic responsibilities. Samuel Brosius, the IRA's Washington lobbyist, interpreted the bill as a significant step toward ending "the tribal relation" and moving Indians toward citizenship. Montezuma was not convinced. He rose to ask why full-blooded Indians were not included in the provisions. When Brosius answered, "It is believed that they are not sufficiently competent," Montezuma shouted, "All bosh!" Then turning away from the associate members in the audience, he explained, "You know these Indian friends, they want us to believe they are helping us when instead of helping us they are playing with us." At this particular gathering, with many members absent owing to the disruptions of the war, Montezuma's position finally gained the ascendancy, and new officers took control of the society.[67]

Lindquist's personal attitudes about the conflicts within the SAI may be reasonably inferred from the response of his close associates. Arthur Parker (Seneca), who later authored a booklet with Lindquist, wrote a friend, "The Society of American Indians is getting into bad company, I fear."[68] He believed Montezuma's position mistakenly equated Indians with European immigrants, who had no treaty relationship with the federal government and whose cultures were more "civilized" than those of the Indians.[69] Matthew K. Sniffen of the Indian Rights Association—another coauthor with Lindquist—denied charges from Charles Eastman that friends of the Indian "tend to follow the Bureau rather than act independently." "We hold no brief for the Indian Bureau," he wrote back. "We regard it as a temporary expedient." But he thought that abolishing the bureau at that time would only lead to the creation of another administrative body in its place. Sniffen continued, "It seems to us that the present system, with all its defects, is preferable to any scheme that would open the bars to the horde of attorneys" who, through contracts to manage Indians' business affairs, would exploit them with "exorbitant fees."[70] According to Sniffen, "Most of those who shout the loudest [about abolition] . . . belong to a clique that has been exploiting the Indians, or would have done so had it not been for the activities of the Indian Bureau."[71] For Sniffen and the IRA, civil service reforms and other modifications could free the Indian bureau from the rankest forms of political influence, but so long as there were treaty obligations to be met and Indians unprepared to protect their interests in business transactions, the BIA would fulfill a necessary function.

By 1919, with the society's abolitionists still gaining power, associate members were advising each other to pay their last dues to the SAI and remove their names from the membership roll.[72] Parker and Roe Cloud abandoned ship one year later. Meanwhile these like-minded reformers returned to their various annual meetings under other auspices, such as the "Friends of the Indian" and the ecumenical Joint Indian Committee. At none of these gatherings did abolition of the BIA appear as an item on the agenda. Each meeting promoted a cooperative relationship with the federal government while remaining silent about that remote prospect when the BIA would no longer be needed.[73] Despite their occasional falling-outs with the BIA, reformers and missionary administrators largely viewed the BIA as somehow their bureau, with the assimilation process being their responsibility to guide and shape. Of course, the very logic of assimilation, as they understood it, required that the abolitionist appeal would reappear from time to time. But in the 1910s, their sense of both compassion and custodial control positioned them in the refinement of a patronizing but fair-minded middle ground.

Lindquist no doubt identified himself with that middle ground. In the early twenties, he summarized his approach to Indian affairs with a call for "gradual release from governmental supervision," arguing that "unrestricted citizenship" should be granted only after individual Indians met the prerequisites of "education and demonstrated ability."[74] Of course, he insisted that "tribalism cannot long endure," but he feared the social and economic disruptions that a rapid assimilation might bring. His attitude, it seems, was no isolated or superficial opinion. Virtually every facet of his life drove in the direction of this patient gradualism and its protective paternalism—life in an immigrant community, the mentor relationship with the Roes, his friendship with one of the brightest Indians of his generation, his educational work with Indian boys, and his participation in the small group of missionaries and reformers who held a proprietary interest in Indian affairs. For the time, at least, Lindquist could be an ardent assimilationist without being a radical one.

2 Indian Dances and the Defense of Federal Guardianship, 1920–1933

On a brisk December day in 1923, G. E. E. Lindquist should have been basking in the glow of his newfound status in the circles of national power. The secretary of the interior had invited him to participate in an unprecedented conference on Indian affairs in Washington, D.C., and Lindquist's friends planned to present his book, *Red Man in the United States,* to President Coolidge the next day in a ceremony at the White House. But Lindquist was smarting from a well-coordinated campaign against missionaries and the BIA for the federal policy on Indian dances and ceremonies. "Mr. Chairman," Lindquist announced during the conference deliberations, "those of us who have been maligned and misrepresented because of our attitude toward the Indian dances in recent months refuse to be . . . placed in the category of reformers." Denying any indiscriminate attempt to prohibit all dances and ceremonies, he nevertheless insisted on suppressing certain practices among tribes in the desert Southwest. As he waved BIA reports of alleged Pueblo and Hopi dance obscenities high in the air, Lindquist stated emphatically, "We take our stand on the matter of secret dances." If those dances were not prohibited, he concluded, then the entire federal system for Indian welfare should be abandoned for consistency's sake.[1]

By taking a close look at the controversy over Indian dances, this chapter explores how the BIA–missionary partnership handled its biggest single test before John Collier became commissioner in 1933. What made the controversy unique was that it polarized federal policy debates in a new way. By bringing a new, anti-assimilationist voice into the arena, Collier and his sympathizers conflated Lindquist's more moderate approach to assimilation with radicals who advocated the complete annihilation of Indian cultures. But this polarizing impact did not break things wide open at the time, because the major players in the debate were divided differently on another question—whether to support the BIA as the guardian of the Indian's interests. In fact, for both the BIA and most Protestant leaders, Collier was interpreted largely as yet another in a long line of agitators attempting to discredit and abolish the BIA. It may seem counterintuitive, to be sure, but Lindquist and his peers saw Collier, the opponent of assimilation policies, as working hand-in-glove with the anti–BIA goals of radical assimilationists like Carlos Montezuma. As a result, missionaries responded to the dance controversy by closing ranks with the BIA and trying to maintain an increasingly tenuous hold on their more liberal sympathies with Indian cultures.

The chapter begins with an examination of the record on Indian dance suppression in the years leading up to the controversy. Throughout the 1910s, I argue, Protestant leaders worked carefully with federal officials to avoid entangling the BIA in a moralistic crusade against Indian dances. But in 1922 when Commissioner Charles Burke felt particularly vulnerable to radical critics, he took hold of the dance issue as a way to rally the missionaries and their large church constituencies behind his administration. Missionaries like Lindquist took the bait. In his widely publicized book, *Red Man in the United States,* and in his participation in the high-profile Advisory Council on Indian Affairs in 1923, he stood up against allegedly immoral "secret dances" while defending the BIA from outside agitators and "sentimentalists."

But Burke's strategy backfired. His decrees against Indian dances gave momentum to Collier's coalition of reformers, while Protestant missionaries began to lose their credibility as benevolent advocates for the Indians' welfare. Burke's own misgivings did not help matters for the missionaries either, for even though he asked them to publicize allegations of Pueblo dance immoralities, he retreated from enforcing the policy on dances and left the missionaries holding the bag.[2]

Nevertheless, in the following years, Protestant support for the BIA endured. In spite of their sense of Burke's betrayal, Lindquist and other church leaders continued to defend the BIA as the guardian of the Indians' interests. This becomes especially clear in the chapter's concluding discussion of Lindquist's 1930 appointment to the Board of Indian Commissioners, where he became a leading voice in advocating the Indian bureau's benevolent authority over Indian tribes.

Thus, while Collier's entrance into Indian affairs threatened to destabilize the missionary–BIA partnership, missionaries responded with an even stronger defense of the BIA's guardian role. In just a few short years, of course, Lindquist would completely rethink his support for guardianship, but until then, his support for the BIA showed no signs of wavering.

Origins of the Indian Dance Controversy

To place the Indian dance controversy in the larger context of the BIA–missionary partnership for assimilation, it is important to understand how the controversy developed. For the principal irony of the dance controversy was that in the years leading up to Burke's dance circulars, BIA opposition to most Indian dances had become somewhat more compromising and more responsive to the local politics of Native resistance. The flagrantly repressive measures of the late nineteenth century, when white settlers associated Native dances with militant uprisings, had been replaced with a dependence upon the education of the Indian race as the best cure for pagan ceremonials. With boarding schools in place, the Indian office expected that traditional dances would die out with the passing of the older generation. Truant officers and school disciplinarians succeeded armed soldiers at the coercive edge of the "civilizing process."

The legal basis for suppressing Indian dances and ceremonials was the Religious Crimes Code of 1883, a law largely formulated with "hostile" and ration-dependent Plains tribes in mind. It sought to suppress Native traditions on military and economic grounds. The intertribal sun dance, which involved the shedding of blood, was banned because it was "intended and calculated to stimulate the war-like passions of the young warriors." Likewise the code penalized the "giveaway," which often attended ceremonies among the Sioux and other tribes on the Plains. The giveaway was part of a system of gift exchanges that tied communities together through reciprocal obligations and helped to distribute material wealth to those in need. But the BIA suppressed it because it undercut the enlightened self-interest thought to be at the heart of hard work and economic security.[3]

As the rations program evolved into a full-blown system of guardianship, the Indians' ward status became the basis for still further assaults on tribal practices. Economic concerns about the giveaway expanded to justify regulating all Indian gatherings, whether religious or recreational. BIA agents kept an especially close watch on the frequency and duration of Indian dances, fearing that the time attending such tribal gatherings might lead to a pauperizing neglect of livestock and crops. That, in turn, would require more federal expenditures for rations and welfare relief.[4] This economic factor might have been an easy excuse for violating the Indians' religious freedoms, but it was treated quite seriously at the time. In 1918, the Indian office even contemplated canceling a series of prolonged religious gatherings by Christian Indians, backing off only after loud protests from missionaries.[5] So while dance regulations were culturally prejudiced against Native traditions, they had the added force of an equally problematic pattern of Indian wardship. The federal government's expenditures in Indian education and welfare gave it the presumptive authority to regulate virtually every aspect of Native life to achieve the most efficient use of federal funds.

Enforcement of restrictions against dances, though, was varied. Many agents in the field service saw Indian dances as harmless social gatherings and even participated in organizing them.[6] Moreover, by the turn of the century, dance policies ran into serious conflict with the Dawes Act of 1887, which granted citizenship to Indians who held individual title to their own lands. Habeas corpus laws thus prevented the BIA from imprisoning citizen Indians for dance offenses.[7] Lacking legal authority and the full support of many in the field service, the BIA dealt with Indian dances as much through grudging compromise as it did through open conflict.

Through the 1910s, the Protestant missionary establishment took its cues from the BIA's own political realism in the area of Indian dances. A petty quarrel with Commissioner Francis Leupp in 1909 set the tone for the decade to come. Catholic and Protestant representatives called upon the commissioner to take more effective steps against the sun dance and other dances that were "immoral in their tendency." Leupp's response was short, if not indignant, accusing the church leaders of forming a resolution without investigating the many obstacles to its execution. Rather than pressing the issue, the missionaries backpedaled. They meant no criticism of the commissioner, they said; in fact, they harbored no "prejudice against dancing as dancing." One missionary even gave a qualified endorsement of toleration, saying, "I believe in [Indians] keeping up social customs of their own so far as it can be done regardless of whether it suits our fancy or not. They have as good a right to their tastes as we have to ours perhaps." Nevertheless, in their effort to sound the keynote of cultural tolerance and sympathy, no one met Leupp's challenge to offer specific suggestions on how to regulate or prohibit Indian dances. The missionaries had learned their lesson: a cordial and effective relationship with the Indian office would require choosing their policy battles well.[8]

Still other pragmatic and theological factors helped to quiet agitation about Indian dances. First, within establishment circles, missionary attitudes toward

Indian cultures in the 1910s were somewhat more charitable than at the height of the radical assimilation drive two or three decades earlier. Liberalizing trends in Protestant theology in the early twentieth century led some missionaries toward an increasing emphasis on God's pervasive, revelatory presence in all human cultures.[9] They began to express a limited but marked admiration for certain intangible qualities in Native faiths, such as the Indians' capacity to saturate even the most mundane activities with religious meaning. Thus a Congregational missionary told a conference in 1918 that the Indians' own religious training should be used as the basis for their Christianization. Missionaries should convince Native peoples that they "don't come to tear down but to build up." Say to them, she advised, "'I will do the building up and let you do the tearing down.'"[10]

Moreover, for some missionaries and reformers, too much publicity about alleged Indian dances and immoralities would undermine assimilation goals. Negative images of Indian cultures might perpetuate stereotypes of Indian savagery, delay white acceptance of Indians as fellow citizens, and give ammunition to critics who claimed Indians could never be assimilated in the first place. If the American public concluded that the Indians were, after all, inassimilable, then funds for missionary and philanthropic endeavors would dry up, leaving the Indians even more vulnerable to disease, vice, and fraud.[11]

So between 1909 and 1919, when isolated field missionaries pressed the BIA to take a more aggressive stand against dances, missionary leaders typically managed to minimize the problem and relieve the commissioner of any responsibility for it.[12] Moreover, concerns about Indian dances were most often expressed not in prudish condemnations, but in the context of larger humanitarian concerns. Dances were problematic, they argued, not because they were innately evil, but because they stood in the way of economic self-sufficiency and made the Indians open to exploitation by surrounding whites.[13] In their dialogue with BIA officials, then, missionaries shaped their activities and public pronouncements on dances to be consistent with the bureau's own professed objectives for the Indians.

What happened, then, to make Indian dance policy one of the biggest controversies in modern Native American history? What contingencies, what miscalculations of public sentiment, left image-conscious missionaries and the BIA exposed to adverse publicity and ridicule?

Several disparate events converged over the course of three years to bring the controversy into existence. The first concerned the creation of a "secret dance file," which the BIA later circulated among missionaries to whip up sentiment against Indian dances. That infamous collection of documents grew out of a small disturbance in northern Arizona in 1920, when a group of Hopi leaders complained about the disruptive activities of a local Mennonite missionary.[14] Two inspectors for the BIA soon arrived to investigate. What followed, though, was a highly irregular four-month inquiry that rebounded against the Hopis themselves. Instead of looking into the formal complaint, the BIA officials squirreled themselves away with a small group of Hopi Christians with an axe to grind against their tribe's traditionalists.

The content of the report that followed was, by the BIA inspectors' own description, "shocking, revolting, almost inconceivably indecent, unlawful, almost unbelievable"—indeed, an "unprintable slime," a "cess-pool of unspeakable vice and sensuality." In the style of classic countersubversionary polemics, the officials transcribed a collection of affidavits from Hopi Christians charging secret Hopi ceremonies with lewd and lascivious behaviors, including virtually every sexual "perversion" known to humankind.[15] Witnesses told of men and women forming representations of genitalia out of clay or pumpkin rinds and using them to proposition one another for sex. In secret ceremonial chambers known as kivas, according to one Christian Hopi informant, female initiates would "pick up their skirts" and "dance with the lower part of their bodies nude" for male onlookers. Others reported the antics of male katsina (kachina) clowns, who, with crowds watching, appeared to copulate with burros or with one another. Of course, traditional Hopis never had an opportunity to account for these and other charges. Their objections were scarcely noted, never transcribed.[16]

In Washington, D.C., at least one high-ranking official was eager to make something of the allegations against Pueblo dances. Edgar B. Meritt, a native Arkansan and lawyer with degrees from Georgetown and George Washington Universities, had become assistant commissioner in 1913. In an apparent attempt to strengthen his job security during a change in administration, Meritt drafted Circular No. 1665, which spoke out against the "elements of savagery and demoralizing practices" in Indian dances. The letter noted that dancing per se "is not inconsistent with civilization," but it asserted that dances were harmful "under most primitive and pagan conditions." Commissioner Cato Sells signed the letter before he left office in March, but for some reason decided against issuing it. Thus it was incoming Commissioner Charles Burke who issued the letter several weeks later on April 26, 1921. There was no public outcry. Meritt kept his job for eight more years. And the inspectors' report, which would later turn up as the bulk of the "secret dance file," was tucked away for a time in the labyrinth of the BIA bureaucracy.[17]

Meanwhile, more than a thousand miles away from the high plateau of northern Arizona, another series of events helped to bring the dance controversy into existence. For while sensational reports were drawing the BIA's attention to Indian ceremonies in the Southwest, an economic crisis in South Dakota prompted a marked increase in missionary agitation against Native dances on the Plains. During World War I, many Indian farms were weakened by government pressure to sell livestock in support of the war effort. At the same time, so-called competency commissions from the BIA granted hundreds of Plains Indians full citizenship and control over their lands. In most cases, that led to the rapid dissipation of Indian properties as landowners either chose to sell for cash or had to liquidate to pay taxes and mortgage debts. Then, early in 1920, the federal government removed wartime price supports for agricultural products, allowing commodity prices to drop by as much as 80 percent. According to economic historian Paula M. Nelson, farmers in western South Dakota—many of them Native Americans—were hardest hit of all. "For west river farmers" in South Dakota, Nelson writes, "the big shakeout came in the twenties and not in the Great Depression."[18]

According to missionary and BIA reports from the northern Plains, Indian dances and giveaways increased dramatically as the economic crisis hit. Of course, it is possible that their reports were skewed by widespread fears of a decline in public morality; prohibition, the red scare, new restrictions on immigration, and the move to suppress Indian dances all bore the stamp of the nation's postwar jitters.[19] But in light of economic conditions on the northern Plains, reports of an increase in Indian dances seem entirely plausible. For among the Sioux tribes and others in the region, dances and giveaways were traditional responses to hardship and the social disintegration that often attends economic decline. Giveaways in particular helped to redistribute material wealth to community members most in need, while binding the community in a web of reciprocal gift exchanges and criss-crossing obligations.[20]

But while increased ceremonial activity was for the Indians a response to economic decline, dances were, for Euro-Americans, the very cause of that decline. Consequently, in 1920 dancing among the Sioux became the subject of an increasing volume of correspondence among missionaries, the Protestant reformers in the Indian Rights Association, and the BIA. The Joint Indian Committee, which consisted of the Home Missions Council and the Council of Women for Home Missions, also delivered its first formal pronouncement on the dance problem in 1920 as well. Members voted to express their "commendation and praise" for Commissioner Sells' "consistent stand . . . in opposition to the continuance and exploiting of uncivilized dances." But this pronouncement, it should be noted, was too cautious to be the stuff of a new antidance crusade. It drew attention to Indian dances without publicly criticizing the commissioner and without calling for any new initiatives. It also sought to blame the dance problem in part on the exploitation of surrounding whites. As an indication of the low priority the committee placed on Indian dances, the 1920 annual report of the Home Missions Council made no mention of the subject in its twenty-page bulletin on Indian missions.[21] Once more, factors that later came into play in the dance controversy might easily have faded into obscurity.

The third set of circumstances that triggered the controversy revolved around the response to a comprehensive survey of Indian social, economic, and religious conditions conducted by G. E. E. Lindquist. The study was funded by John D. Rockefeller Jr.'s Institute for Social and Religious Research and later published as *Red Man in the United States*. As the massive survey neared completion in 1922, Lindquist and the Home Missions Council organized twelve regional conferences with Protestant missionaries to publicize the results. Curiously, at the vast majority of the conferences, missionaries ignored the question of Indian dances.[22] But the economic crisis on the northern Plains prompted the conferees at Sioux Falls, South Dakota, to focus much of their discussion on dances as an obstacle to Indian self-sufficiency. They ended their meeting by asking to meet with area BIA agents to follow up on their concerns.[23]

When the Washington office received a copy of the records from Sioux Falls, Commissioner Burke decided to do the missionaries one better and convene a meeting himself the next fall in Pierre. His own motives were clear. The Indian Office had been under heavy attack lately from radicals trying to abolish the BIA. In the past year, Carlos Montezuma and his lawyer, Joseph Latimer, had gained a sympathetic hearing with President Warren Harding. Referring to Montezuma, Latimer, and others, Burke told the gathering at Pierre that false propaganda had been "sowing seeds" of "dissatisfaction" that threatened the bureau's congressional appropriations. But through "the ministers and missionaries all over the country," he hoped to "get to the public information that will be true . . . and in this way build up a sentiment" in favor of the bureau's work.[24]

The transcript of the meeting shows how Episcopal Bishop Hugh Burleson and other church leaders moved cautiously so that they might support the commissioner without stepping too far out in front of him. For example, they knew that Burke was unlikely to issue a complete ban on Indian ceremonies and dances, so they followed his cue and developed a series of proposals for limiting the problems associated with Indian gatherings. To keep dances from taking Indians away from their farms for prolonged periods, they recommended that dancing be limited to one day per month and suspended altogether during months of planting and harvest. They also called for better enforcement of regulations against persons under the age of fifty participating in the dances—a position they justified by the claim that the current dances were not traditional, but a far worse set of hybrids spawned by Indian youth borrowing from surrounding whites. And they called for a ban on the giveaway, which they saw as an impediment to individual prosperity.[25]

After allowing for some variance in enforcement, Burke made these recommendations the basis for his Supplement to Circular No. 1665 on February 14, 1923. Then, as a model for the "tact and persuasion" he wanted superintendents to exercise in the matter, he issued an appeal directly "to all Indians" to stop their "useless and harmful performances." "I do not want to deprive you of decent amusements or occasional feast days," he wrote, "but you should not do evil or foolish things or take so much time for these occasions." One missionary publication called the letter "brotherly advice to the Indians." The tone was far more paternal than fraternal, however, treating the Indians, according to one contemporary observer, as if they were "children of not more than elementary school age."[26]

With the exception of a brief allusion to the Hopi Snake Dance, all the details of Burke's letters pointed to alleged problems among the Plains tribes, not the Indians of the desert Southwest. Many observers took the letter's regional focus at face value, and when they did, Burke's circular appeared to have accomplished its purpose. It strengthened missionary support for an embattled Bureau of Indian Affairs, kept up administrative pressure against the secret dances of tribes in the Southwest, and yet diverted attention toward the Plains, where few white activists were concerned with protecting the Indians' cultural heritage.

Yet even if Burke was not looking for a public fight over Pueblo cultures in the Southwest, his Supplement to Circular No. 1665 nevertheless landed him one. In the months between the original circular in 1921 and its supplement in 1923, a loose coalition of artists and writers in New Mexico had begun to organize itself into a powerful political force. Through their publicity skills and access to major newspapers and periodicals, they began to turn public opinion against the BIA and its long-standing policy of cultural assimilation.

As early as 1882, artist Frederick Remington had recognized the possibilities New Mexico held for painters with interests in landscape and Indian themes. Unlike the Plains tribes, who endured military defeat and the near-total loss of their economic base, the Pueblos maintained their economic independence and tenaciously preserved their cultures intact, thus making them attractive subjects for artists and writers. With the advent of World War I and the collapse of European society in its aftermath, New Mexico's elite social circles swelled with dozens of cultural exiles, such as Mary Austin, D. H. Lawrence, Elizabeth Shepley Sergeant, and John Collier. To one degree or another, they all sought an escape from the bankrupt civilization of the modern West and found in the small-scale Pueblo civilizations a source for their own spiritual renewal.[27]

Under Collier's leadership, the New Mexico bohemian colony gained national attention when it organized to fight the Bursum bill in 1922. The bill sought to determine title to Pueblo lands that had been occupied by Hispanic squatters for several decades, but its provisions overwhelmingly favored the squatters' claims against the Pueblos. Protestant reformers from the Indian Rights Association (IRA) geared up to fight the bill through congressional lobbying, but the new reformers flooded the nation's major newspapers with letters and broadsides. And Collier introduced direct action techniques into the arena of Indian reform by organizing Pueblo villages to voice their own opposition to the bill. The campaign worked. Wrangling over Pueblo land claims would continue for some time to come, but by February 1923 the Bursum bill was a dead letter.[28]

It was just at the peak of the controversy over the Bursum bill, when Collier and his allies were heady with the knowledge of the bill's likely defeat, that Burke issued his Supplement to Circular No. 1665. This time, what Burke had to say about Indian dances quickly caught the attention of an informed and thoroughly engaged crowd of Pueblo sympathizers. With Collier's collaboration, the *New York Times* and *New York Tribune* published articles sharply criticizing Burke for prohibiting the ancient rites of the Hopi and Pueblo Indians.[29]

Attempting to rise above the fray, Burke turned to members of the Protestant missionary establishment in April 1923 to whip up public sentiment against Pueblo and Hopi customs. Through the Indian Rights Association, he sent copies of the secret dance file to the ecumenical Joint Indian Committee and other leading missionaries across the country.[30] Setting aside any doubts they might have had about the file's veracity, they quickly rallied behind Burke's stand for Indian progress in industry and morality. In a published letter to the *New York Times*, Edith M. Dabb, head of Indian work for the YWCA, compared the Pueblos' secret dances to forced childhood marriage and widow immolation in India. "Primitive beauty," she reminded her readers, "is frequently found in close company with primitive cruelty and primitive ugliness." Dabb urged her "Christian nation" to support the commissioner and grant "ambitious" Indians the education they needed to triumph over "the weight of tribal tradition."[31]

Thus, through the convergence of a series of loosely related incidents, the

BIA veered from its earlier caution in suppressing Indian dances and embroiled itself in an unfavorable controversy. For their part, the missionaries probably would have avoided a good deal of the adverse publicity if they had stuck to the more humanitarian and economic concerns about Indians on the northern Plains. But they were more than willing to gather around a commissioner who took some risks to improve, as they understood it, the moral climate among the nation's indigenous peoples. They gladly interrupted their own modest trend toward tolerance and respect for Indian cultures in order to preserve their sense of custodial responsibility for the moral dimension of federal Indian policies. But while their attitudes toward Indian cultures vacillated between charitable tolerance and rank hostility, they remained constant in their quest for political legitimacy with the BIA.

Red Man and the Committee of 100

As major newspapers became fully engaged with reporting the burgeoning dance controversy, two important events—a book publication and a national forum on Indian affairs—kept missionaries and Native religions in the spotlight. Taken together, they show how Protestant leaders tried to interpret Collier and his allies as part of a broader threat to the very existence of the BIA. As I argued in chapter 1, since the turn of the century, the primary opponents for Lindquist and other missionary leaders had been radical assimilationists who wanted to abolish the BIA and remove federal guardianship over Indian lands. Missionary leaders, on the other hand, positioned themselves as patient guides who would, in cooperation with the BIA, protect Indian "wards" from unscrupulous land interests and grant them at least some measure of economic self-sufficiency and cultural pride as they endured the transition into Euro-American society. So when Collier began challenging the policies of the BIA, Protestant reformers interpreted him largely as yet another threat to the BIA and its services. To be sure, attitudes toward Indian cultures marked a dividing line between Collier and most missionaries. But for Protestant leaders, an equally important issue was at stake—the future of the BIA and the Indian wards who depended on it.

Even without the dance controversy, the publication of Lindquist's survey, *Red Man in the United States*, would have been regarded as an important event. Weighing in at a hefty 460 pages, it was the first comprehensive survey of Native American communities ever conducted—church-funded or otherwise—with more than 90 percent of the data compiled from field visits by survey personnel. As a sign of its quasi-official status, the book was enveloped by endorsements from the highest offices within the BIA, with a foreword by Commissioner Burke and an appendix by Assistant Commissioner Meritt. Burke commended missionaries and welfare societies for their "elevating" work among the Indians. He recognized certain "beautiful" traditions in the Indians' ancient "spirituality," but he nevertheless noted the retarding presence of many "benighted and . . . degrading" practices that require "kindly and persuasive" reform. The BIA and the churches' "humane" service for the Indian, he concluded, "cannot be done hurriedly or harshly," even if "short-sighted" critics grew impatient with the slow progress of assimilation.

Likewise, Lindquist cast missionaries and the Indian bureau together as the Indians' "fast friends," in contrast to the "sentimentalists" and other friends from whom "the 'original American' may well pray to be delivered." Those who wished to "preserve the Indian permanently as a museum piece" were for Lindquist no better than others who regarded Native Americans as "hopelessly degenerate." Both would withhold "education and civilizing influences" from the Indians—the one to justify white encroachment on Indian lands, the other to satisfy a "romantic fancy."[32] Lindquist also defended his gradual approach to assimilation on racial grounds. For part of his rationale behind a patient, cooperative approach by both church and state came from his view that Indians possessed their own "racial weaknesses" to be taken into consideration, as well as racial strengths to be preserved and enhanced.[33] Lindquist does not appear to have conceived of Indians in the hardwired terms of biological determinism.[34] But he did use the language of racial difference to justify both the promise of assimilation, whereby every group makes a contribution to the national character, and the more gradual approach favored by the BIA.

For most readers, though, the hook lay not in Lindquist's defense of a measured approach to assimilation, but in an advertiser's claim that the volume contained timely information on the recent dance controversy.[35] On that score, Lindquist reiterated familiar missionary objections to the commercialization of Indian dances, the "all night camps" with their "many temptations," the "undesirable features" introduced from certain "white man's dances," and the potential interference with industrial pursuits. When he turned to the more "religious" dances of the Pueblos and Hopis, he spoke vaguely of "obscenities" and "barbaric cruelties" documented in BIA files.[36] For Lindquist and his cohorts, the "present cooperation of Government and missionary agencies," once again, promised to resolve these and all other social problems.[37]

Reviews of the book appeared in dozens of the nation's papers and periodicals, amplifying an already sizeable public debate on Indian dances. The most scathing review flowed from the illustrious pen of Mary Austin, the Santa Fe novelist. She scolded Lindquist for spreading "a thin veneer of scientific data" over a very unscientific bias against all things Indian. If missionaries had their way, she wrote, the Indian would have no future but to be made into "a lower middle class . . . imitation white man." For her, the book lacked even "a glimmer of a notion" that in Indian cultures there was something "precious" worth preserving for the sake of "our own culture." "Altogether," Austin concluded, Lindquist's book "summarizes, often unconsciously, the bigotry, ignorance, and cupidity of our dealing with the Indian."[38]

Peter Phillip, the reviewer for the *New York Times,* offered a more mixed evaluation. He commended Lindquist's book for the useful information it provided to philanthropic work among Indians, and he hoped that its repeated accounts of white avarice and neglect "will spread the story of the injustice that the Indian has received at our hands." He also sympathized with Lindquist's rebuttal of the unrealistic sentimentalists. But he faulted Lindquist for promoting a "desperate policy of assimilation." For Phillip, the Indians should be granted "some vestige of racial integrity," just as ethnic Europeans preserved their "national music and folk dances."[39]

The rich irony of these reviews is that in Lindquist's critiques of radical reformers like Richard Pratt, Lindquist himself sought to give full measure to the "Indian's contribution" to American civilization. In previous debates, it was always Lindquist who opposed any "desperate assimilation policy" that would, in his words, "ram . . . our Anglo-Saxon civilization" down the Indian's throat.[40] His own experience as an assimilated Swedish-American had already provided him with the immigrant analogy for Indian assimilation that Phillips invited Lindquist to consider. And like Mary Austin, Lindquist and his peers worried that any attempt to push assimilation too quickly would merely result in Indians adopting the lowbrow culture of dime novels and moving pictures.[41]

But the common ground that Lindquist shared with his critics could not last in view of the emerging tectonic shift in public attitudes about assimilationist Indian policy. For even as Lindquist lumped Collier and Austin together with radical assimilationists in the threat they posed to the BIA, Lindquist's critics lumped his own more moderate views about assimilation with those of his radical opponents. This polarizing trend, which became full blown during Collier's administration, ultimately began in these debates over Indian dances.

That same tension between Lindquist's moderate views and the pressures toward polarization were particularly apparent in the deliberations of the Advisory

Council on Indian Affairs in December 1923. Convened by Interior Secretary Hubert Work, the Committee of 100 was Work's attempt to have prominent non-government figures set aside their hostilities and formulate some kind of consensus on which federal policies might be founded.

When the advisory council met on December 12, though, the sharp divisions among participants threatened to overshadow the entire gathering. In the all-important vote for the council chair, Arthur Parker—the missionaries' choice—was elected over Collier's pick by the razor-thin margin of thirty to twenty-nine.[42] As council members began considering the topic of "tribal life," Presbyterian missionary and Joint Indian Committee Chairman Thomas Moffett tried to build some consensus by proposing a mildly worded resolution on Indian dances. It commended Commissioner Burke for his circular letters on Indian dances and sought to clarify the limits of the government's intrusions in Native cultures. For example, the resolution stated that the government should not "curtail or infringe" upon the Indians' "lawful ancient ceremonies, rites, and customs." Also, the resolution "thoroughly commended" the Indians' "native arts and crafts" such as basketry, pottery, and blanket weaving. But it insisted that when Indian ceremonies "contravene the laws of the land, or the interests of morality, by concurrence of Indians and whites," they should be "discouraged and discontinued."[43]

With the motion on the floor, the discussion exploded in impassioned debate. Lindquist drowned out other voices as he introduced the documents that had come to drive the controversy. He proclaimed, "We do not take the attitude of prohibiting all dances and Indian ceremonials, but we take our stand on the matter of secret dances; and we do feel that we have the authority in the shape of testimonials and affidavits on file in this Indian Office, copies of which I hold in my hand, that [have] substantially the attitude that we hold." "If we want to maintain . . . the [Indians'] old life as it was hundreds of years ago," he added, then "let's do away with education; let's do away with the industrial program, the whole matter of land tenure, etc. Let's be consistent in the matter."[44]

Then John Collier rose to speak. He called the Pueblo tribes' religion "a system of ascetic expression" that was "older than Christianity." Comparing the "cooperative dramatic art" of Indian dances to Europe's Gothic cathedrals, Collier criticized the assimilationists' focus on the "alleged accidental immoralities that may flow from the expression of a great art." In his view, defending Pueblo cultures involved no inconsistency with his support for land and educational initiatives. For it was the preservation of the Indians' sacred communal life that spurred Collier to protect Indian lands in the first place. For the moment, though,

Lindquist's side emerged victorious when Moffett's compromise resolution passed on a voice vote.[45]

As the council meeting came to a close, a singular incident stole headlines about the gathering and further steeled Collier's resolve to uproot the Protestant missionary establishment in Indian affairs. For some months, the Institute for Social and Religious Research had been planning to present a decorated copy of Lindquist's survey to the president in a formal ceremony. Ruth Muskrat (Cherokee), a young poet and protégé of YWCA Indian Secretary Edith Dabb, was called upon to craft a brief address. But just days before the council met, the editorial secretary of the institute stumbled upon the idea of making the presentation later that week, when the council planned to meet at the White House. He quickly obtained Commissioner Burke's cooperation in arranging it.[46]

So on the afternoon of the council's last day, when the entire contingent of dignitaries met at 1600 Pennsylvania Avenue, this otherwise unscripted social event was interrupted by Muskrat's brisk march to the president's side. Attired in leather skins and beaded headdress, the Mount Holyoke College student offered Lindquist's book to Coolidge "in behalf of the many Indian students of America." The book, she stated, contained "an intelligent and sympathetic understanding of our needs and our longings," and it was sure to facilitate their quest to adapt to the world of "the white man" while "preserv[ing] the best that is in our ancient civilization."[47] When journalists questioned her about Indian dances, Muskrat quipped, "We have no patience with those sentimentalists whose cry is, 'Keep the Indian in his primitive state!' . . . We do not exist for artists to look at or slushy writers to misrepresent." After she finished speaking, Muskrat joined the entire council in posing with the president for press photographs. Then President Coolidge—who scarcely met members of the council, much less bothered to address them—whisked Muskrat away for a private luncheon.[48]

For Collier, this incident epitomized everything that went wrong with the Advisory Council on Indian Affairs. It positioned the Indians as grateful supplicants of the BIA and reinforced public sentiment for Indian assimilation. In an article for *Sunset* magazine, Collier sardonically described Muskrat as a "vision . . . beautiful and soft-voiced," and dismissed Lindquist's survey as "a book crowded with defects."[49] Privately, he called the book "absurd" and denounced the presentation as a "cheap trick," adding, "The President himself thought, as the reporters did, that we, C. of 100, were presenting the Lindquist book through our charming (tho to us unknown) spokeswoman."[50] Indeed, photographs of Muskrat and the book ceremony filled newspapers across the country, dominating reports of the council's proceedings.[51] In this event, at least, Collier found himself trapped by the behind-the-scenes maneuvering of a missionary establishment still close to the commissioner's ear.

Overall, however, the Indian dance controversy served more as an oracle of the difficulties that lay ahead. Even before the debate subsided, dozens of reservation superintendents flouted Burke's dance circular by failing to report on their progress against the "dance evil."[52] And by August 1924, the IRA was accusing Burke of making a complete surrender to Collier and the Pueblo traditionalists on the issues of Native religions.[53] Burke left his Christian supporters in the indelicate position of rallying in his defense, only to have him wilt in the face of opposition.

If Burke had intended his dance circular to strengthen the hand of the "true" friends of the Indians, then his attempt badly misfired. Publicity about the secret dance file, which Burke and the missionaries assumed would trump all opposition, did not really help the cause. The file's inaccessibility to public scrutiny left missionaries open to charges of sectarian prejudice in their evaluations of indigenous cultures. Missionaries themselves might have backed into the dance controversy through largely economic concerns about the Sioux Indians, but they readily followed Burke's lead to attack Pueblo and Hopi cultures as "barbaric regimes" of "unbridled license" and "cruelty."[54] The dance controversy laid bare the missionaries' thirst for legitimacy as the national custodians of the Indians' welfare.

Even more, the dance controversy began to alter the shape of Indian policy debates by adding to the dialogue a new, anti-assimilationist voice that would ultimately paint radical assimilationists and Lindquist's gradualists with the same broad stroke.[55] For Collier, the missionaries were scarcely different from the more culturally aggressive reformers they had been quarreling with for the previous twenty years. But in 1923, the lines of debate still fell along the older argument of whether to cooperate with the BIA or attack it from the outside. At the Committee of 100, the Protestant missionary establishment was pitted against both Collier, who generally opposed the BIA's policy of cultural assimilation, and the radical assimilationists, who faulted the BIA and missionaries for holding Indians back from full social integration. Indeed, at the end of the advisory council meeting, a last-minute alliance between Collier and the radical assimilationist Thomas Sloan (Omaha) drove home the compatibility of those two seemingly irreconcilable visions of reform. Sloan proposed that the BIA make definite plans to dismantle its programs within the next twenty years. Collier supported the move, not because he wanted to remove federal guardianship over Indian lands (as Sloan did), but because he wanted to bring new approaches into Indian affairs and could see little way to do so in the face of an entrenched bureaucracy.[56]

Lindquist and his associates defeated the proposal, but for them, the two extremes of the continuum on Indian affairs had just embraced in a common—and reckless—objective. Crowded between two other visions for reform, the missionaries continued to elbow their way toward what they regarded as a compassionate middle ground. Nevertheless, only the most perceptive visionary could have foreseen that twenty years later—at the time when Collier and Sloan would have the BIA brought to an end—Collier would already be the longest-serving Indian commissioner in the bureau's history, and Lindquist would be the gadfly seeking to discredit and abolish the Indian bureau. In 1923, conflicting agendas kept cultural pluralists, radicals, and missionary gradualists relatively distinct. But the dance controversy foreshadowed the day when Lindquist's approach to assimilation would be almost indistinguishable from that of his radical antagonists.

Guarding the Status Quo

At the close of the advisory council in December 1923, Lindquist returned to his position as religious work director at Haskell Institute in Lawrence, Kansas. For a time, personal factors seem to have distanced him from the national stage. His work required him to devote most of his time to administering a busy schedule of religious activities for students at Haskell. Then, in 1925, he spent several months in Sweden as a representative of the Congregational Church at the conference of the World Council of Churches. While there, he also toured the country lecturing to church audiences on Indian missions. Later that same year, tragedy struck when his son, seven-year-old Harvey, died of pneumonia, thus drawing Lindquist more deeply into his family and away from national politics.

Meanwhile, the Indian Rights Association responded to Collier's growing influence with a mixture of opposition and compromise. They carried on the fight for Protestant interests in Indian affairs by actively defending Commissioner Burke against Collier's more volatile accusations of corruption and neglect.[57] But the IRA's officers also cooperated with Collier and his American Indian Defense Association (AIDA) on the numerous causes they shared. With AIDA's support, the IRA drafted legislation granting citizenship to the last one-third of the Indian population who were not yet citizens.[58] The two organizations worked together to expose graft in Oklahoma's probate courts, where lawyers and judges had taken possession of valuable Native lands. They also found common ground in legislation to grant the Navajos and other tribes a more equitable share of oil and mineral royalties. In fact, the health, education, and social needs of American Indians were so overwhelming, and the exploitative pressures of western land interests so aggressive, that Collier and the IRA had surprisingly little difficulty putting their differences aside to improve Indian welfare.[59]

By contrast, Lindquist moved in circles where he would not have to show the slightest pretense of respect for Collier's agenda for reform. He could harden to the point of describing Collier as "ten times worse than the KKK."[60] Significantly, his period of withdrawal distanced him from the voices that were shaping a different policy direction. That became particularly apparent in 1930 when Lindquist reentered national politics through his appointment to the Board of Indian Commissioners (BIC). The BIC's intransigence in the face of pressures for reform helped to alienate Lindquist from the Indian Rights Association and the Home Missions Council, which tended to be more accommodationist in their approach to Collier.

The years from 1924 to 1933, then, represent a period of transition. Collier's drive to reform the BIA gathered juggernaut speed. Protestant and BIA executives increasingly pushed for moderate reforms in an attempt to head off a full-blown revolution. And Lindquist, confident that the BIA had been making reasonable progress all along, cast his lot with the defenders of the status quo.

Scholarship on this period has typically focused on Collier's reform efforts and the less radical adjustments supported by administration figures and many Protestant leaders. But a finer portrait can be drawn by attending to a third force represented by the Board of Indian Commissioners, most Protestant missionaries in the field, and a majority of BIA employees outside of Washington, D.C. Both contemporary observers and present-day scholars have commonly referred to this third force as the "Old Guard." And for that period, the term has a certain appropriateness. But this Old Guard ultimately provided the nucleus of a creative and effective opposition to Collier's administration. A closer examination of Lindquist's activities on the Board of Indian Commissioners, then, will help to uncover the social and institutional roots of a significant movement to overturn Collier's reforms in the 1930s and 1940s. Finally, attention to Lindquist's policy positions on the eve of Collier's appointment will show the persistence of his commitment to the BIA and the doctrine of Indian wardship in the early 1930s.[61]

By his own account, Lindquist's appointment to the Board of Indian Commissioners in 1930 came as a complete surprise.[62] His selection, however, was not altogether improbable. The BIC's chairman, Samuel A. Eliot, was also on the board of the Society for Propagating the Gospel (SPG), the missionary agency that had employed Lindquist since 1927.[63] Eliot, a Unitarian minister and son of

Harvard president Charles William Eliot, was familiar with Lindquist's work and knew that, although Lindquist lacked the wealth of other board members, his SPG position would give him the flexibility to carry out obligations to the BIC.[64]

Established by President Grant in 1869, the BIC was a ten-member citizen panel responsible for fighting corruption and agent malfeasance in the Indian service. Serving without pay, members were typically Protestant, wealthy, and personally invested in Indian affairs through church and philanthropic work. The board carried out its commission through firsthand investigations into reservation conditions and independent reports submitted to the secretary of the Interior. Its influence on legislation peaked in the late nineteenth century when it played a key role in formulating the assimilation policies of land allotment and education that dominated Indian affairs until the 1930s.[65]

By the 1920s, the BIC had joined other reform groups in supporting a prolonged period of federal guardianship over Indian properties.[66] That guardianship, of course, meant a more deeply entrenched role for the BIA, a rise in congressional appropriations for BIA expenditures, and yet another indefinite delay in the ultimate assimilation of the Indians. For radical reformers in the 1910s and 1920s, the BIC's support for an enlarged bureaucracy made the board appear to be little more than "an uncritical ally of the Indian Office." For the BIC, though, the federal government was the only thing that stood between the Indians and further economic devastation, and the humanitarian logic of assimilation required that Indian property be protected until the Indians had learned how to hold on to their property for themselves.[67]

Lindquist spent most of his three years on the Board of Indian Commissioners defending the BIA's educational and welfare programs from reforms inspired by Collier. Within days of his appointment, for example, he entered a formal protest against a proposal to place health and education services for California Indians in the hands of the state government. Collier supported the move as a way to break the BIA's hold on Indian affairs. BIA Commissioner Charles Rhoads (1929–1933) also supported the measure as an intermediate step toward assimilating California's Indians.[68] But, in a position he would reverse in the 1940s, Lindquist argued for keeping educational and health services in the hands of the federal government. "The history of California's treatment of her Indians," he wrote, has been "a black page on the nation's escutcheon." According to Lindquist, the Indians of California opposed such proposals because they feared that state-run schools and hospitals would refuse to serve them.[69]

Another issue that drew Lindquist's attention was the effort to improve BIA personnel along the lines recommended by the famous Meriam report published in 1928. Named for Lewis Meriam, a forty-three-year-old Harvard graduate and professional statistician who "epitomized the Progressive faith in scientific administration," this nine-hundred-page report became the blueprint for reforming Indian affairs under President Herbert Hoover between 1929 and 1932.[70] Among the recommendations actually implemented was the requirement that new employees in educational and supervisory positions hold college degrees, while existing employees who did not meet the standards were forced to retire or take lower-paying positions. Lindquist believed these changes worked a hardship on existing employees and invited the new hires to look with scorn upon senior personnel.

These complaints were both personal and philosophical. The former supervisor of the BIA's education system, Hervey B. Peairs—a close friend to Lindquist who had given him his first job at Haskell—was forced abruptly to retire in 1931 after forty-four years of service in the BIA. The new education supervisor, W. Carson Ryan Jr., did not so much as attend the retirement ceremony. Peairs's replacement at Haskell held a Ph.D. but had no prior experience in Indian education, and, true to Lindquist's expectations, he ran into so many problems that students vigorously protested his administration.[71]

Lindquist's misgivings over personnel reform also included concerns about the prospects for Indian employees, who constituted one-third of the BIA's payroll. For Lindquist, an important part of the BIA's guardian role was to give young Indian school graduates jobs in the Indian service, where they would not be required to compete directly with better educated white applicants, but still had opportunities for professional advancement. He treated Indian employment in the BIA as a form of "affirmative action," but the new personnel policies threatened to push Indian employees down into menial labor. "In view of the arbitrary raising of standards which involves academic degrees even for band masters," he wrote Chairman Eliot, "a great many worthy Indian people are automatically shut out of service to their own people. I, for one, deplore this situation."[72] In response to one of Lindquist's complaints, the head of the BIA's school system, W. Carson Ryan, insisted that "for the Indian's own sake it is important that he be held to the same standards as whites," or else the BIA might inadvertently foster a sense of racial inferiority.[73] "This sounds very lovely in theory," Lindquist replied, but it failed to take into account the Indians' lack of educational opportunity. By the time Indian students finished high school, financial pressures typically prevented them from "secur[ing] the college degrees required." As for current Native employees who lacked advanced schooling, Lindquist said that many had entered the BIA "under the impression that they met all qualifications and would be in line for promotion, all things being equal."[74] But without any allowances to grandfather in existing personnel, Ryan's policies threatened to stifle precisely those ambitions that assimilation policy sought to promote.

This conflict came to a head at a large conference of BIA employees in Oklahoma City in October 1931. Lindquist was attending as the official representative of the BIC, and fellow board members expected him to raise his personnel concerns in a face-to-face exchange with Ryan and other high-ranking officials. But Lindquist received specific instructions on how to go about it. When Lindquist addressed the conference itself, one BIC officer told him, he should do a "good talk" on cooperation and loyalty to the BIA, "but when you get with the inside group then you can go the limit . . . on the peril of Indian employees, the low morale . . . the discrimination in the way of salaries, etc., in favor of the new people."[75] Apparently, Lindquist did just that. He told Ryan that the new policies "work injustice to Indians" and disproportionately valued formal education over life experience. New employees, he complained, "enter the Service with a preconceived notion that everything in the Service . . . is wrong and that nothing short of radical change will satisfy the exigencies of the situation." Reporting on the meeting, Lindquist asserted that the BIC's "agitation" on personnel standards "will be productive" in the long run, but Lindquist's exchange with Ryan offered little hope in the immediate future.[76] The eastern educator feared that personnel changes were moving too slowly rather than too quickly, and Lindquist could only conclude that the BIC and the BIA's executives "do not see eye to eye in the matter of qualifications."[77]

Even more than personnel policies, the issue of federal guardianship over tribal assets loomed large over Lindquist's BIC engagements. One of the key factors that prompted Lindquist and many of his peers to assume a gradualist approach to assimilation after the turn of the century was their fear that whites and assimilated Indians of mixed descent would exploit full-bloods, who were thought to be less savvy in protecting their private property on an open market. So while assimilated Indians often pushed for legal changes that would liquidate tribal assets and remove federal restrictions on the sale of Indian property, more conservative tribe members preferred to keep those restrictions in place to avoid the dissipation of tribal resources. On the face of it, assimilationists like Lindquist would seem likely to support the approach of the assimilated Indians, since continued property restrictions might perpetuate the political, cultural, and social differences that separated Indians from whites. But in fact, Lindquist's gradualism placed him on the other side. He knew that this also committed him in favor of a larger, more costly federal bureaucracy, but, as he argued:

Too much of the speeding up process in seeking to push back the frontiers is foredoomed to failure. Our Government can well afford to ally itself with forces of time, which . . . will do a perfect work if not rushed. Should the Indian continue to be a federal responsibility another twenty-five years— what then? No doubt the federal treasury will still be intact. A rich Government will not be poorer. If the Indian is to be absorbed and assimilated into our body politic let it be a benevolent assimilation. Let us hope that this philanthropy will mean an enrichment of life to all concerned.[78]

With the ultimate assimilation of the Indians a foregone conclusion, Lindquist had no qualms about maintaining property protections that ran counter to assimilation in the short term, so long as they helped to make the process "benevolent."

A case in point was a dispute over the Klamath Indians' vast timber holdings in southern Oregon. Wade Crawford was a leader among the assimilated members of the tribe and a vocal critic of the BIA who sometimes worked with Collier to publicize his grievances. He wanted to sell the timber and divide the money among individual tribe members. A full-blood faction, on the other hand, viewed Crawford and his followers as a disgruntled group who had sold their individual land allotments, spent the income recklessly, and turned to tribal forests as a potential cash cow. With a vote of 102 to 68, the tribe voted to authorize Crawford as the tribe's formal representative in a delegation to Washington.

According to Lindquist's observations of the council meeting, there might have been a few voting irregularities as the full-bloods charged, but the real reason for Crawford's victory was the political sophistication of the educated tribe members who ran the council. "It was interesting to me to see how closely the tactics and methods which are practised by white men in political meetings were followed," Lindquist wrote. "There was the use of key speeches at the psychological moment, the well-timed applause . . . the advantageous confusion when the first vote was taken, the reading of telegrams and letters at the right moment, all nicely calculated to arouse enthusiasms and confuse the opposition." Since the Klamath tribal council was in the hands of an aggressive minority, Lindquist concluded that it was incompetent to manage the tribes' valuable timber for the collective good. So he recommended that the Department of the Interior disband the council and assert its authority to act as guardian over the Klamath reservation. Lindquist wrote, "The Department alone is charged with the responsibility of guardianship and should not be hampered by a few Klamath Indians who go to Washington . . . to embarrass the administration." Recognizing that his proposal ran counter to the ultimate goal of assimilation, he continued, "Permit me to remind you that the Indian Service is committed to the policy of individualizing and humanizing the Indian problem. . . . Any effort to individualize the Indians' property must take the human equation into account." The BIA's first goal, in Lindquist's view, should be that of "changing a way of living." If it succeeded in that slow educational process, he concluded, "perhaps the matter of individualizing the property will take care of itself."[79]

In this and dozens of similar reports, Lindquist resorted to federal guardianship as a means of easing the Indians' transition into American society. Bracketing egalitarian principles in the BIA's hiring and promotion practices, he called for continued preferences for Indian applicants and employees. Likewise, he used the BIA's authority over its wards to protect tribal properties.[80] His program for assimilation was fraught with inconsistencies and contradictions, but in the early 1930s, he was unwavering in the vigorous defense he mounted for the institution of the BIA itself. This point is important because it reveals that on the eve of Collier's appointment as Indian commissioner in 1933, Lindquist was still fighting the same policy battles he had fought since first entering the Indian field— struggles not against Collier's style of cultural pluralism, but skirmishes over the BIA's moral and legal obligation to protect the Indians' interests. Under Collier's administration, Lindquist would charge that BIA hiring preferences and protections over Indian lands patronized the Indians, perpetuated white racism, and thwarted assimilation. But until 1933, Lindquist was among the most aggressive in supporting the BIA's guardian responsibilities.

Unfortunately for Lindquist, who took great pride in serving as a commissioner, the election of Franklin D. Roosevelt to the presidency spelled the end of the BIC. Roosevelt appointed Collier to head the very Indian Office that he had attacked for more than a decade.[81] And as a longtime symbol of the Protestant establishment in Indian affairs, the BIC was one of Collier's first targets.[82] Lindquist and other board members tried to fend off the BIC's dissolution, but to no avail. At Collier's request, President Roosevelt ordered the sixty-four-year-old board to terminate its activities in June 1933. A revolution was about to begin.

In tracing Lindquist's involvement in the Indian dance controversy and the Board of Indian Commissioners, this chapter has sketched something of the political landscape of federal Indian policy before 1933. It has shown that missionaries and other reformers were divided over two different issues: whether to continue a policy of cultural assimilation, and whether to reform the BIA, dismantle it, or vaunt its existing authority as the most reliable guardian of Indian lands. I have argued that, in the polarizing wake of the Indian dance controversy and Collier's attacks on the BIA, Lindquist attempted simultaneously to maintain a moderate approach to cultural assimilation and a more rigid defense of the BIA itself as the guardian of the Indians' interests. This approach was viable so long as Lindquist remained on the inside, with close access to BIA officials. But with Collier's appointment, it could not survive the events that were soon to come.

3 Collier's New Deal for the Missionaries, 1933–1934

In characteristically vivid prose, Collier once told a *New York Times* interviewer that his goal as commissioner was to "plow up the Indian soul."[1] He wanted to bring to light the "spirit of oneness with nature" that lay hidden beneath decades of government hostility toward indigenous cultures. For Collier, knowledge of the Indians' "reverence for the web of life" could redeem the Western world from a "bleak winter" of self-seeking materialism and dissolve the unfortunate marriage of Christianity and nineteenth-century individualism. In fact, it was his repulsion at the federal policy of suppressing Native traditions in the early 1920s that convinced him to devote the rest of his life to reforming Indian affairs. Other activists, he recognized, had long been involved in protecting Indians from economic exploitation, but they shared in the government's view that Indian religions were, in the final analysis, an obstacle to the Indians' survival in American society. Collier hoped to turn that equation around, to show that Indian religions could serve as the very basis for the survival of American society itself, as well as enabling the Indians' own survival in the modern world.[2]

But to do that, he admitted, he would have to confront the "complex interdependent relationship of the Indian Service and various missionary bodies."[3] So how did Collier begin to translate his mystical insight into concrete, bureauwide reforms? What measures did he take, and what was their impact on Native cultures and missionary programs?

This book devotes the next two chapters to answering these questions. Chapter 3 examines Collier's reforms that sought specifically to dismantle missionary prerogatives and restore Native religious autonomy. Chapter 4 examines the controversies surrounding the Wheeler-Howard Act of 1934, which encapsulated Collier's overarching program for tribal self-government and land tenure. Taken together, these two chapters form the pivot on which the rest of the book hinges. For while missionary executives tried to take Collier's leadership in stride, Lindquist clearly saw the crisis that Collier's changes would bring, both to the activities of the missionaries and to the long-term prospects for Indian assimilation. The early months of Collier's administration marked a period of intense travel and lobbying for both Lindquist and Collier, and they deserve extensive treatment for the turmoil and uncertainty they created. Indeed, much of Lindquist's life must be viewed as his attempt to find an effective counterresponse to the changes Collier initiated in 1933 and 1934.

It would take some years, to be sure, before Lindquist moved away from an ad hoc response to Collier and toward formulating a more enduring strategy, particularly in his 1940s' drive to end what he called "Indian wardship." In fact, Lindquist's early efforts might well have been enough to minimize Collier's impact had his administration lasted only a few years. For, as this chapter shows, Collier's reforms were slow to take root as the skepticism and resistance of both Native Americans and BIA bureaucrats retarded Collier's progress toward his goals. But even in the first full year of Collier's administration, we can see Lindquist and others struggling with approaches that they would later develop to greater effect. Two of those approaches stand out in the chapter that follows. First, Lindquist stepped into a leadership vacuum as the strongest advocate for the scattered corps of field missionaries, who felt the brunt of Collier's changes on religious issues and were repeatedly frustrated by the accommodations of their missionary executives on the East Coast. Second, he formed new alliances at the national level with more radical reformers, such as Elaine G. Eastman and Flora Warren Seymour, who shared his antipathy to Collier and eventually drew Lindquist into a deeper opposition not just to Collier, but also to the BIA itself.

In this chapter, we will see how these changes began to grow from the aftermath of Collier's executive reforms on religious freedom—specifically his Circular Number 2970, which reversed BIA prohibitions on dances and other traditions, and his new regulations governing missionary activity in federal boarding schools. In the face of these two administrative policies, the consensus of missionary support for the BIA came into question as alliances became strained and new coalitions were formed. The chapter ends with a discussion of the more ideological dimensions of the religious conflict between Lindquist, his cohorts, and Collier.

Circular Number 2970

Issued in January 1934, Circular Number 2970 vigorously reasserted Indians' freedom to practice their religious traditions under the guarantees of the First Amendment. The policy statement instructed agency superintendents to grant Indians "the fullest constitutional liberty in all matters affecting religion, conscience and culture." Even more, Collier called upon all BIA employees to maintain "an affirmative, appreciative attitude toward Indian cultural values," while Native arts and crafts were to be "prized, nourished and honored." Reversing the pattern of the past several decades, Indian leaders were no longer expected to obtain permission for many of their dances and ceremonies, nor need they compromise the timing and duration of the events to meet government pressures toward hard work and self-sufficiency. Native languages, which had previously been proscribed in government schools, were now sanctioned as "vital, beautiful and efficient."[4]

If religious history were purely the product of formal, political power, then we might expect Collier's circular to have revolutionized the religious lives of Native Americans across the country. But instead, response to the circular stood mired in many of the habits and patterns that Collier sought to counteract. Native traditionalists, for example, were slow to react. Indigenous traditions that had long been suspended, modified, or pushed underground did not suddenly reappear in the bright light of day. In part, official policies of assimilation and Christianization had taken their toll in eroding Native practices. The late-nineteenth-century Ghost Dance, for example, had been effectively abolished. And an order from Washington could not guarantee its own enforcement in the field, especially among civil servants hired under previous administrations. Yet it is also true that Indian religions had persisted through resistance to official intent. What one writer said of tribes in the Southern Plains applied to other areas as well: "There is no renascence of Indian culture in central and western Oklahoma, because Indian culture there never died in order to be reborn." Collier's circular, then, did not precipitate dramatic reversals in the practice of indigenous religions. In 1934, Native Americans continued the complex negotiation of religious identity and practice that had characterized the previous several decades, only now with the promise of a sometimes-remote federal tolerance.[5]

There was at least one tangible sign, however, that some Native Americans began early on to take advantage of the circular's guarantees. Leaders of the Native American Church, an organization formed to protect the ritual use of the hallucinogenic plant peyote, revised their charter in 1934 to create room for a more distinctly non-Christian interpretation of their piety. When they first chartered the church in 1918, peyotists in southwestern Oklahoma described their worship as "the Christian Religion with the practice of the Peyote Sacrament." To be sure, not all peyotists understood their practice as a form of Christianity, but James Mooney, an anthropologist for the Bureau of American Ethnology, suggested that the Native American Church stress its continuities with Christianity in order to gain public tolerance. In April 1934, however, Collier's new policies emboldened Native American Church leaders to omit any references in their charter to the Christian religion, describing their worship instead as "the sacramental use of the earthly plant known as Peyote with its teachings of love of God and right living." While many Native Americans might have taken Collier's support for their traditions as yet another transitory phase of Washington policy, the new charter of the Native American Church demonstrated that at least some began to act on the promise of religious freedom.[6]

Like Native Americans, BIA employees had to feel their way toward a full understanding of what Collier's new policy would entail. Of course, the short-term fallout placed career field agents in something of a bind. Ten years earlier, they had been expected to comply with Commissioner Charles Burke's circulars against Indian dances, and now they had to convince a new commissioner that they could honor his positive stance toward Native cultures. For those already sympathetic with Collier's attitude, the new regulations provided the opportunity to carry out their own convictions. For others, finesse was the order of the day. Since at least some measure of compromise with indigenous customs had been a necessary part of administering BIA agencies anyway, most field agents were able to point to their begrudging toleration of Indian religions as if it were a positive sign of affirmation. Thus agents from North Carolina to California acknowledged Circular 2970 by evincing their appreciation for tribal customs and material art. They spoke of Indian decorations in homes and offices, their active participation in Navajo "sings" and Indian fairs, and the various occasions in years past when they had protected their charges from overzealous missionaries.[7] However, W. O. Roberts, superintendent of the Rosebud Indian Agency in South Dakota, was more candid than most when he told Collier that he was complying with the circular on religious freedom, but he feared repercussions from influential Christian Indians on the reservation. If they stopped cooperating with his administration, he indicated, his ability to carry out other policy initiatives might be sharply curtailed.[8] Situated between Collier's orders on the one hand and powerful Christian factions on the other, BIA agents sought to keep the peace—and their jobs.

For most of those missionary executives who made up the ecumenical Joint Indian Committee, Collier's new directive was received with expressions of "concern" but surprisingly little protest.[9] They had long regarded themselves as members of a de facto religious establishment, uniquely positioned to maintain a productive dialogue between church leaders in Indian missions and government figures in Indian affairs. Their relative silence, then, betrayed the strength of their conviction that a cooperative approach to Collier would gain more for missionary interests than outright public opposition. That silence also owed something to the influx of a new group of committee members who were sensitive to growing pressures in favor of the Indians' civil liberties. For example, Mark Dawber, a Methodist expert on rural churches and a rising member of the Home Missions Council, conceded that religious freedom for both Native Christians and Native traditionalists "is all we have a right to ask."[10]

In contrast, missionaries in the field typically viewed Collier's reforms with reproach, if not outright alarm. For them, Collier bore the brunt of responsibility for what they perceived as a steep rise in reservation drunkenness, violence, and immorality. Lindquist spoke for them when he complained to the Indian Rights Association of there being "more drinking and general carousing than ever before."[11] One of his informants, a tribal court judge with strong missionary ties, reported that Indian dances were now taking place "every two or three weeks" around Yuma, Arizona. Since the sponsors of the dances "are not obliged to ask permission," the informant stated, "there is no [police] protection for the younger generation." Marriages were breaking up, law enforcement was lax, and underage Indian girls were being victimized by the predatory lusts of syphilis-infected men. This moral chaos, he continued, had nothing to do with a genuine revival of pre-Columbian traditions. Rather, Collier's support for Indian religions was being manipulated as a cover for moral license, the likes of which would never have been tolerated under "the old custom."[12] Some observers blamed the increased alcohol abuse and vice on the repeal of Prohibition and the cash earnings that many Indians enjoyed through work for government agencies during the Depression.[13] But others looked to the "devil" as the root of government sanction for Indian dances, along with the orgy of sex and drunkenness that purportedly followed in their wake.[14]

Along with sparking reports of a decline in Indian morality, Collier's Circular 2970 also threatened to poison the working relationship between missionaries and BIA agents in the field. Rumors spread about a wave of anticlericalism in the Indian bureau that mirrored ominous trends in Mexico and other parts of the world.[15] Baptist workers among the Crow Indians in Montana, for example, reported to Lindquist that a recently employed BIA agent had ridiculed them at a large public gathering, suggesting that their work was no longer in line with federal policies.[16] Reservation superintendents in some areas evicted missionaries who, through ad hoc arrangements, had been allowed to occupy agency housing without paying rent. And in a few boarding schools, administrators put an immediate halt to missionary activities on campus.[17]

With the federal government controlling the spaces and institutions where the vast majority of missionary contacts with the Indians occurred, Christian workers felt unusually susceptible to the caprice of an Indian commissioner who seemed hostile to their endeavors. Indeed, Circular 2970 on religious freedom highlighted a weakness in Indian missions that had been present for decades but only now became a full-blown vulnerability. George Hinman, a Home Missions Council liaison with the BIA in the early thirties, contemplated that weakness on the eve of Collier's appointment when he wrote, "The work of present-day missionaries among Indians can never be wholly free from dependence on the Indian Service." At the most fundamental level, it was the Bureau of Indian Affairs that possessed the authority to grant or deny land to missionary agencies for new missions. Moreover, for reasons of expedience, "a considerable portion" of missionary work was "based on some Indian agency or government institution." Why, most missionaries had thought, would they want to build a mission church at some isolated point when a church near the BIA agency headquarters and boarding school would guarantee them the greatest possible exposure to the Indian population? It was far better, they believed, to meet the Indians where they conducted official business than to track them down one household at a time on their far-flung reservations.[18] However, a strategy that made sense in an era of missionary-government cooperation had, with Collier's appointment, become seriously flawed.

The "Golden Calf": New Regulations on Religious Instruction

The missionaries' vulnerability can be seen with greatest clarity by examining the issues surrounding Collier's new regulations on missionary activity in federal boarding schools, which he released just days after Circular 2970. At the same time, a close look at the issue of religious instruction also shows once more the enormous difficulties Collier faced in making substantive changes in the widely dispersed field offices of the BIA. Even more, the controversy over religious instruction revealed a growing rift between field missionaries and their denominational leaders on the East Coast. And it was that rift that allowed Lindquist to assume an influential mediating role in opposing Collier.

Before I describe the new regulations and the deliberations that produced them, it is important to note that the boarding school system for Indian children grew out of the late-nineteenth-century push to assimilate the Indians as rapidly as possible. Bureau officials and Protestant leaders believed that by training an entire generation of Indian children in the ways of civilization, the "Indian problem" could be solved in just a few short years. By the 1920s, the early optimism had waned under the influence of scientific racism and the ongoing resistance of both Native children and their parents. Rather than a gateway into the world of public schools and industrial occupations, federal boarding schools became part of an entrenched bureaucracy, more isolating than assimilating in their impact on Indian children.

Despite their problems, federal boarding schools were—from a logistical point of view—an important point of contact between missionaries and Indians. With thousands of Indian youth concentrated in a dozen or so large boarding schools, missionaries had a form of access to the Indians unparalleled on sparsely populated reservations. Moreover, important BIA officials had long supported the churches' involvement in the everyday work of Indian education. Hervey B. Peairs (1866–1940), a close friend of Lindquist's who served as superintendent of the BIA's school system for more than twenty years, believed that if the churches cooperated in their boarding school ministries, school graduates could "become the best missionaries to their people."[19]

So when Collier assumed the reins of the Bureau of Indian Affairs, he faced a long-established and stable code of collaboration between Indian educators and Christian missionaries. In fact, the official regulations governing missionaries on school campuses had remained virtually unchanged since 1910, when conflicts between Catholic and Protestant missionaries forced the BIA to intervene against sectarian proselytizing. According to those regulations, parents indicated their denominational affiliation on the school application, while pupils with no church membership were "encouraged to affiliate with some denomination" upon arrival at boarding school, with the exact form of that encouragement left open to local interpretation. For their part, missionaries and local pastors were allowed one or two hours per week for weekday religious instruction in the students' respective traditions. Schools also offered space for denominations to organize Sunday school and worship services on weekends. And on Sunday evenings, all students in a given school—whether they claimed a denominational tradition or not—gathered for a "nonsectarian" assembly, with hymns and scripture readings carefully chosen by the Washington office so as to avoid factional grumbling.[20]

For Collier, these regulations unfairly favored Christianity over traditional forms of Native religious practice. They excluded instruction in indigenous traditions, and they contained no safeguards against compulsory attendance at programs of Christian worship. In fact, the plenary "nonsectarian" assembly on Sunday evenings explicitly offered a Christian message of moral uplift as one of the formal components of boarding school education. Moreover, the existing regulations assumed that, once a student's denominational affiliation (if any) had been determined, the child's parents would automatically want him or her to be enrolled in weekday religious instruction by a denominational representative. Collier believed, however, that in the interest of religious liberty, consent to religious instruction should not be taken for granted. Many Native parents might make some kind of claim to denominational affiliation because that was part of the student application process—not because they identified themselves that closely with any particular brand of Christianity or expressly desired to see their children receive Christian training.[21]

But before Collier could make any changes, he had to deal face-to-face with the Protestant missionary leaders who represented a powerful missionary and Native Christian constituency. So, in the late summer of 1933, Collier did not issue a new set of regulations as a fait accompli. Instead, perhaps in an effort to build bridges or assess his opposition, he introduced a tentative draft of new regulations to the Joint Indian Committee, and asked for advice from the executives who made up the committee. The draft began as the committee might have wished, by crediting Christian missionaries for the "contribution of good" they had made throughout the history of Indian-white relations. But it rather abruptly reminded readers that the federal government held jurisdiction over the lands and buildings in which most missionary work took place. "As a privilege but not as a right," therefore, missionaries were to be permitted access to boarding school facilities in order to contact students and carry out devotional and educational programs. Compulsion, the draft continued, was strictly forbidden. And weekday religious instruction was limited to students whose parents "knowingly and voluntarily" registered a direct request in writing before their superintendent, a requirement significantly more restrictive than filling in a line on an enrollment form. Finally, the draft allowed "any representative of a native Indian religion" the same privileges as Christian missionaries.[22]

The Joint Indian Committee acquiesced in Collier's desire to remove the compulsory elements of religious instruction from federal boarding schools. Committee members had come to accept at least some of Collier's changes as inevitable.[23] After conceding the question of compulsion, though, the Joint Indian Committee voiced two concerns about the tentative draft of regulations. First, it asked Collier to remove the menacing statements about the BIA's authority over missionary activities. Once again, missionaries were vulnerable on this point, and the committee wanted some assurance that that vulnerability would not be used to antagonize church workers. Accommodating their request, Collier struck the objectionable clauses and added a statement instructing school officials to "cooperate with the missionaries" in carrying out parents' requests.[24]

The Joint Indian Committee proved less successful with a second concern: their objection against granting school privileges to practitioners of Native religions. Their inconsistency should be readily apparent. Whereas committee members resisted Collier's assertions of federal authority over their own religious activities, they nevertheless called upon government officials to flex that authority against Native traditionalists. Despite an apparent double standard, they called for amending the original draft to grant school privileges only to those whose activities were "helpful in the character development of the pupils." According to their proposal, school superintendents—who typically were friendly toward Christian missions—would be responsible for judging the value of Christian and Native programs. Although committee members were willing to subject Christian missionaries to the same approval process as Native traditionalists, their recommendation still indicated that they were not willing for the federal government to give up its control over indigenous traditions. In their view, school superintendents were more competent than non-Christian parents to determine whether training in tribal traditions contributed to "character development."[25] But in this case, Collier rejected the committee's proposed amendment, leaving judgments about the qualifications of a religious representative up to Indian parents.

This inside look at how the new regulations were developed clearly shows that in dealing with the leadership level of the BIA, missionary executives were pragmatic in their aspirations. They understood the general direction of Collier's administration, and they adapted accordingly. And even though they did not win concessions from Collier on every point, they nevertheless seemed content with Collier's acknowledgment that they belonged with him at the bargaining table. Engagement in some kind of reciprocal relationship with Collier was, for them, perhaps as important as the outcome of the negotiations. In fact, when field missionaries complained bitterly about the new regulations, the Joint Indian Committee defended them on the grounds that they had had a hand in writing them.[26]

Missionary executives had more working in their favor, however, than a symbolic concession or two from Collier. And that may help explain their satisfaction with the results. For in practice, many of Collier's changes in religious instruction had little effect on the everyday workings of the school missionaries. Several key factors appear to account for this.

First, missionaries in BIA schools faced very little competition from indigenous traditions because tribal religious leaders apparently did not take advantage of the liberty Collier's new regulations offered them. Given the BIA's history, many of them might have been skeptical about the true scope of the new privileges in government schools. It is possible, too, that many tribal communities had already developed relatively effective ways of reincorporating their children into Native traditions once they returned to their communities.[27] Also, indigenous religions tended to articulate their views of the sacred in ritual and spatial terms, making it difficult to adapt meaningful religious training to a Western classroom setting, where Christian doctrine and catechesis by contrast were well suited. And among many tribes, such as the Hopi in Arizona, religious rituals were embedded within a multigenerational network of clans and religious societies. That network of relationships and obligations, like the rituals themselves, could hardly be replicated in residential schools.[28] However well intended, the extension of school privileges to Native religions proved an empty victory for Collier—a strike for freedom in principle, but a relative failure in practice.

Skepticism and reluctance on the part of Native Americans were not the only problems Collier faced in implementing his executive order. A second factor in obstructing Collier's new regulations was the antagonism of the BIA's civil service employees. Many subordinates in the BIA viewed Native religions as an obstacle to the Indians' moral, intellectual, and physical well-being. For example, the superintendent of the Pine Ridge Agency in South Dakota feared that members of the Native American Church, who used the hallucinogenic plant peyote in their sacrament, would request permission to "teach the peyote habit" to school children. He had already compromised his convictions when, in accordance with Collier's earlier circular on religious freedom, he permitted peyote services to take place on the reservation, even though state law prohibited the drug. But his conscience would not allow him to recognize the Native American Church as a "legitimate organization" for instructing Indian children.[29]

More common than overt opposition was BIA employees' passive resistance to the new regulations, particularly with regard to the ban on compulsion. A wealth of evidence suggests that school superintendents used administrative drag and confusion to preserve existing arrangements with missionaries and alleviate the hassles involved in gaining explicit parental consent for religious instruction. Henry Roe Cloud, Lindquist's friend and former missionary partner, was superintendent of the BIA-run Haskell Indian Institute in Lawrence, Kansas, when Collier issued the new guidelines from Washington. Roe Cloud informed Collier that most of the compulsory Sunday assemblies at Haskell dealt with "student morale and student organizations," not religion. And when the meetings did stress religious themes, "equal opportunity has been given to all denominations to listen to the various speakers respectively." With this assurance, which took no account of students' commitments to indigenous traditions, Roe Cloud believed he had obviated any possible objections.[30]

Other school administrators saw no compelling reason to alter arrangements that seemed to satisfy everyone involved. After stalling for over a year, the superintendent of a Navajo school in Arizona finally asked Collier whether the regulations were indeed meant to apply to his jurisdiction, since "there is but one missionary here and the Indians have not at any time protested against his activities."[31] According to F. W. Boyd, superintendent of Warm Springs Agency in Oregon, church attendance had been routine for so many years that his students were "accustomed" to it and lacked any "feeling that they were being forced to attend religious services against their will."[32] At Salem Indian school in Oregon, James T. Ryan believed he could fulfill the intent of the regulations by excusing from church attendance only those students whose parents expressly asked that they be excused. Besides, he added incredulously, nothing in the Protestant program "would interfere with anyone's religious ideas" after all, since it dealt primarily with what he called "character building."[33]

Even for those superintendents most determined to free the Indians from missionary domination, changes in the school program were difficult to implement without causing all kinds of scheduling and personnel headaches. For example, church attendance at Sherman Institute in Riverside, California, dropped by as much as one-half following announcement of the new regulations.[34] And that kind of fluctuation could ripple across any school's program. Children choosing not to attend church services or religious instruction would require added supervision by an already overworked faculty, and new programs would have to be developed to occupy those students' time. Imagine the frustration of Alida Bowler, who entered the Indian Service as one of Collier's most enthusiastic supporters. She sternly informed the Episcopal missionary at her Nevada school that his compulsory program "was absolutely contrary to present policies" and that she was certain many parents would prefer their children "not receive the Christian teachings which he was prepared to give." Yet the contingencies of school administration forced her to tell him that no changes would take place until the school was more adequately staffed.[35]

A third factor that slowed implementation of Collier's new regulations on religious instruction was confusion over parental consent and the limits of religious compulsion. Did the principle of in loco parentis mean that school officials must compel children to go to church if their parents wanted them to be compelled? Should children be allowed to go to church if they were willing but their parents were not (or had not given express consent)? These questions and many others were too numerous and detailed for Collier and his top advisors to answer with uniformity. And when they did intervene to correct local misinterpretations, their recommendations were often inconsistent and liable to still more differing interpretations.

The general direction should have been clear: Collier was changing the fundamental orientation of the BIA toward Native religions and restoring the authority of Indian parents to resist the Christianization of their children. But the BIA's educational system, however hierarchical its authority structures might have been, was too large and unwieldy to change quickly. Existing relationships between missionaries and school officials—and the precise arrangements for religious instruction they had made—were the product of a process of adaptation that had taken place slowly and with different results in various locales. It would take some time for the revolution at the top of the bureaucracy to create the desired evolution at the bottom.

For these reasons, missionary executives took Collier's new regulations in stride. They had seen Indian commissioners come and go, and they probably expected Collier's tenure to be just as transient as the others. They were confident that they could represent their field missionaries' interests in an ongoing dialogue with the commissioner, and do so with minimal disruptions in the missionaries' work. And to some extent, their instincts were right. But on some issues, the Home Missions Council proved unresponsive to missionary concerns, and on those issues, it was Lindquist who played a key role in redressing grievances against the new policy.

The problems involved with obtaining parental consent for religious instruction offer the best example of Lindquist using his field connections to effect a change in policy. As noted earlier, Collier required that parents register their consent to religious instruction at their respective agency headquarters, in the presence of the local bureau superintendent. It requires little imagination to appreciate the Herculean task missionaries faced in abiding by the new requirement. They resented the days and weeks involved in contacting their parishioners, informing them of the new regulations, and following up to see if consent had in fact been given. Indian parents frequently lacked access to means of transportation, and the agency office could be as far as two or three hundred miles away. For missionaries and Christian parents already wary of Collier's appointment as commissioner, the new regulations seemed calculated to drive Christianity out of government schools.[36] Indeed, a few superintendents put an immediate halt to missionary activities on campus in February 1934, confirming the fears of local Christian leaders. And although school officials promised to resume the program of religious instruction in the next school year, after parental consent had been obtained, missionaries bitterly denounced the lengthy interruption of their work.[37]

Missionary workers in federal boarding schools might have felt more at ease about matters if they trusted their own missionary executives on the Home Missions Council to lobby for their interests in Washington. But their representatives on the East Coast focused instead upon calming their fears and downplaying their complaints. Impressed by Collier's skills of persuasion and unwilling to disturb their working relationship with him, missionary administrators repeatedly expressed their trust in Collier's goodwill. In a circular letter to the Joint Indian Committee's religious work directors in federal boarding schools, Ann Seescholtz from the Council of Women for Home Missions and William R. King from the Home Missions Council insisted that Collier did not intend to "handicap" their work or break up the Indians' "church life." They defended the new regulations, saying that Collier had amended the new policy according to their wishes, and they stressed that Collier positively instructed BIA personnel to cooperate with the missionaries in carrying out parents' instructions.[38]

But most field missionaries went unconvinced. For a more sympathetic ear, they turned to G. E. E. Lindquist, a Home Missions Council member, to be sure, but a field representative who was in closer touch with their concerns than the dismissive executives in New York City. Lindquist had been a key figure in helping the Home Missions Council organize religious instruction in boarding schools since the 1910s, and he believed his associates on the interdenominational council had been too quick to sanction Collier's revised regulations. On his own copy of the final draft, in fact, Lindquist indicated his sense of alienation from the deliberative process when he scribbled, "They put it in the fire and out came this calf."[39]

In October 1934 Lindquist cosponsored a meeting of thirty Oklahoma missionaries to voice concerns about Collier's apparent hostility to Christian activities.[40] In a series of "findings" most likely penned by Lindquist himself, missionaries argued that the ban on compulsion contradicted the government's responsibility to fulfill parents' wishes about their children's religious instruction. For them, government compulsion of Indian children did not deny religious freedom if it was based on the voluntary faith of Indian parents. And in opposition to the opportunities Collier granted to Native religionists for religious instruction, the Oklahoma conferees called for a study "of the effects of certain religious ceremonies on the moral, physical, and mental life of the children." They had no intention of violating the Indians' religious freedom, they insisted, but as missionaries, they sought to build up Native societies by offering, implicit within the gospel, "what is best in [indigenous] culture and present well-being."[41]

Collier's response was swift and bitter. In a press release the next day, he claimed the missionaries at the Oklahoma conference were a small minority of extremists whose missionary boards had already given their approval for the new regulations. Surely, he concluded, it was only because these missionaries' "arts of persuasion" were "weak or nonexistent" that they needed the help of official coercion to carry out their work among Indian children.[42]

Knowing that his own Home Missions Council was not likely to take up the missionaries' cause, Lindquist sent the conference findings to Matthew Sniffen of the Indian Rights Association (IRA), a leading Protestant reform organization with offices in Philadelphia and Washington, D.C.[43] But before the IRA could conduct an investigation, Collier preempted some of their concerns by revising the regulations in two ways. Whereas previously parents made their written requests in the presence of the superintendent, Collier made it possible for them to register their requests before an official representative of the superintendent. That slight revision allowed missionaries to travel across reservations with an authorized witness close by to gather parents' written requests. Collier also allowed parents to make a verbal request for religious instruction in those cases where parents could not read English and where they had resolved, after years of dealings with non-Natives, never to trust anything in writing.[44]

With these revisions, the prospects for religious instruction became somewhat better than before. Parents were better able to procure religious instruction for their children if they wished, and missionaries could better cope with the logistical problems created by the requirement of parental consent. Moreover, as long as sympathetic school superintendents still dominated the BIA, missionaries could count on some flexibility in local interpretations of the rules.

But Collier's regulations had replaced in principle, if not yet in practice, the inherited prerogatives of Christian education with the broader tolerance of religious pluralism. In the area of federal Indian education, Collier transformed the churches' role from a cooperative partner in the common task of cultural assimilation, into a special interest group with narrow, self-preservationist goals.[45] Rather than a collaborator in racial uplift, missionaries were deemed a threat to individual and collective freedoms. And the louder they objected to this change, the more they seemed to prove Collier's premise that missionaries had been coddled all along. That no doubt is why most denominational executives on the Home Missions Council refused to protest the new regulations, choosing instead to jump at the bone of cooperation Collier offered in their formulation. Up against accommodationist leaders who left them exposed to Collier's charge of extremism, aggrieved missionaries fell back upon the assistance of Lindquist and their working relationships with school personnel to preserve their opportunities for religious instruction.

In Defense of Christian Civilization

These more or less technical debates over school regulations did not encompass the full scope of the Protestant response to Collier's cultural pluralism. Of course, they tell an important part of that story, for in the field, the ultimate test of the missionaries' quasi-establishment was a practical one: to what degree would the federal government discourage tribal religions and encourage missionary access to BIA institutions? But there was another battle engaged against Collier's executive reforms that did not restrict itself to behind-the-scenes negotiations over administrative protocols. That battle took place in the public forum of the national religious media, where the belligerents fought, in their minds, for the very future of Christian civilization.

In shifting the discussion from institutional to rhetorical matters, it is important to recognize that most of the people who joined Lindquist in the media charge against Collier's religious pluralism were reformers with affinities for the radical version of assimilation policy. Until 1933, Lindquist had remained at arms' length from most radicals. He even accused them of trying to "ram" American civilization down the Indians' "throat" without regard for their dignity and the positive cultural contributions Indians might make to a composite national way of life.[46] But in the face of Collier's administrative stance toward indigenous traditions, Lindquist saw that this was no time for the ambivalent attitudes of the gradualist approach. He therefore gravitated closer to the small network of the nation's best-known radical reformers.

One of the more formidable radical assimilationists to team up with Lindquist was Flora Warren Seymour (1888–1948), author of several popular books on the historic frontier. A resident of Chicago, she was also a lawyer well qualified to tease out the legal implications of Collier's proposals. In 1922 she became the first woman to serve on the Board of Indian Commissioners, where she met Lindquist upon his appointment to the board in 1930. With Lindquist, she had resisted the moderate reforms of the Rhoads-Scattergood administration and deeply resented Collier's decisive move to abolish the board when he became commissioner.[47] But until 1933, she and Lindquist had frequently been at odds on the issue of federal guardianship. While Lindquist favored maintaining government protections over Indian lands and slowing the assimilation process in order to protect less assimilated full-bloods, Seymour advocated the more hard-nosed "sink or swim" approach characteristic of radical assimilationists.[48] Lindquist's friends in the Indian Rights Association called her "rather extreme" and "erratic," but over the course of Collier's twelve-year career as Indian commissioner, Lindquist would forsake his gradualist leanings and join with Seymour to take part in a sizeable reaction against Collier's policies.[49]

Seymour's most widely read attack on Collier's religious pluralism appeared in the *Missionary Review of the World,* a middle-of-the-road digest of features and news from around the Protestant world. In her alliteratively titled article, "Federal Favor for Fetishism," she argued that Collier had betrayed the nation's Christian past by "fostering . . . primitive ritualism" as if it were the "law of the land." In a pattern that would fit Lindquist's radical allies more than Lindquist himself, Seymour attacked Collier in large part by attacking Indian cultures themselves. The BIA, she argued, had a legal obligation to limit the religious freedom of its Indian wards, especially when Native cultures (allegedly) sanctioned such patently immoral activities as "ritual prostitution" and polygamy. Public health problems on Indian reservations likewise betrayed for her the absolute necessity of making critical judgments about the overall value of Native traditions. She described cases where young children had reportedly been killed by the ministrations of medicine men and where tribal curing ceremonies had done little more than spread contagious disease, without relief for those originally infected. In short, she argued that Commissioner Collier, the nation's guardian of Indian health and welfare, could not possibly improve the lives of American Indians and, at the same time, protect and promote their adherence to traditional cultures. Missionaries caught in the cross fire of Collier's conflicting goals, she advised, should stand firm in the knowledge that they had "something of value to offer"—namely, the "fellowship of faith and the ways of Christian civilization."[50]

Another important public advocate for the missionaries was Elaine Goodale

Eastman (1863–1953), a septuagenarian author from western Massachusetts. Unlike Lindquist, Eastman had been brought up in Indian affairs during the time when radical assimilationists like Richard Pratt dominated the scene, before missionary gradualists helped swing the reform establishment toward a slower, more selective approach to Indian assimilation. She taught Indians at the Hampton Institute in Virginia, which pioneered in Indian education. Later, she served as a teacher and school inspector for the BIA in South Dakota. There she married Charles Eastman (Ohiyesa), a Santee Sioux physician with Dartmouth credentials. In 1890 the two met in South Dakota on the eve of the Wounded Knee massacre. And, after witnessing firsthand the ineptitude and rank political patronage that thrived in the Indian administration, they became lifelong advocates for the abolition of the BIA and with it, the removal of government protections over Indian lands. By the 1930s, Elaine had become estranged from her husband, in part over his end-of-life attempt to recapture the folkways of his tribal childhood. For Elaine, though, any compromise on the total cultural assimilation of the Indians smacked of racist doubts about the Indians' full capacity for civilization. As a result of the estrangement, Elaine shifted her writing energies toward her own projects and away from editing her husband's popular books on Indian folklore. Creating public opposition to Collier became her primary ambition toward the end of her life, and she seemed to relish the opportunity to revive the strong racial egalitarianism that had once inspired so much optimism in the assimilationist project.[51]

Eastman took her case to *Christian Century,* a prominent liberal journal with editorial sympathies for Collier's reforms.[52] Like Seymour, she spent a good bit of time detailing Native customs almost certain to offend the journal's well-to-do Euro-American readers: the "bloody ordeal" of the Sun Dance, the self-mutilations of grieving widows, and the "trance-like stupor" of the peyotists. For that majority of Native Americans who had been exposed to Western education and Christian missions, she argued, Collier's desired restoration of pagan religions would be a curious imposition. For those wavering between two cultures, Collier's efforts would most likely lead to the unfortunate creation of more syncretic or "bastard religions," like the ill-fated Ghost Dance or the quasi-Christian peyote cult. And for those southwestern tribes who offered the most promising laboratory for Collier's desired "Red Atlantis," Eastman saw a future of social degeneration as American civilization crowded around them. The only prospect Native religions held, in her view, was in the tawdry world of "tourist attractions and commercial enterprises." A Pueblo ceremony might be "financially profitable," she quipped, "but is it spiritually edifying?" Collier's policy, she argued in conclusion, "tends not to the promised full enfranchisement, but rather to a perpetual twilight of insincere praise and actual inferiority."[53]

In his reply, published directly below Eastman's article, Collier sardonically thanked Eastman for making his case so plain by her virtual admission that Indian religions were not, in her view, religions at all. According to Collier, Indian religions contained all the components of the most exalted human spirituality—mystical experience, moral vision, ritual art, and an enlarged consciousness of "the world-will." Indian religions therefore deserved constitutional protections no less than Eastman's own Episcopal tradition.[54] Elsewhere, Collier argued that rather than favoring paganism over Christianity, he was "seeking to encourage every life-giving factor, ancient as well as new, in the experience of the Indian." If the Indian can be sustained "in his *whole* self," according to Collier, he "can take more . . . from the white world . . . than the Indian who has been bereft of his own past or who has chosen to renounce it."[55]

Not willing to let the debate end with Collier's reply, Eastman further countered by insisting on her attitude of deep respect for indigenous religions, at least in their pristine forms. As she pointed out, she had collaborated with her husband on *The Soul of the Indian* (1911), a glowing tribute to precontact Siouan spirituality.[56] That in itself proved, in her mind, her sensitivity toward "the important values of the primitive faith and worship—*for the primitive* [emphasis added]."[57] The larger question for her was whether a primitive faith could remain free from degradation in the context of a superior, aggressive civilization. She thought not. Indeed, she doubted whether the "poetic mysticism" of Indian religions would long survive without the artificial support of "external suggestion and official encouragement."[58]

Lindquist chimed in his support to Eastman's argument with a letter of his own to the *Christian Century*. Without quite indulging in the polemics of Seymour and Eastman, he underscored Eastman's claim that a near majority of American Indians were already Christians. For them, he noted, a "revival of tribalism" would only be a bizarre "anachronism." The culture of the Plains Indians in particular "vanished with the buffalo," making Collier's efforts there "foredoomed to failure." "All Indians," Lindquist concluded, "must be saved 'by a process of Christian assimilation to American life' and not by a carefully guarded and subsidized segregation."[59]

Recognizing that as Euro-American Christians, their own authority in tribal religions could be called into question, Seymour, Eastman, and Lindquist worked to publicize the views of Native Americans themselves who rejected Collier's policies on Indian religions. Eastman, for example, was able to convince J. C. Morgan (1879–1950) to join her in writing against Collier in *Christian Century*.[60] Morgan was a missionary for the Christian Reformed Church and the leader of an important political faction within the Navajo tribe. He feared that Collier would isolate the Indians by sending them "back to the blanket" and transforming the Navajo reservation into a "monkey show" for gawking tourists and anthropologists.[61] Speaking as a Navajo who "should know the inside life of my own people," he condemned the backwardness of Navajo living conditions and singled out the healing ceremonies of medicine men as a deadly form of "pagan surgery."[62] Collier responded by calling Morgan "a victim of theological bias" against Navajo traditions. He wrote that he opposed "that form of blindness which sees no virtue except in one's own doctrines, conventions and superstitions. The Navajo religion is a lofty one—lofty in the ethical and in the esthetic meaning. So is Mr. Morgan's religion. The Navajo religion is infinitely tolerant of its competitors. . . . I wish that Mr. Morgan could learn tolerance from his fellow Indians."[63]

But in the tense atmosphere that surrounded Indian affairs in 1934, it was difficult to see how any position at all on Indian religions could be truly free from bias. And with so many Native Americans themselves holding leadership positions within Indian churches, the debate could scarcely be understood as a conflict between Indians and Euro-Americans. Christianity had become indigenized, and Collier's policies would have no choice but to take that into account.

For Lindquist, Morgan, and other Christian writers, then, Collier erred in his patent denial of the essential unity of Christianity and civilization, missions and moral uplift, Protestantism and progress. The scaffolding that held these dualities together for them consisted not of a sophisticated, discursive theological argument. Rather it was built out of an empirical judgment that the Christian religion had been the driving force behind America's power and prosperity. As the dominant religion of the nation, the midwife of Western science and technology, and the guiding light for assimilation policy itself, Christianity deserved, in their view, continued cooperation from America's federal institutions.

Collier, though, used the executive powers at his disposal to begin unraveling the web of Christian influence within the BIA's educational and welfare programs. With his vision rooted in a commitment to cultural pluralism generally and a devotion to the communal traditions of Native American societies in particular, Collier sought to revitalize American culture through the preservation of the Indians' close-knit, ritually based, pre-industrial communities. Christian missionaries, in his view, still had a role to play in Indian affairs through community service, but they would no longer be the bureau's collective arbiter of religious and moral authority.

This chapter has looked carefully into the changes of policy with regard to Indian culture and religions that Collier instituted when he became commissioner. I have argued that those changes significantly undercut the quid pro quo relationship that had long existed between the bureau and the missionaries. In that relationship, missionaries offered their political support for the ongoing work of the BIA in exchange for the BIA's extension of unique privileges to Christian workers. This relationship was further grounded in a larger belief that America enjoyed a unique calling as a beacon of Christian civilization. But Collier vigorously asserted the authority of the BIA to proscribe missionary activities, thereby placing the future of Christian missions among the Indians in jeopardy. In response, missionaries split along the lines of whether to oppose Collier publicly, with members of the Joint Indian Committee choosing to maintain a working relationship with Collier, while field missionaries—with Lindquist as their most visible advocate—treated the situation as a full-blown crisis. At this point, Lindquist would adamantly argue that the problem resided in Collier, and not in the missionaries' dependence on the BIA. But as the next chapter shows, Collier's effort to redirect the BIA toward his vision of tribal self-government sowed the seeds for a new missionary attitude toward the BIA.

4 Battle over the Wheeler-Howard Act, 1934

The early months of 1934 were charged times. The most momentous new departure in the history of federal Indian policy hung in the balance. Debate started in February when Collier introduced the initial draft of the Wheeler-Howard Act—his revolutionary proposals for tribal self-government and land tenure. And it subsided June 16 with the final passage of a drastically revised bill of the same name. In the meantime, all of Indian country was thrown into turmoil. Each tribe struggled to understand how the new legislation would apply to its own unique situation.

Protestant missionaries and reformers certainly did not watch the debate from the sidelines. They were already primed for controversy by Collier's efforts to protect Indian cultures, and they quickly saw that his executive reforms on religion were only one part of his plan to transform the work of the BIA. For even if Collier could end federal support for the Christianization of the Indians, there remained an entire range of missionary-supported bureau activities that Collier threatened to overturn. To change the future course of Indian communities, Collier had to do more than limit the proselytizing activities of missionaries within BIA institutions. He had to redirect the agency's sweeping goal of individualizing and Americanizing the Indians as well.

And here, no less than in his promotion of indigenous cultures, Collier encountered intense opposition from missionaries and reformers. As R. Scott Appleby has argued, the "competition for souls" in American home missions "was cast not only in religious but also in civic terms."[1] Sacred interests bled over into the secular because missionaries assumed, as a matter of course, that preparing the Indians for citizenship and economic independence was inseparable from presenting them with the gospel. Indeed, the civic dimension of Indian missions inspired a kind of parallel orthodoxy alongside the historic creeds, only instead of Trinity, Christ, Church and Spirit, the watchwords were Assimilation, Education, Citizenship, and Private Property. But what Collier proposed through the Wheeler-Howard Act of 1934 was nothing short of civic heresy, for rather than merge Indians into the mass of the American citizenry, Collier sought to foster and protect tribal sovereignty and corporate ownership of property.

These objectives pressed far-reaching questions about national identity and the universality of America's egalitarian and democratic ideals. What would it mean for national unity, missionaries wondered, if several hundred thousand of America's citizens governed themselves and their corporately held lands not through the usual means of state and local government, but through councils established for people exclusively of Native descent? And what if the federal government not only tolerated those pockets of Indian sovereignty but actually fostered and sanctioned them as a permanent and obligatory part of America's civic landscape?

For most Protestant missionaries and reformers, there was, to be sure, a limited sense in which Indians possessed aboriginal rights based on the legacy of federal treaties. But they typically regarded those indigenous rights as transitory and inferior to the rights of citizenship and private property. As Native Americans came to enjoy the full rights and privileges of American citizenship, they presumably would no longer want or need the guarantees of indigenous rights from the federal government. Until the 1920s, the Indian Rights Association defended Indian treaty rights to protect Indian land claims or maintain federal services, but its officers did not view indigenous rights as a perpetual arrangement or as a permanent marker of tribal existence.[2] Collier and his advisors, however, seemed to contemplate the possibility of an indefinite future for indigenous rights—alongside, and unsurpassed by, the rights of American citizenship.[3]

For Lindquist and the many missionaries and reformers like him, Collier's civic heresy caused at least as much grief as his religious pluralism. Indeed, Collier's proposals for tribal self-government touched a nerve in Lindquist that purely cultural questions never did. Lindquist had long argued that Christian conversion could go hand in hand with a vital sense of Native identity. The civic conversion he envisioned, by contrast, boiled down to a mutually exclusive choice between the separatism of tribal sovereignty and the national unity of American citizenship. His blueprint for the Indians' civic and economic integration could not countenance a permanent federal recognition of tribal sovereignty, no matter how limited that sovereignty might be. According to Lindquist, once Indians passed through the preparatory gray zone of wardship, they should be treated under the law strictly as individuals, without consideration of race or aboriginal ancestry. But Collier threatened to turn what Lindquist viewed as temporary expedients— treaty rights, land protections, and exemptions from property taxes—into a permanent liminal world of uncertainty and confusion.

This chapter describes the original version of the Wheeler-Howard Act that Collier introduced in February 1934, and it posits Lindquist as the leading missionary in a concerted effort to oppose the bill. As before, Lindquist found himself struggling on two fronts: against Collier directly, and also against a small but influential group of missionary executives who interpreted Collier's revolutionary proposals more mildly as yet another mechanism for the Indians' slow entry into American society. With the vast majority of field missionaries on his side, Lindquist engaged in three months of tireless lobbying, which, together with a chorus of other voices, led Congress to pass a new version of the bill that became law in June. While the new draft contained enough of Collier's original vision for him to claim it as his own, Lindquist and his peers entered the summer of 1934 calling the new bill a victory for themselves. In their view, they had slowed Collier's juggernaut and forced him to accept legislation that was largely compatible with their assimilationist and humanitarian goals. Along the way they plumbed the depths of their power, but sometimes at great personal cost, and at the risk of alienating some of the powerful missionary allies they would need to thwart Collier in the long run.

Collier's Program for Land Tenure and Self-Government

To set the stage for Collier's legislative proposal and the debates that surrounded it, some background on the land crisis that made those proposals feasible in the first place is needed. For more than four decades, the Dawes Act of 1887 served as the legal blueprint for Indian assimilation. It sought to break up Indian tribes by taking communally held lands and dividing them into allotments for the individual members of the tribe. To give individual Indians time to learn the skills necessary to make a living off their land, the allotments were to be held in trust by the federal government for twenty-five years. Then, at the end of the trust period, landholders would receive a patent in fee simple for their allotments and assume the rights and obligations of a much-vaunted American citizenship. Western legislators supported the law because the allotment process promised to free up "surplus" reservation lands for white settlement. But the driving force behind the Dawes Act was the Christian humanitarians who made up the Protestant reform organizations. Their optimism for allotment stemmed from their belief that the mere possession of private property would engender among Indians the enlightened self-interest necessary for civilization. According to reformers, as long as the Indians held an interest in tribal property, they would remain within the constraints of their tribes' social, cultural, and religious norms. But the private ownership of valuable property would, reformers believed, instill an ambitious and healthy self-interest in individual Indians, prompting them toward industrious habits and respect for the laws that protected their own property as well as that of others. Cultural assimilation, then, was expected to follow inevitably from this change in economic interest from the tribe to the individual.[4] That was the theory.

But in practice, numerous problems arose, particularly when the BIA issued patents for individual allotments. In the large majority of cases, individual Indians lost their lands: some sold for quick cash, others forfeited their lands to mortgage debt or tax liabilities, and still others were the victims of swindling Indian agents and land-hungry whites. By the early twentieth century, legislators and administrators took measures to prevent such wholesale losses of land by expanding the government's guardian responsibilities over those deemed "incompetent" to protect their estates on an open market. The trust period was extended for thousands of Indians, and the BIA assumed greater control over Indian lands through leasing arrangements and management of probate cases. Without these guardian functions, reformers feared, land allotment and citizenship would bring not assimilation and full incorporation into American life, but impoverishment at the hands of aggressive speculators. Indeed, after the Meriam Report published its criticisms of land policies in 1928, allotment and the issuance of fee patents slowed to a near halt.[5]

A growing guardianship over Indian properties, however, brought its own set of problems—a burgeoning bureaucracy and a virtually limitless federal involvement in the Indians' economic affairs. An Indian owning an allotment in trust, for example, could not sell or lease the allotment without official approval. Nor could he or she spend the money gained from leasing without making a formal request to the superintendent, since even the money from leases was held in trust by the government. Ironically, the vested interest that allotment policy succeeded most visibly in creating was not that of individual Indians, but that of the Bureau of Indian Affairs itself. Yet the bind seemed intractable. The harder the BIA pushed the Indians to assimilate and accept their allotments, the more likely the Indians were to lose their lands and bring further condemnation upon the BIA from reform-minded gradualists. But the harder the administration pushed to protect Indian properties, the more they thwarted Indian self-initiative—the very trait reputedly needed to cross the bridge into American society—and the more vulnerable the government became to charges of bureaucratic and institutional self-interest.[6]

Other problems dogged the implementation of the Dawes Act. For example, the allotment policy left Indian heirs practically landless. After a couple of generations, a 160-acre allotment—which just might have supported a single family in 1887—ended up in the hands of numerous descendants, who could not support themselves on their shares and often liquidated to get at least something from their holdings. Many reservations became hopelessly checkerboarded with plots alternately owned by white settlers, Indians with patented lands, and Indians with lands held in trust by the government. Those conditions made it impossible for tribes to use their lands effectively in grazing, timber, and agricultural pursuits. All told, Collier estimated that Native Americans lost eighty-five million acres of land as a result of the allotment policy—almost two-thirds of the landed estate tribes held when the Dawes Act was enacted in 1887. While observers in 1934 still disagreed over the merits of the original vision that prompted allotment policy, all agreed that the administration of Indian lands stood in desperate need of reform.[7]

Collier's proposed solution to the catch-22 of guardianship and land loss was a radical restructuring of Indian land tenure and the role of the federal government in tribal affairs. In February 1934, soon after he released his executive orders on Indian religious freedom, Collier introduced an administration measure called the Indian Reorganization Act. Also known as the Wheeler-Howard Act (for the legislators who sponsored it), Collier's forty-eight-page legislative proposal sought to preserve and expand Indian land holdings, promote Indian self-government over the direct rule of the BIA, and restore the tribal social structures that had been debased or destroyed by assimilation policies under the Dawes Act.[8]

In its initial form—that is, before it was significantly revised and passed in June 1934—the Wheeler-Howard Act contained four major sections. Title I provided a voluntary mechanism for establishing Indian home rule. Patterned after British "indirect rule" in colonial Africa, Collier's proposal would allow tribes to adopt charters of incorporation as "federal municipalities." They could develop

Indian properties such as sawmills and agricultural cooperatives—indeed, properties of any type and description—and operate them according to rules and customs as modern or as traditional as they wished. Those properties would be held in trust by the federal government (meaning they could never be sold to non-Indians), and they would be exempt from state property taxes. Since properties held in trust could not be used as collateral for bank loans, the bill was quickly amended to provide for a multimillion-dollar wheel of credit for tribal development. Over time, as Collier envisioned it, tribal corporations would take over all the health, education, welfare, land management, and law and order responsibilities that the federal government was providing. Meanwhile, chartered communities would acquire the authority to remove BIA agents from their reservations, and new regulations would make it possible for Indians to obtain jobs in the BIA without satisfying civil service requirements.[9]

To prepare the Indians to assume their responsibilities, Title II authorized expenditures for Indian education in the myriad skills required for self-government. Scholarships and student loans were to help Indian students attend college. And the BIA's education division would be required to develop curricula on "the social and economic problems of the Indians" and "the history and problems of Indian administration." Moreover, Title II would reinforce the substance of Collier's executive order on religious freedom by making it the declared purpose of Congress to "preserve and develop" the "arts, crafts, skills, and traditions" of Indian civilizations.[10]

Title III restructured federal policy on Indian land tenure. It prohibited future land allotments and prevented, apart from direct congressional action, the issuance of fee patents on allotted lands still held in trust. Beyond maintaining the status quo on land holdings, it authorized appropriations for enlarging reservations and consolidating those that had been checkerboarded by sales to non-Indians. Then, in order to give the chartered communities land units that were large enough to be of some use, it required those allotment owners whose lands were still held in trust to exchange ownership of their land for an equitable share in the tribal corporation. Landowners would be allowed to remain on their allotments and to pass any improvements down to their descendants, but individual land inheritance itself would be eliminated. Land that had been hopelessly fractionalized by heirship would likewise be sold back to the tribe.[11]

Title IV addressed the problem of legal jurisdiction over Indian tribes and reservations. Since the late nineteenth century, the BIA had granted tribal courts authority to decide most civil and criminal matters on Indian reservations, with the exception of several major crimes. Collier feared, though, that the tribal courts were under the thumb of agency superintendents and they possessed too much latitude in their judgments. So Title IV proposed that a Court of Indian Affairs be created, with Indian judges to be appointed by the president, to hear criminal, civil, and probate cases from chartered communities.[12]

The way that Collier went about hawking the bill was at least as important as its details. His most frequent claim was that Indian self-government would end the demoralizing effects of wardship, or what the bill called "federal tutelage." This claim was crucial for the bill's passage because, as Collier knew, it could never become law without support from at least some assimilationists. By stressing the devolution of the Indian affairs bureaucracy, then, Collier hoped to tap into the anti-BIA sentiment harbored by many who saw the Indian Service as an obstacle to assimilation, not a means of accomplishing it.[13] In fact, he insisted in House hearings that the bill could be interpreted as a humane way to merge the Indians into American society. Through indirect rule, he argued, Indians would gain experience in the administrative and educational tasks required to govern democratic communities. And with the powers granted by self-government, they could determine for themselves when and under what conditions they might be assimilated.[14]

But Collier's core vision was not assimilationist—or not assimilationist in its conventional sense. For one of the key features in assimilation policy had been the assumption that allotment and citizenship would ultimately lead to the end of the special federal relationship with the Indians. That special relationship can be traced to the United States Constitution, which treated Indians as members of semi-autonomous nations. Through treaties, for example, Indians interacted with the United States government not as individuals but as tribe members who, in exchange for land, received protections over their reservations, as well as educational and welfare services from the federal government. Even after Indians received citizenship in 1924, the BIA continued to guard their resources (with inconsistent results, of course) and to provide basic social services that other citizens received from their individual states. Assimilationists, though, still looked toward the day when Indian citizens would, legally speaking, be indistinguishable from all other citizens. Assimilationists might have differed somewhat over the extent to which Indians could preserve their cultural identities, but the ultimate termination of federal obligations to Indians *as Indians* had been the central political objective of assimilation policy.

What Collier proposed, though, was an end not to the unique federal relationship with the Indians, but to its most oppressive and intrusive features. That still left open the possibility of an enduring *legal* distinctiveness for the Indians.

In Collier's plan, tribes would continue to own their lands as tribes, not as individuals. Lands would still be held in trust by the federal government and be exempted from state and local property taxes. And all social services and law-and-order institutions on Indian reservations would come within the oversight of the tribal corporation and, ultimately, the secretary of the interior. In the end, Collier's proposal might have claimed neutrality with regard to the Indians' cultural assimilation, but it reinforced the legal bases for the Indians' perpetual differentiation from the body politic. Underneath the conventional rhetoric of a gradual assimilation, Collier was moving in the direction of Indian nationhood—the political antithesis of assimilation.[15]

Lindquist's Blueprint for a Fervent Opposition

To gain some understanding of how the Protestant missionary establishment responded to the proposed Wheeler-Howard Act, it is useful to turn once again to G. E. E. Lindquist. Lindquist had invested the past twenty-three years of his life in Indian assimilation. Moreover, as an assimilation gradualist, he had been a leading supporter of the BIA's guardian role, in opposition to radical assimilationists who worried more about government paternalism than white exploitation of a still vulnerable Indian minority. In his fight against Collier's proposals, though, Lindquist's own views became radicalized. The paternalistic bureaucracy he had once supported as a temporary expedient, he now began to reject as a means for Collier's own heterodox ambitions. Seeing through Collier's claim for the assimilating possibilities in the Wheeler-Howard Act, Lindquist became the leading missionary defender of the original vision of the 1887 Dawes Act.

Although Lindquist published at least one article against the Wheeler-Howard Act while it was still under deliberation, a franker and ultimately more influential assessment appeared in his "Items on the Proposed Collier Policies." Hastily written and loosely organized, Lindquist's catalog of objections was dubbed the "Fourteen Points," an allusion to Woodrow Wilson's similarly numbered, but significantly more irenic, wartime peace proposals. This mimeographed list quickly became the blueprint for much of the grassroots missionary agitation against the proposed Wheeler-Howard Act.[16]

In the document, Lindquist began his analysis of Collier's land reforms by conceding that the allotment policy had contained "certain grave errors." True to his gradualist leanings, he argued that allotment had been pushed too rapidly, with too little appreciation for the time involved in educating individual Indians to protect their estates from debt and fraud. Lindquist also granted that something needed to be done about the problem of heirship lands and the numerous landless Indians created by poor administration of the allotment policy.

But he insisted that the principles of "individual ownership" and "personal initiative" were "forward-looking" and based on "humanitarian motives." To be sure, Lindquist thought, Collier's plan might increase the total Indian landholdings, but only at a very high price. For by compelling successful allotment holders to relinquish their land to the community, Collier would effectively "abolish the holding of personal property." Even more, Lindquist continued, since the plan promised to give landless Indians a share in the tribal corporation, it suffered the inherent weakness of making its strongest appeal not to stable, industrious landowners, but to the "shiftless . . . agitators" who had already "run through with what little property they had."[17]

Along with criticizing the land policies in Title III, Lindquist fumed against the provisions for self-government and the Indian court system in Titles I and IV. He argued that Collier's plan would create "'Nations within a Nation,' segregated and isolated minorities with an elaborate, intricate and expensive administrative set-up." Collier touted this setup as an end to government paternalism, but in fact, Lindquist pointed out, ultimate control over tribal charters and community services still rested in the hands of the Interior Department and the BIA. "Both church and state," Lindquist argued, "should join forces to . . . set [the Indian] on his own feet and sever forever the ties that bind him to the [federal] government." Otherwise, according to Lindquist, Indians might never find acceptance among their Euro-American neighbors. For by providing "special privileges, gratuity appropriations" and exemptions from state and local taxes, the bill would inevitably exacerbate white prejudice and racial misunderstandings.[18]

As if to confirm Lindquist's fears, a group of commissioners from Rollette County, North Dakota, presented a series of resolutions to the House Committee on Indian Affairs in favor of the bill. Embittered by having to provide indigent support for about two thousand Indians in the Turtle Mountain Reservation, they interpreted Collier's proposal as a way to segregate the Indians politically and free their county from any obligation to provide social services to the Indians. They explicitly commended the compulsory feature of the bill requiring restricted allotment holders to exchange their lands for a share in the tribal corporation, because it helped to broaden the legal distance between Indians and non-Indians in the county. Then, in the final step of the trajectory they sought, they asked that the bill be amended to prevent Indians from voting in county or state elections, since all the Indians' legitimate rights, the county commissioners believed, would be vested within their chartered communities.[19]

Lindquist argued for the defeat of Collier's legislative reforms, then, on the twin principles of private property and national unity. And tying those principles together was Lindquist's assertion that the bill enhanced rather than lessened the patronizing and segregating influences of the BIA. In view of Collier's reforms, Lindquist's typically gradual approach to assimilation became less viable as an option. For he had long supported special legal protections and programs for the Indians, such as tax-exemptions on Indian lands, preferential hiring of Indians in the BIA, and the entire federal bureaucracy for Indian education and welfare. But what assimilation gradualists intended as interim measures toward assimilation, Collier posited as permanent obligations to America's aboriginal inhabitants. Lindquist, then, would have difficulty supporting special protections and programs for the Indians without Collier turning those assimilationist means toward separatist goals. Collier might have defended his bill as a potential step in the direction of economic recovery and assimilation, but for Lindquist, the Wheeler-Howard Act doomed the Indians to the ghetto of racial hatred, cultural isolation, and economic impoverishment.

A Divided Protestant Response

Of course, not all Protestant leaders interpreted Collier's proposal as Lindquist did. Some took Collier at his word and favored the bill as a bona fide step toward Indian integration into American society. J. M. Somerndike, executive secretary of the Presbyterian Church (U.S.A.) Board of National Missions, praised Collier's plans for land tenure and defended the self-government provisions as a move toward the Indians' full realization of the citizenship they had gained in 1924. "If wisely and successfully administered," he wrote, the new bill "should win them the respect of their fellow Americans, regardless of race."[20]

Somerndike's fellow missionary executives on the ecumenical Joint Indian Committee apparently shared the sentiment. At an exceptionally large, specially called meeting of the committee in New York, more than sixty Protestant home mission representatives spent an entire day examining the bill. They expressed "whole-hearted and sincere appreciation" for Collier's devotion to the Indians' welfare, as well as "general agreement" with the "spirit and purpose of the Bill." His proposals, they believed, offered a potential solution to the "stultifying reservation system," while also helping the many Indians who, for the foreseeable future, would be best served by continuing to hold their properties under tribal auspices rather than individually. Although some executives reported receiving letters of opposition from field missionaries, most saw the bill as a unique opportunity to bring a sizeable infusion of capital and economic development to impoverished Indian reservations.[21]

Lindquist himself could not attend the extraordinary meeting, but upon his copy of a typed report of the proceedings, he wrote, "Apparently scant attention paid to protests of missionaries themselves who are on the firing line and are up against these problems daily." Lindquist's anger was palpable. He had played a key role in organizing the Joint Indian Committee in the 1910s, when it focused primarily on preventing competition among Protestant denominations involved in Indian missions. In the intervening years he had supervised numerous Joint Indian Committee activities, coordinated meetings with BIA officials, and written or cowritten the bulk of the committee's field surveys and publicity. But now the committee offered no help in resisting Collier's far-reaching proposal. Denominational executives seemed willing to dissolve their differences with Collier in the presumption of mutual goodwill.[22]

Yet another obstacle in Lindquist's fight was the inability or failure of his Indian friends and associates in the BIA to oppose Collier's initiatives. Under normal circumstances, concerns about job security would have been enough in most cases to quiet an employee's dissent. But in April 1934, Interior Secretary Harold Ickes published a circular letter to BIA employees informing them that if they wished to oppose the new policies, they would have to do so "outside of the Service." "Any other course" besides resignation, he wrote, would be "unscrupulous and detrimental to the Indians."[23] Since many Christian Indian leaders held positions in the BIA, Lindquist lost the possibility of gaining strong public support from some of his best Indian allies.[24]

Ruth Muskrat Bronson was one of those potential allies. She had presented Lindquist's book *Red Man in the United States* to President Coolidge in 1923 and defended his stand against Indian dances at the height of the dance controversy the same year. After studying at the University of Kansas and Mt. Holyoke College, she joined the BIA in 1925 and taught English at Haskell Institute, while Lindquist served there as Religious Work Director. In 1934, Lindquist met with Bronson at least once in New Mexico while he was organizing Navajo opposition to Collier's legislative initiative.[25] He apparently hoped to use her influence for his own countercampaign, but Bronson assiduously kept her true attitude toward Collier's plan out of the public record.[26]

If Bronson's silence on the Wheeler-Howard Act could be explained by Ickes's infamous "gag order," Henry Roe Cloud's enthusiastic support for the bill proved more difficult for Lindquist to stomach. Roe Cloud was a charismatic, well-educated Presbyterian minister who had attended seminary with Lindquist at Oberlin. Together in 1915 they founded the Roe Indian Institute in Wichita, Kansas, with plans to offer a college preparatory course for promising Indian students. Roe Cloud and Lindquist began to part ways in the late 1920s, though, when Roe Cloud served as Indian adviser for the famous Meriam survey of Indian administration and later joined the Indian Service as a special agent in 1930. In 1934, Collier came directly between Lindquist and Roe Cloud when he asked Roe Cloud to take the lead as the foremost Indian lobbyist behind the Wheeler-Howard Act. Roe Cloud accepted the invitation, thus becoming Collier's personal proxy at tribal meetings across the country.

Once again, Lindquist's marginalia—this time on a copy of Roe Cloud's address at Martin, South Dakota—betrayed the strain in a relationship in which Lindquist was deeply invested. Lindquist's question marks and exclamation points punctuated Roe Cloud's observations.[27] In part, Roe Cloud reconciled himself to Collier's policies by stressing those features that perpetuated traditional assimilationist goals, such as educating and cultivating strong Indian leaders, expanding medical and social services, and inculcating values of economic independence and self-governance.[28] But in taking such a large share in Collier's campaign, Roe Cloud, in Lindquist's view, betrayed the common ideals that brought them together at the beginning of their now divergent careers.[29]

Lindquist, then, found himself in something of a predicament. Collier had the authority to squelch dissent among assimilationist employees in the BIA, and he had successfully co-opted the talents of one of the Native leaders with close ties to Lindquist and the Protestant missionary establishment. He was a skilled propagandist with ample access to national news media. And through several highly publicized regional "Indian Congresses," he was bringing the entire weight of his reform movement directly to the reservations to win Indian support for the bill. Lindquist, on the other hand, was a member of the now-defunct Board of Indian Commissioners, and he was quickly losing influence among the newer members of the interdenominational Joint Indian Committee. What recourse did he have for defeating Collier's sweeping legislation? Without being overly schematic, it is possible to say that Lindquist mounted his attack by moving in two directions simultaneously—upward into national centers of power and reform sentiment and outward to his numerous contacts in the field. He intensified his engagement with a small network of urban reformers who, like himself, were strongly committed to the assimilation program for the Indians. Chief among those contacts were Flora Warren Seymour, the Chicago lawyer who had served with Lindquist on the Board of Indian Commissioners; Matthew K. Sniffen, secretary of the Philadelphia-based Indian Rights Association; and Elaine G. Eastman, a radical assimilationist in Massachusetts with roots in the first generation of Indian reformers. As a group they had once ranged across the spectrum between gradualism and radicalism in the assimilation debates of the previous several decades. But under Collier's administration, they increasingly took their cues from the more radical, anti-BIA elements among them.[30]

Moreover, Lindquist used the freedom of movement he enjoyed as Missionary-at-Large for the Society for Propagating the Gospel to cover thousands of miles in the Indian country agitating against Collier's proposals. Within his small circle of reformers, in fact, that was his chief contribution. While others remained in Chicago and Philadelphia and published articles and open letters to the president, he rode the rails from South Dakota to Arizona, organizing Christian constituents and gathering field intelligence for other reformers to use in their own publications. Several of Lindquist's allies no doubt have drawn more attention from historians for their fight against the Wheeler-Howard Act, but it was Lindquist who served as the guerilla leader for the effort.

Lindquist's field activism centered on the regional Indian Congresses Collier scheduled to explain the bill and win tribal support for the initiative. As Collier trekked across the country to convene his open forums, Lindquist shadowed his every move. He organized side meetings with Indians and Protestant missionaries and established contacts with the local press. He made speeches and crafted resolutions with local ministerial groups and Indian chapters. And he slogged through hours of debates and strategy meetings, all in an effort to slow what threatened to be a Collier-driven juggernaut of reform. Indeed, it would be difficult to exaggerate the energies Lindquist poured into this endeavor. But who else could have taken up the task as he did? Flora Warren Seymour attended one Indian Congress, but financial considerations probably kept her, as well as Matthew Sniffen and Elaine G. Eastman, from carrying the mantle in the field. A number of Native American leaders vigorously opposed the Wheeler-Howard Act, but their influence extended only to their tribe or region at most. The same could be said of field missionaries as well. But Lindquist made his living by traveling from reservation to reservation, speaking with missionaries and Christian Indian leaders and convening countless small meetings. Working from his centrally located home base at Lawrence, Kansas, Lindquist was uniquely positioned with the financial and political freedom, as well as the necessary contacts in the field, to facilitate Indian and missionary opposition on a transregional scale. His behind-the-scenes activism helped tie together a significant portion of the grassroots campaign against Collier's reforms.[31]

Collier himself knew that Lindquist could not be ignored. He tried at first to counter Lindquist's propaganda at the Plains Indian Congress in Rapid City, South Dakota, on March 5. According to an Associated Press wire report, Lindquist had called Collier's bill "communism in the rankest sense." Collier countered by telling the Indians gathered at the congress, "It is not communistic to extend to you the right to organize for mutual aid. It is not communistic to allow you to have the same instruments of power which are possessed by all of the other people." Lindquist called the press report "absurd," and with the help of Roe Cloud, who was presiding over the congress, he obtained the floor long enough to insist that he himself had never claimed the bill was communistic. It seems that Lindquist was merely repeating the claims that he had heard Indians make, but that distinction meant little to Collier or to many whom Lindquist was trying to influence.[32]

So just a few weeks later on March 23, Collier turned again to neutralizing Lindquist's mobile campaign, this time devoting an entire morning to the task while stumping through Oklahoma. Lindquist, Collier noted, had dogged him step-by-step across Indian country, sowing seeds of misunderstanding and falsehood. His "Fourteen Points," Collier continued, was "the most vicious propaganda in existence"—worse even than the lies and distortions of the predatory lumber and cattle interests who likewise opposed the bill. With most opponents to the bill, he noted, selfish interests were transparent, but Lindquist's antagonism came dressed in the guise of Christian benevolence. According to Collier, people like Lindquist "believe in working for and with the Indian but have no faith in the Indian. They seem to believe there is no good in him and that it is their Christian duty occasionally to rescue one from his no-good race. Lindquist has no faith in the Indian, and where there is no faith, there can be little love."[33]

Collier's charges notwithstanding, Lindquist could still tap into considerable opposition to the Wheeler-Howard Act. Most field missionaries opposed the bill because they saw it as the logical extension of Collier's attempt to obstruct their activities and reestablish pre-Columbian tribal life.[34] Some even feared that Collier was moving toward eliminating Christian missions altogether—something he had the implicit authority (though certainly not the political support) to do.[35] The Indian self-government features of the bill added yet another layer of anxiety to that concern. For, as Matthew Sniffen of the Indian Rights Association wrote, the secretary of the interior could ultimately give chartered communities "unlimited power to handle their internal affairs, and perhaps power to eject any person or persons whose presence was considered undesirable." He believed missionaries were "unduly alarmed" about this threat, since he doubted that any tribe would take so radical a step as to ban missionary work, "but it would be possible for that to be done," he conceded.[36] Others expressed fears that some traditional societies like the Pueblo Indians of New Mexico might use their authority to limit the rights of assimilated or Christian tribe members.[37]

Some missionaries even took their opposition to the bill to a level beyond the war of words. In May 1934, when the Indians at Standing Rock were scheduled to vote in a referendum on the Wheeler-Howard Act, they found they could not do as planned. Percy Tibbetts, a Native missionary at the local Congregationalist church, had locked the doors of the YMCA building where the vote was to be held, and left town on a conveniently timed vacation.[38]

Besides fellow missionaries, Lindquist could also depend on the support of a large number of allotted Indians who were particularly hostile to the provision that allowed the secretary of the interior to transfer title to their lands over to a tribal corporation. Many saw it as Lindquist did, as a way to benefit landless Indians at the expense of landholders. They suspected that the bill was one more in a long line of externally imposed schemes to rob them of their property. One of the ironies of this suspicion, as historian Kenneth Philp has argued, is that it signaled the extent to which assimilation policies had indeed taken effect. In opposing the new bill, many allotted Indians were zealously protecting their vested interests in private property, just as allotment policy intended.[39]

Yet not all Indian opposition was premised upon the ideals of American citizenship. Leaders from Fallon, Nevada, pleaded with Collier to take remedial measures for destitute and starving Indians before approaching them with the less tangible benefits of experimental legislation. "All winter," they wrote, "we have asked your office for food and clothing for our old Indians who have been forced to beg from door to door." But instead, Collier was sending them "an idealistic law" that gave no relief.[40]

Equally important were tribal fears that the new legislation would threaten cherished treaty rights and delay the settlement of outstanding claims against the federal government. For example, one Oklahoma Cherokee group, the Keetoowha Society, wired Collier to say bluntly, "What we need is for your government to keep the treaties or agreements that they now have with the Indian and make less laws." Of course, Lindquist was lukewarm toward this form of Indian opposition, for he feared that treaty rights could themselves become the basis for a permanent segregation of the Indians from the body politic. But in the frenzied agitation against the Wheeler-Howard Act, Lindquist suppressed such ideological differences to carry out a more effective campaign.[41]

Some of the most fertile ground for Lindquist's activism was Navajo country at the time of the Fort Defiance Indian Congress in March 1934. There Lindquist hooked up with J. C. Morgan (1879–1950), an articulate Native missionary for the Christian Reformed Church and leader of an important political faction within the Navajo tribe. Morgan believed that the Wheeler-Howard Act undercut constitutional guarantees for citizens, treating Indians instead as aliens who lacked the full rights of citizenship.[42] According to Lindquist, Morgan was actively involved in frustrating Collier's efforts at the Fort Defiance Congress. He "rendered yeoman service" in helping Lindquist circulate his mimeographed "Fourteen Points" as widely as possible. He also helped persuade the Navajo tribal council to postpone a referendum on the bill until the tribe had had more time to evaluate it. That decision struck a blow to Collier's entire campaign, because it undermined Collier's claims for widespread Indian enthusiasm over the bill.[43]

Everywhere Collier turned, there was Lindquist, working his connections, talking to reporters, passing out leaflets, and fomenting all-around ill will toward Collier's administration. For the most part, Collier could do very little to stop him. Lindquist was too deeply embedded in a rich network of relationships both in Indian country and in urban centers in the East for him to be easily discredited. And he was too coy to give Collier the satisfaction of going head to head against him when he had his chance at Rapid City. Like the buffalo, Lindquist was a large and obvious target, but surprisingly agile and elusive to Collier's grasp.

In one situation, though, Lindquist left himself and one of his allies vulnerable to Collier's retribution. The incident occurred at Sherman Institute, a federal boarding school in Riverside, California. Through his lobbying efforts in southern California, Lindquist inadvertently set in motion a chain of events that led to the firing, at Collier's insistence, of a Home Missions Council missionary of good standing. The story is worth examining, because it provides a window into the kind of low-level organizing that Lindquist carried out in his fight to defeat Collier's proposals, and its outcome reveals the complex political landscape that Lindquist and like-minded missionaries faced in the early years of the Collier administration.

The first sign of trouble at Sherman came on April 30, 1934, when rumors reached Collier that someone at the school was printing material adverse to the Indian Rights Bill and organizing employees and students for a hostile campaign.[44] He quickly telegrammed school superintendent Donald H. Biery to determine whether the rumors had any basis. Biery reported that the reports had nothing to do with any of his employees, but stemmed instead from the activities of the Rev. Floyd O. Burnett (1896?–1950). Burnett was a Methodist minister of Native descent from Oklahoma, serving under the auspices of the Joint Indian Committee of the Home Missions Council as Sherman's religious work director.[45] He had recently published a lengthy broadside against the Wheeler-Howard Act in the local paper, where he referred to himself as "Director [of] Religious Education, Sherman Indian Institute." His title obviously left the false impression that he was himself a BIA employee at Sherman, and that BIA employees were clamoring against Collier's reforms.[46]

That alone would have been enough to capture Collier's attention, but Burnett's agitation against the Indian New Deal did not stop there. From interviews with Sherman students and employees, Biery discovered that two weeks earlier, Burnett had joined with G. E. E. Lindquist to visit several southern California churches and distribute materials against the Wheeler-Howard Act. On several of those local church visits, Burnett and Lindquist took Sherman students with them, thus implicating the students in their lobbying. Going back even further in time, Biery's inquiries revealed that on March 14, six weeks before Lindquist's visit, Burnett and a student assistant had used the school mimeograph machine to run off about fifty copies of political propaganda one evening when the school was practically vacant.[47] The material Burnett copied, it turned out, was none other than Lindquist's "Fourteen Points." And he had copied the material just two days before the Riverside "Indian Congress"—one of the series of regional meetings that Collier had convened to promote the Wheeler-Howard Act. Finally, Biery learned that at the time of the Riverside Congress, Burnett had invited all the school's Indian employees as well as many of its older students and local graduates to his home, where he distributed his propaganda and pressured them to spread the word on their respective reservations about the evils inherent in the bill. Biery had apparently uncovered the plan that Lindquist had worked out for coordinating a grassroots campaign against Collier's proposed policies. Lindquist had carried out similar adverse activities himself during the congresses at Rapid City, South Dakota; Santo Domingo, New Mexico; and Fort Defiance, Arizona. But since he could not personally attend the Riverside Congress, he worked closely with Burnett to counteract the administration's propaganda there.[48]

When Superintendent Biery confronted Burnett about his activities, Burnett argued that he had the backing of his employer, the Home Missions Council, since the material he had been distributing came from Lindquist. And he insisted that he had not used Sherman students to advance his agenda when he made visits to area churches; their only role, he stated repeatedly, had been to provide music for worship services. In his response, Biery targeted the behaviors he found most offensive: he forbade Burnett from using the school mimeograph machine for "adverse" purposes, and he prohibited Burnett from taking Sherman students with him to church meetings where he planned to speak against the Wheeler-Howard Bill. Burnett assured Biery that he would avoid implicating the school in his political activities, but added that he would continue to exercise his right as a citizen to oppose Collier's bill.[49]

Superintendent Biery's primary goal in reporting to Collier, it should be noted, was not to condemn Burnett, but to remove any question in Collier's mind that Sherman employees and students supported his new policies. Motivated in part by Interior Secretary Harold Ickes's so-called gag order, Biery was simply protecting himself and his subordinates. But he had no thought of forcing Burnett off campus, even if he believed Burnett had "taken undue advantage of the privileges accorded him" as a missionary on campus. Biery's correspondence with Collier, then, attempted to close the entire episode with a summary of the new restrictions he had placed on Burnett and an expression of his view that his investigation "satisfactorily removes any implication regarding our school and its activities."[50]

But when Collier received Biery's correspondence he took immediate and drastic action. He wired Biery and William R. King, Secretary for the Home Missions Council, with instructions to withdraw Burnett's privileges at Sherman Institute. According to Collier, Burnett had abused his privileges in a surreptitious political campaign, adding rather vaguely (and unrealistically) that "political activity by missionaries cannot be allowed."[51] The commissioner had a moral obligation to Sherman students, Collier explained, to make certain that a person of Burnett's character not be "forced upon the Indian children" in his charge.[52]

In a direct appeal to Collier, Burnett reiterated his contention that he had not used Sherman students to promote his political views in area churches. And with regard to his access to school facilities, he admitted to having used the school mimeograph to make copies of the "Fourteen Points." But he noted that in past years, he had always been given liberty to use the machine so long as he provided his own supplies. Moreover, this liberty had been granted in an informal exchange that allowed the school to use chairs, tables, and other equipment owned by the Protestant chapel situated just off campus. Burnett's access to the mimeograph machine was not so much a favor from the school as part of a reciprocal set of obligations between two organizations that were both somewhat strapped for resources. After further denying that he acted surreptitiously or with the intention of deceiving school administrators, Burnett requested that Collier reverse the decision to withdraw his campus privileges.[53]

When Burnett's wife became ill and needed surgery, his pleas became urgent. Forsaking his earlier defense of his right to free speech, he promised Superintendent Biery that if he were given back his job, he would henceforth refrain from political activity altogether. Biery, in turn, wrote another letter to Collier, noting this time that Burnett's account of the facts, as far as he could determine, was accurate. He also downplayed the extent of Burnett's political activities on campus and indicated that with only one exception regarding the mimeograph machine, Burnett's use of school equipment and facilities had been unobjectionable. He nevertheless pledged his support for Collier's original decision.[54]

For several more months, Burnett made further appeals and asked supporters to write Collier and the Home Missions Council on his behalf, but to no avail. The Home Missions Council, for its part, thoroughly endorsed Burnett's religious work at Sherman, calling him "one of our best religious work directors." But the council never challenged Collier's authority or judgment in the matter.[55] Apparently, Lindquist's position was too compromised for him to be of any help to Burnett, but some of his close associates took up Burnett's defense. Elaine G. Eastman, for example, attempted to persuade the editor of *Christian Century* to publish a story on the Burnett incident.[56] But the journal kept its misgivings about Collier's decision off the record, while giving strong editorial support to Collier's new policies.[57] Flora Warren Seymour directed her considerable energies against the Home Missions Council itself. "If the Home Missions Council submits to this," she told one of its officers, "the way will be paved for getting rid of any and all missionaries in Indian work." She pleaded that the council not allow the missionaries' long record of service among the Indians to end with "a feeble submission to an unwarranted and despotic order."[58] Despite the efforts of Burnett and his friends, Collier stood firm in expelling Burnett from Sherman Institute.

In the Burnett incident then, the disestablishment of missionary privilege in Indian affairs went hand in hand with Collier's attempt to unravel the policies of Indian assimilation. He sought to restrict the oppositional influence of Protestant missionaries and mark out the newly limited roles that they could play within Indian affairs. Working in his favor, of course, were the Indian service personnel's compelling interest in keeping their jobs, and the Home Missions Council's studied refusal to depart from its general pattern of public support for BIA policies. For Lindquist, on the other hand, his liberty to oppose Collier reached its limit at Riverside, California, where he was still dependent upon the Home Missions

Council's backing if he wished to minimize the risks to his missionary friends. In his contacts with field-workers and Christian Indian leaders, he found a large constituency loyal to his own assimilationist views. But in the long term, he would need to develop new and more stable ways to mobilize their energies and force Collier to reckon with them as players in the world of Indian affairs.

If Burnett was the first martyr in Lindquist's crusade against Collier, Lindquist believed he could at least claim that the sacrifice went to a triumphant cause. For at the same time that Collier was wielding his autocratic authority against Burnett at Sherman Institute, he was also losing control over the legislation he had originally proposed. During the week of May 17, Collier went back to the Senate and House committees on Indian affairs to hammer out legislation that stood a reasonable chance of passing through Congress. By the time they were finished, the bill—shrunk to one-third its size—bore only a modest resemblance to the original draft.[59]

Lost in the rewriting were Collier's proposals for a Court of Indian Affairs (Title IV) and the declaration of Congress's intention to preserve indigenous cultural traditions (Title II). From Title I, legislators removed the granting of municipal powers to tribal councils, while leaving in place the creation of "Indian chartered corporations" for economic development. Further changes excluded the large Native populations in Alaska and Oklahoma from the bill. Collier also was forced to amend the section that would compel allotment holders to exchange their land for a share in the tribal corporation, making it more difficult for him to consolidate tribal lands into manageable units for timber, agriculture, and grazing purposes. Like the previous bill, though, the new version ended the policy of land allotment and appropriated the hefty sum of ten million dollars as a revolving fund to stimulate tribal economies.[60]

Public responses to the new bill treated it largely as a defeat of the old one. On the floor of the House, Representative Edgar Howard (Nebraska) claimed that the new bill was actually written by the congressional members who had "objected most strenuously" to the original bill.[61] Lindquist joined Matthew Sniffen of the Indian Rights Association in gleefully proclaiming the Wheeler-Howard bill officially "abandoned." And together, they declared themselves in favor of "ninety percent of [the new draft's] provisions."[62] Flora Warren Seymour interpreted the new bill as an attempt by Collier to "save face" and avoid the appearance of a legislative defeat.[63] Indeed, by favoring the revised bill, Lindquist, Sniffen, and Seymour were claiming bragging rights on the success of their counter-campaign.

Their celebrative mood, however, was a bit premature. Despite the drastic revisions, the Wheeler-Howard Act remained the most important Indian affairs legislation since the Dawes Act of 1887. Under the guise of economic rehabilitation, Collier managed to strengthen the legal basis for federal relations with Indian tribes and actually shift that relationship toward the restoration of tribal sovereignty. The driving questions now had to do with how the bill was to be administered. Like the Dawes Act before it, the Wheeler-Howard Act was porous and open-ended. In the hands of a commissioner with assimilationist sympathies, its rich funding could provide a mechanism for Indian integration into American society through economic development and educational opportunities.[64] But in Collier's hands, the act could still be used to accomplish much of his original vision of cultural and civic pluralism. Lindquist the gradualist might have seen the final version of the Wheeler-Howard Act as a temporary measure along the road to assimilation, while Collier the pluralist saw its provisions as part of a distinct and enduring federal obligation to America's aboriginal inhabitants. The difference would hinge on how the new law was applied.

By the end of 1934, then, everyone's gains and losses remained as ambiguous as the Janus-faced qualities of the bill itself. Collier held the discretionary power to apply the landmark legislation according to his own purposes. His executive reforms set the stage for protecting Indian religious traditions and limiting missionary authority in BIA institutions; and the Wheeler-Howard Act, when read in terms of Collier's intent, directly opposed the program of Americanization, individualization, and citizenship that missionaries had long supported. But Collier was dealing with a stubborn bureaucracy and an Indian population that was justifiably skeptical of BIA innovations. Without lasting reforms, a succeeding commissioner could reinstate federal prerogatives for missionaries and subvert Collier's self-government proposals through administrative neglect. On the other side, Lindquist was just beginning to plumb the depths of hostility toward Collier among his hundreds of contacts in Indian country. With their help, Lindquist might still be able to keep Collier's crusade in check.

5 Struggle to Redeem the BIA, 1935–1942

Although G. E. E. Lindquist congratulated himself with a sense of triumph against Collier's legislative program in 1934, by May 1935, he had already settled into a deeper realization of the challenges he now faced. Ruminating over the events of the past twelve months, he spoke forlornly of "drastic new experiments" and "reactionary proposals" from the Bureau of Indian Affairs. The Indians were being treated as if "they were incapable of becoming civilized." Missionaries, too, had become the "targets" of "drastic regulations." Stepping back for a moment, Lindquist concluded that the previous year had been "one of the most difficult and perplexing" in his twenty-five years as a Christian missionary.[1]

At the heart of his bewilderment was an unwelcome and unfamiliar experience of powerlessness. Throughout his career, Lindquist had maintained cordial and close relationships with BIA officials. He had met with powerful politicians and worked with esteemed scholars and educators. He had published a groundbreaking book on Indians that was reviewed in major newspapers and journals. And President Hoover had appointed him to the prestigious Board of Indian Commissioners in 1930. In short, he had been the quintessential insider to Indian affairs. And as a result, he had bought into the power of the BIA as a protective and guiding force in the lives of America's indigenous peoples. But now he found himself estranged from the institutions and positions of power where he had once made himself at home.

Faced with this situation, and with no question of resigning himself to the sidelines, Lindquist looked at several choices for how to proceed. First, he could cooperate with the BIA in those settings where cooperation was still possible. Second, by organizing field missionaries and fostering negative publicity about Collier, he could try to wrestle the BIA away from Collier and back into friendlier hands. Or third, he could cut his ties to the BIA altogether and seek to achieve the Indians' assimilation by working *against* the BIA, rather than with it or through it.

This chapter shows that in the seven or eight years after Collier gained control of the BIA, Lindquist opted largely for the first two approaches, and he used them steadily and effectively to preserve missionary access to BIA institutions and create problems for Collier's administration. The chapter begins by discussing missionary programs in BIA schools, which, in spite of new regulations, remained strong through Lindquist's strategy of bold cooperation with school administrators. Then I discuss Lindquist's leadership in founding a new national organization for field missionaries, specifically for the purpose of leveraging their influence against Collier's policies. In both of these cases, Lindquist was working strategically to make the most of the clout and authority that missionaries and Christian Indian leaders already enjoyed. In the latter half of the chapter, we turn to a consideration of Lindquist's role as an outside agitator, where he played a key part in publicizing Collier's missteps and failures. In case studies of Collier's dealings with the Navajos and the Taos Indians, we will see how Collier's much-vaunted goal of tribal self-government ran into conflict with other priorities, such as economic rehabilitation and religious freedom. These administrative inconsistencies gave Lindquist the ammunition he needed to question Collier's professed commitment to tribal self-rule.

In these attacks on Collier, though, a transformation was slowly taking place in Lindquist's attitudes toward the BIA. At first, Lindquist's primary target was Collier, not the BIA. But Lindquist could only accuse Collier of using the BIA to patronize and dominate the Indians for so long before he would have to change his own approach to the BIA for consistency's sake. For if a disempowering paternalism lay at the core of his opposition to Collier, then he could no longer support the paternalistic vision of the BIA that he had advocated either. Paternalism was still paternalism, whether it claimed to be assimilating the Indians or not. And the only way to eradicate federal paternalism in Indian affairs, Lindquist ultimately concluded, was to abolish the BIA altogether.

But that gets us ahead of our story. This chapter focuses on the years before Lindquist was ready to take that more radical step, a period when his hostility was directed more toward Collier than toward the existence of the BIA. For now, faced with the choice between abandoning the BIA and attempting to redeem it, Lindquist remained committed to redeeming it.

Capitalizing on Missionary Strengths

As Lindquist surveyed the field of Indian missions and the crucial interface between missions and the BIA, he saw that one of the most important assets he could draw upon in resisting Collier's administration was the long-standing tradition of church activity within federal boarding schools for Indians. In 1934, Collier tried to break up the missionaries' monopoly in Indian education by opening school doors to Indian traditionalists and prohibiting compulsory school programs of worship and denominational instruction. But Lindquist was able to maneuver and direct missionary resources so that in spite of Collier's formal policy, religious work directors continued to enjoy virtually unrestricted access to Indian children.

The larger reason for Lindquist's success can be traced to the tradition of service that missionaries provided within Indian schools and the sense of obligation, in turn, that school superintendents often felt for supporting missionary work. Missionaries had long embedded themselves in the day-to-day workings of many federal boarding schools, creating patterns of reciprocity and exchange with school administrators. And by giving much-needed support to the operations of the school, missionaries helped to ensure that they would preserve their unusual privileges. Even if they grumbled about Collier's policies at the national level, they could nevertheless support, through voluntary and even extraordinary assistance, the particular schools they served.[2]

Lindquist encouraged this pattern and turned it into an effective strategy for preserving the missionary establishment in Indian education. Living next door to Haskell Institute in Lawrence, Kansas, he supervised almost a dozen school missionaries employed by the Home Missions Council. His seasoned advice to those under his charge was simple: be loyal to boarding school programs and excel in the doing of good deeds for staff and administrators. In fact, the regular reports that religious educators sent to Lindquist began, according to his specified format, not with the expected summary of worship programs and religious instruction, but with a narrative account of how they had contributed positively to their respective school's overall program.

This strategy should not be surprising. It has been said that the best job security is to make oneself indispensable, and that is precisely what religious workers did. Many of the schools were geographically isolated, staff turnover was high, and parents were typically too far away to pitch in with volunteer service. Meanwhile, religious work directors stepped into the gaps. They substituted periodically when teachers were sick, and for prolonged periods when schools had difficulty filling openings. To take pressure off of overworked school counselors, they ran weekly programs about dorm life, helping homesick and disoriented students make the adjustment to boarding school routines. They served as regular members of school committees, planned extracurricular activities, attended teachers' meetings, chaperoned socials, drove buses, wrote general interest articles for school papers, assisted in school hospitals, served as "squad leaders" for morning calisthenics, punched tickets at athletic events, and led programs at staff parties. This work was voluntary and unpaid. And it had nothing directly to do with religion. It was commonplace school labor that the school itself was responsible for performing. But the Home Missions Council subsidized school activities through the salaries of their religious work directors. Churches kept their foot in the door of Indian schools in large part by giving them support in the numerous areas where school programs and personnel fell short.

From the school administration's point of view, missionary assistance in nonreligious activities proved too attractive to pass up. Every job that missionaries took on represented one less burden for the school's regular staff. At the Chilocco Indian School in Oklahoma, for example, the task of organizing Saturday evening socials fell to religious workers not because it was their responsibility, but "largely because they have the time and energy to do it." And with regard to substitute teaching, administrators naturally turned to religious work directors who, because they often held master's degrees, were far better qualified than most other available candidates. Even after discounting the pro-missionary attitudes of many superintendents, the sheer constraints of time and money made missionary service an attractive auxiliary labor pool to school administrators.[3]

If religious educators' work within school programs went unpaid, it did not go unrewarded. What missionaries received in exchange was the extension, largely undisturbed, of their extraordinary privileges in the BIA's schools. Of course, they continued to plan Sunday schools and worship services, and during the week they provided their usual hour of religious instruction. But in many places they were allowed to do a good bit more. Missionaries at several schools taught courses in religion and biblical studies as part of the schools' for-credit curriculum.[4] In Flandreau, South Dakota, the school assigned student labor to make repairs on the local Methodist and Episcopal churches.[5] Moreover, the larger boarding schools typically gave missionaries office space, while at the Chemawa

Indian School in Oregon, school officials allowed missionaries exclusive use of two abandoned dorm buildings. The Protestant religious work director at Chemawa actually resided in one school building rent-free with his entire family.[6] Religious work directors were so thoroughly enmeshed in the daily life of many federal boarding schools that students, according to A. Willard Jones at Chilocco, had accepted them as "normal member[s] of the employee group."[7]

In sum, at the local level of federal boarding schools, the missionary establishment still held. Collier's new regulations in 1934 sought to dismantle the religious establishment, but well into the 1940s, religious work directors continued to bear the marks of a state-sponsored religious favoritism. Of course, that favoritism could not be taken for granted. Unlike during the nineteenth and early twentieth centuries, the BIA itself provided no federal mandate to Christianize the Indians. And missionaries preserved their privileges more through a process of mutual exchange with school administrators than through an inherent or presumptive religious authority. But they nevertheless could maintain, as far as Indian children were concerned, the appearance of official status. Yet another generation of Native American children would have reason to perceive Christianity as America's state religion.

Even if missionaries could preserve their access to BIA institutions at the local level, there remained the far more difficult question of how to parlay their collective influence on Collier and national policy debates. Field missionaries lacked a reliable organizational medium for forcing Collier to reckon with their concerns. In most circumstances they would have depended upon the executive secretaries of the missionary boards to help them advocate their causes. But the Joint Indian Committee, which consisted of missionary executives from the ecumenical Home Missions Council and Council of Women for Home Missions, had proved more willing to represent Collier's new policies to a skeptical missionary force than to leverage the widespread missionary resentment against Collier. According to Mazie Crawford, Presbyterian missionary to the Nez Perce tribe in Idaho, the capitulation of the mainline denominational boards had placed field-workers "in an exposed position and tak[en] away their weapons."[8]

Lindquist took this problem to heart. He had seen reformers and missionary executives lose touch with the sentiments of field-workers before. When he first entered Indian missions during the early twentieth century, field missionaries such as his mentors, Walter and Mary Roe, had helped to persuade an influential Protestant establishment in the East to adopt a more gradual approach to assimilation—an approach more consistent with missionary concerns for the social stability of Indian communities and their churches. And now missionary executives seemed to be allowing their proximity to Collier to blind them to the problems Collier's policies created for missionaries in the field. If the Protestant establishment in Indian affairs were to continue to exist at all, it would depend upon the combined strength of both field missionaries and their representatives in the East.

Moreover, Lindquist needed an organized voice for field missionaries in order to shore up his own eroding reputation among upper-level missionary administrators. After his aggressive campaign to block the Wheeler-Howard Act, the Joint Indian Committee began limiting Lindquist's exposure to administration officials. In December 1934, committee members like Anne Seesholtz pulled strings to remove Lindquist from the program of a meeting where Collier might be present, and they used back channels to assure Collier that Lindquist's hostility, while faithful to some missionaries in the field, did not represent the collective mind of the committee itself. To save face personally and begin to restore assimilation policies nationally, Lindquist would need to find or create an organization of field missionaries large enough to earn the respect of the Joint Indian Committee and Collier as well.[9]

A still larger issue motivated Lindquist to consider creating a national organization for field missionaries. By his own reckoning, nearly half of all Indians were affiliated with Christian churches. And many of those congregations were led by Native Americans themselves. Out of 438 ordained Protestant ministers on Indian reservations in 1923, more than 260 were Native Americans.[10] An organization of Euro-American missionaries and Christian Indian leaders, Lindquist believed, could turn Collier's vision of Indian self-government against itself, by displaying the strength of Indian sentiment in favor of political and cultural assimilation.

In the fall of 1934, a diverse group of Indians formed a new organization that held some initial promise for funneling Christian Indian attitudes into a politically significant movement. Called the American Indian Federation (AIF), this loosely knit coalition of Indian leaders represented the most militant wing of opposition to Collier's reforms. Collier called the group a bunch of "warped witchburners" and spent considerable time and energy refuting their allegations. He used BIA personnel to infiltrate the group's meetings and even went so far as to persuade the FBI to investigate its leaders.[11]

Not surprisingly, given his extensive travels, Lindquist himself had connections with several of its early officers.[12] He was personally acquainted with the organization's president, Joseph Bruner, a Creek businessman in Sapulpa, Oklahoma.

During the late twenties, he and Bruner had been frequent contributors to a small Indian-owned magazine named *The American Indian,* which was published in Tulsa.[13] The AIF's vice president was J. C. Morgan, the Christian Reformed missionary and tribal leader who put Lindquist's "Fourteen Points" to powerful use against the Wheeler-Howard Act on the Navajo reservation. And the rather active chaplain of the new group was Floyd O. Burnett, whom Collier banned from Sherman Institute following his and Lindquist's political agitation in southern California. Lindquist also knew Alice Lee Jemison (Seneca), the AIF's most effective congressional lobbyist.[14]

Borrowing from the rhetoric of Protestant fundamentalism and the red scare movement of the 1920s, AIF leaders argued in broadsides and House hearings that America was a "Christian Nation," and that Collier had subverted its highest principles through the imposition of "Atheism and Communism" upon Indian tribes.[15] They charged that "Christian activities among the Indians are being hampered and hamstrung," and they sent circular letters to missionaries in the hopes of strengthening the AIF's sometimes-fragile base of support.[16] On at least one occasion, Nez Perce church leaders in Idaho used House hearings with the AIF to call for Collier's removal from office on the grounds, in part, of his proposal to "resurrect the old religious ceremonials."[17]

Several problems prevented the AIF from becoming the organizational vehicle Lindquist was looking for in his fight against Collier. First, the AIF's red-baiting and guilt-by-association indictments of Collier and other government officials did not suit Lindquist's style or the collective attitude of the Home Missions Council. Second, President Bruner transgressed Lindquist's personal ethical code by using peyote and advocating racial segregation for African Americans.[18] Third, several AIF members in the Pacific Northwest allied the group with the German-American Bund and other fascist and anti-Semitic organizations.[19] And finally, the single objective that held the AIF together—the abolition of the BIA—was still too far-fetched for Lindquist and most other Protestant leaders in the midthirties. As historian Laurence Hauptman has argued, the guiding spirit of the AIF was the abolitionist Carlos Montezuma, one of the Protestant missionary establishment's most bitter enemies. In the 1910s and 1920s, in fact, Lindquist had supported the Home Missions Council and the Indian Rights Association in opposing Montezuma's attempt to gain control of the Society of American Indians, fearing that he and his supporters would "set the Indians free" from the BIA's paternalistic protections only to have them destroyed by western land interests. Under Collier, it is true, Lindquist and other missionaries began to rethink their opposition to abolitionist radicalism, but the AIF was still too extreme on this and other counts to acquire an enthusiastic following from most Christian Indians and Euro-American missionaries and reformers.[20]

With no alternative in sight, but still committed to amplifying the voices of missionaries and Indian pastors, Lindquist founded the National Fellowship of Indian Workers (NFIW) in 1935. Beginning with thirty missionaries at a meeting in Madison, Wisconsin, the group quickly grew to include six regional conferences and approximately four hundred active members by 1942.[21] Although the term *fellowship* in the title hinted at the religious and ecumenical character of the organization, Lindquist clearly intended for the group to act as a political lobby in Indian affairs.[22] The NFIW's original statement of purpose bore this out, for the organization would, it claimed, "give a ready and authoritative voice to the scattered body of Indian missionaries" in the United States, and "bring to public attention in a forceful way the sentiment of Indian missionaries on any matters affecting the welfare of Indians and Indian missionaries."[23]

Throughout the 1930s, regional and national meetings published resolutions that criticized Collier's administration on numerous counts. NFIW members deplored the government's "zigzag policies" and called for assimilation to "go forward as rapidly as possible." They opposed the federal subsidies that Collier acquired for Indian arts and crafts. They fretted over the liberties Collier extended to peyote use among Native Americans. They charged the BIA with perpetuating a "blight of dependency" upon federal economic support.[24] And they faulted Collier for the autocratic manner in which he handled Navajo affairs.[25] Some of the most active members, moreover, were among Collier's staunchest critics. Floyd Burnett, chaplain for the American Indian Federation, was a charter member and the chair of the fellowship's important Findings Committee in 1935.[26] J. C. Morgan, the vocal Navajo critic of the Indian New Deal and vice president of the AIF, was an active member as well. And Flora Warren Seymour, the Chicago lawyer and former member of the Board of Indian Commissioners, made numerous conference speeches and contributed articles to the NFIW *News Letter.*

Along with giving institutional clout to what had previously been a scattered chorus of missionary complaints, the NFIW also promised to provide field missionaries a stronger platform for challenging the accommodating posture of their superiors on the Home Missions Council. In fact, some NFIW members were wary of maintaining any connections at all with the ecumenical body. One person declared at the inaugural meeting that "if the organization is to depend upon the Joint [Indian] Committee of the Home Missions Council not much would be done."[27] So throughout its existence, the NFIW prodded the Joint Indian Committee to take stronger stands on such policy issues as peyote, reservation law and order, and the problem of Indian "wardship."[28]

At the outset, Joint Indian Committee members chafed against a group that purported to speak for field missionaries, especially when they believed the role already belonged to them. Its secretary called upon denominational executives to write cautionary letters to their field missionaries about the NFIW's second meeting in 1936. Missionaries who attended should "do everything possible," according to the Joint Indian Committee, to make the gathering "a fine, construc- tive, forward-looking [conference] and not allow it to deteriorate in criticism of the present or past policies of the Government."[29] Lindquist himself appeared willing to tolerate a measure of compromise with the Joint Indian Committee. He sought not so much to antagonize his fellow committee members as to make them more accountable to the isolated missionaries he encountered on his an- nual round. Thus Lindquist worked for several years to gain the committee's endorsement and financial support for the NFIW.[30] In the process, the NFIW made a few adjustments in its program to ease fears about possible missionary extremism. In 1937, the NFIW toned down its statement of purpose, leaving behind muscular claims about an "authoritative voice" for the "forceful" presen- tation of missionary views, and opting to speak more congenially of "orderly means" to "discuss" Indian policy issues.[31] From the viewpoint of Lindquist's pragmatism, the fellowship could give up its sharper edges in order to bridge the gap between field-workers and missionary board administrators. As long as that gap was bridged, field missionaries could bring their attitudes to bear on the work of the Home Missions Council, and, through it, gain more credibility within the BIA.[32]

Perhaps the NFIW's greatest historical significance lies within the double meaning of its own name. For the fellowship sought to support not only workers among the Indians, but also "Indian workers" themselves. By the 1940s, ap- proximately half of its national and regional conference participants were Indian pastors and community leaders.[33] Also, many long-term officers in the NFIW were American Indians, such as Robert P. Chaat (Comanche)—one of Lindquist and Roe Cloud's first students at the Roe Indian Institute.[34] In the NFIW, then, the Bureau of Indian Affairs encountered the makings of an indigenized church, where Indian leaders were assuming the authority to speak for themselves with- out mediation from Euro-American missionaries.[35] Lindquist's institution build- ing set in motion an indigenizing process within the overarching goal of promot- ing assimilationist ideals. That led to some ironic consequences, as we shall see, especially when the NFIW veered from Lindquist's views in the 1940s and 1950s.

But in its more immediate impact on the Collier administration, the NFIW served to deepen Collier's awareness of the religious and political diversity of America's Indians.

At different levels of the Indian affairs bureaucracy, then, Lindquist adopted different strategies for maintaining missionary influence. At the local level of reservations and boarding schools, where BIA officials were furthest removed from the reform attitudes of Collier and his staff, missionaries devoted themselves to community service as a means to continued access to BIA institutions. At the national level, where missionary representatives on the Joint Indian Committee had largely endorsed Collier's reforms, Lindquist founded an organization to make ecumenical leaders more accountable to field-workers' skepticism and resentment. And with the growing involvement of Native Americans in missionary leadership, church influence in Indian affairs was on its way toward being reconfigured along indigenous lines.

Probing the Ironies of Tribal Self-government

While Lindquist organized missionary and Christian Indian influence, he also worked another angle of attack on Collier's reforms. Here we see Lindquist taking on the role of the outside agitator, the obstructionist—a role he had despised in Collier until 1933 but suddenly found himself forced to assume for himself. Lindquist's method was simple. All he had to do was look for signs of Collier's failures and inconsistencies, publicize them, and use them to build up Native distrust of Collier's sweet promises of tribal self-government. And indeed, Collier's administration gave Lindquist all the ammunition he needed to accomplish his goals. For despite his repeated disavowals, Collier failed to free himself from the BIA's traditionally paternalistic and condescending relationship to Indian tribes.

The gap between rhetoric and reality appeared early on in Collier's administration. When he introduced the Wheeler-Howard Act in February 1934, he claimed it would "curb the hitherto almost autocratic powers of the Office of Indian Affairs over the persons, property, and institutions of the Indians by granting to them the elementary powers of self-government." The legislation, he added, would give the Indians "a chance . . . to shake off the deadening clutch of bureaucratic domination, and to achieve the freedom and dignity which their history and qualities entitle them to."[36] But in reality, while attempting to establish tribal self-government, Collier frequently imposed his policies against Indians' will. He ran roughshod over Indian attitudes and used threats and promises to cajole tribes into accepting his reforms. In doing so, he was repeating the behaviors he had condemned in his assimilationist predecessors. Of course, Collier's administration did promise to grant the Indians a measure of cultural freedom and tribal autonomy that assimilationists never contemplated. But even in the act of granting that freedom, Collier inescapably held the power to revoke it. And he could not resist the temptation to exercise that authority when an Indian group failed to share his view of the higher good.

Scholars have identified several overlapping reasons for Collier's failure in this regard. One has to do with problems in Collier's core philosophical vision. E. A. Schwartz has argued that Collier's preservationist views on Indian culture were a red herring that smoked over his strong commitment to the governing authority of a professional bureaucracy. For Schwartz, Collier failed to foster genuine self-governance because he never managed to overcome the elitist views of his upbringing in the aristocratic circles of the New South.[37] Similarly, anthropologist Thomas Biolsi has argued that Collier's plan for Indian self-government, also known as indirect administration, functioned "not as a new empowerment of Indian people but as a technique of domination." "The Indian New Deal for Collier," he continues, "meant the BIA showing the Indians the light and eventually, theoretically, at some unspecified and mysteriously receding point in the future, turning administration over to Indians. In the meantime, professionals knew what was best."[38] In another account, Russell Barsh attributes Collier's problems to "the steady, guiding hand of bureaucracy." Collier inevitably ran the BIA according to the motive that implicitly guides bureaucracies more than any other— institutional self-preservation. Collier, in this view, succumbed to the inherent pressures involved in leading a large bureaucracy by seeking to expand the BIA's power rather than limit it.[39]

Whether the cause was philosophical or political or a combination of the two, Lindquist and his associates quickly picked up on Collier's problem and constantly used it to their advantage. Their attacks were predatory and, in retrospect, hypocritical. Lindquist and most missionaries had encouraged paternalistic and intrusive BIA policies so long as those policies favored the Indians' Christianization and assimilation. Having supported a gradual assimilation with a lengthy guardianship over Indian societies, Lindquist stood on weak ground when he criticized Collier for his bureaucratic intrusions and patronizing ways. But by making Collier's inconsistencies and failures in tribal self-government the primary point of attack, a more substantial transition was taking place in Lindquist's approach to federal Indian policy. He was beginning to see that the guardianship he had long supported had become the mechanism for the Indians' perpetual differentiation from the body politic. Observing Collier's administration convinced Lindquist and others with him that the solution to the Indian problem lay not with a guarded assimilation—which, by its ambivalence, might still play into Collier's hands—but with a more radical and immediate severing of the federal government's unique relationship with Indian tribes. That point would not become fully apparent until the mid-1940s, when Lindquist identified the BIA—and not simply Collier's running of it—as his primary enemy. Until then, Lindquist's effort to obstruct Collier's administration often seemed as much rooted in opportunism as in principle.

Lindquist began accusing Collier of bureaucratic heavy-handedness with the introduction of the Wheeler-Howard Act in February 1934. As he was fond of noting, the bill made eighty-three references to the authority of the Indian office and the secretary of the Interior.[40] All tribal constitutions and charters of incorporation required approval from the Interior Department. Tribes could not raise taxes, set membership guidelines, or even hire employees without the secretary's oversight. And while the bill envisioned tribes assuming control over their own public services, it nevertheless granted to the federal government the power to decide whether and how to relinquish that control. Even the bill's most popular features—the revolving credit fund and scholarships for education—could be used to bribe Indian groups into accepting the new charters. Or worse, the monies could be used as more stick than carrot by denying federal funds to tribes that voted not to organize under the bill.[41]

Once the revised version of the Wheeler-Howard bill was passed in June 1934, Collier soon came under fire for the one provision that seemed to set his administration furthest apart from his predecessors—the section granting individual tribes the right to veto the legislation that had been written on their behalf. In what some have called a "legal sleight of hand," Collier and the solicitor of the Interior Department, Nathan Margold, manipulated the bill's provision on tribal referenda to guarantee that virtually every tribe would come under the act, simply by counting all nonvoters as positive votes in favor of reorganization.[42] In fact, seventeen tribes had already voted to exempt themselves from the Wheeler-Howard Act by January 1935, but the solicitor's decision brought them under the bill anyway. Matthew Sniffen, secretary for the Indian Rights Association and close friend of Lindquist, immediately called attention to the problem in "Futile Voting." Collier's action, he warned, had rankled Indians "too numerous to ignore." Under pressure, Collier relented and sponsored legislation authorizing the BIA to count only the votes of actual election participants.[43]

Collier's difficulties did not end once the controversy over voting guidelines subsided. Almost a third of America's tribes voted to reject the Wheeler-Howard Act, and of the 181 tribes that accepted it, only half followed through to adopt constitutions by the end of Collier's term in 1945.[44] Many Indians experienced Collier's version of tribal self-government as an externally imposed reform.[45] According to historian Kenneth Philp, the Wheeler-Howard Act "imposed rigid political and economic ideas on tribes that varied in their cultural orientation."[46] As a result, Collier's administration of the Indian New Deal made him an easy target for Lindquist and other missionary opponents.

Two case studies from the Southwest—the Navajos and the Taos Pueblos—help round out the portrait of Collier's problems and the way that Lindquist and other Protestant opponents turned them to their advantage. The high profile of these two groups made Collier's difficulties with them particularly significant. The Navajos were the single largest Native American tribe, with approximately fifty thousand members. They extended across three states—Arizona, New Mexico, and Utah—and their holdings in land, livestock, and oil made them a matter of interest to economic and political forces throughout the Southwest. The Taos Pueblos were equally important to Collier, but for different reasons. They were the ones who first inspired Collier to move into Indian reform. Culturally resilient and economically independent, they should have provided a model for how Collier wanted his reforms to play out. But Native resistance dogged Collier at every turn, and that gave Lindquist an opening for publicizing Collier's missteps to a national audience.

When Collier became Indian Commissioner in 1933, the Navajos were facing their greatest economic crisis in almost seventy years. After undergoing military subjection and forced removal in the 1860s, the Navajos returned to their home-land in the four corners area to subsist on their livestock herds of sheep and goats. As a result of their isolation and economic independence, they enjoyed a period of rapid population growth and relative freedom from BIA interference. But over time, the reservation became too small to support the tribe's growing herds, and the problems of overgrazing and soil erosion began to wash away their prospects for self-sufficiency by the late 1920s. Then, with the onset of the Great Depression, the price of wool dropped from 30.2 cents per pound in 1930 to 8.6 cents per pound in 1932. Opportunities for wage labor off the reservation dried up, and the Navajos stood on the brink of economic collapse.[47]

Collier responded to the crisis by instituting herd reduction regulations to prevent overgrazing and soil erosion. The Navajos, however, strongly resisted Collier's attempts to cut the size of their herds. They believed that land and rain shortages were the true causes of their problems, not the number of animals on the range. But Collier, thinking that he was taking a longer view of the tribe's survival than the Navajos themselves, pushed ahead through a series of complex, poorly administered programs for herd reduction. A sign of how Collier would deal with the Navajos appeared early, in an October 1933 meeting with the tribal council. In language reminiscent of Commissioner Charles Burke's 1923 circular against Indian dances, Collier told the council that he already possessed statutory authority to force tribe members to reduce their herds, but he sought instead to win their cooperation through reason and persuasion. Repeatedly over the next several years, Collier's land management advisors would urge the Navajos to avert disaster through herd reduction, the Navajo tribal council would reluctantly consent, and tribe members would resist.

Unfulfilled promises and unfairly executed programs further provoked Navajo enmity. In 1934, Collier promised that if the Navajos would follow through with herd reduction plans for that year, he would convince Congress to enlarge the boundaries of the reservation. The Navajos carried out their side of the bargain only to find Collier unable to discharge his. Even those who accepted the inevitability of herd reductions were disturbed by the inequities in how they were carried out. Wealthy owners discarded culls from their herds without any sacrifice, while some small owners had their flocks reduced below subsistence levels. Others lost even the goats they needed to provide milk for their children.[48]

Leading the opposition to Collier's administration of Navajo affairs was J. C. Morgan, a Christian Reformed missionary and tribal council member with close personal ties to Lindquist, Sniffen, and assimilation activists Elaine G. Eastman and Flora Warren Seymour. He was also active in the National Fellowship of Indian Workers and served as a vice president in the American Indian Federation. Born in a hogan in 1879, Morgan graduated in 1901 from Hampton Institute in Virginia, a boarding school that trained both Indians and southern blacks in the twin gospels of hard work and Christian morality.[49] There can be little doubt that the animosity between Morgan and Collier ultimately stemmed from the differences in their cultural and religious convictions. Collier called Morgan "a victim of theological bias" whose attitudes were "prejudiced" and "intolerant." Morgan argued, though, that it was Collier whose understanding of traditional Navajo culture was blinded by preconceived fancies. The medicine men whom Collier celebrated, Morgan told readers of the *Christian Century,* practiced "pagan surgery" and spread ignorance and disease through their ministrations.[50] Articulate and highly motivated, Morgan became the leading Navajo antagonist to Collier's reforms.

But as Donald Parman has argued, the cultural debate between Morgan and Collier did not account for Navajo opposition to BIA measures. Rather, Morgan's rise to power grew out of his skillful manipulation of the economic and political problems that Collier struggled to resolve. To most Navajos, cultural pluralism and assimilation dealt with matters that were abstract and somewhat removed from more pressing needs such as keeping their livestock and obtaining clothing for their children. So while Morgan beat the drum of Christian assimilation for a national churchgoing audience, among his own largely unconverted tribe members, he served as an effective mouthpiece for the Navajos' numerous administrative grievances.[51]

Morgan's influence in Navajo affairs continued to grow in the spring of 1935, when the tribe deliberated whether to adopt the provisions of the Wheeler-Howard Act. Collier and top officials from Washington mounted a vigorous crusade to persuade Navajos to vote yes in the referendum. But Morgan and two other Protestant Navajo church leaders actively campaigned for its rejection, saying that the bill's "communistic" proposals violated both American norms and the property traditions of the Navajos themselves. Those charges were linked as well to the issue of herd reduction, which pitted a powerful federal government against the individual property interests of Navajo herders.[52] After a fierce and divisive debate, the tribe voted to reject the bill by a narrow margin, with the decisive votes coming from Morgan's own district.[53]

Collier was convinced, and rightfully so, that Christian religious leaders among the Navajo played a pivotal role in this major failure for his administration. Without mentioning Morgan by name, Collier told the tribe that he honored their decision but regretted its having been based on statements that were "totally and . . . knowingly false." In his petulant letter, Collier went on to list the various financial benefits the tribe's vote had forfeited, inadvertently confirming Morgan's allegations that Collier had tried to bribe the tribe into accepting the Wheeler-Howard Act.[54] There is also evidence that Collier considered taking action against the Christian Reformed Church's (CRC) missions on the Navajo reservation, for he had his staff gather information about the location of their churches and the legal status of their land grants. At the very least, his agents talked with CRC missionaries about Morgan's activities, encouraging them to remain neutral on policy matters and ultimately undercutting their willingness to keep Morgan in his church position.[55]

In summer 1937, matters on the Navajo reservation began once more to come to a head. Collier's drive to reduce Navajo herds accelerated rather than abated as the Indian service began its most systematic program yet to match herd populations with the land's carrying capacity. Federal marshals were brought in to support tribal police in enforcing compliance, and in one case, the federal government initiated a lawsuit against Navajo herd owners to obtain the desired result.[56] For his part, Morgan became convinced that Collier was using herd reduction to punish the tribe for rejecting the Wheeler-Howard Act.[57] He also believed Collier's agents were engaging in a dirty tricks campaign to wear him down. In May 1937 several of his Navajo opponents, reportedly at the instigation of the BIA superintendent E. R. Fryer, attempted to create a disturbance near Morgan's home in Farmington, New Mexico, so that they could trap him and have him arrested.[58] Adding to the tensions, Navajo police arrested and beat Morgan's brother-in-law the following August during a dispute about livestock regulations.[59]

Recognizing the volatility of the situation, Collier made a misguided attempt to reorganize the Navajo tribal council and build grassroots Navajo support for his programs. He instructed an executive committee within the existing tribal council to canvass the reservation and select new council members from among the Navajos' most respected leaders. But because the tribal council was formed through selection, not election, Morgan believed that Collier was attempting to handpick a council that would rubber-stamp his initiatives.[60] By spring 1938, Collier and his Navajo opponents seemed deadlocked in an intractable feud while tribe members lived in constant uncertainty about the fate of their livestock and their livelihoods.

At just that moment of vulnerability for Collier, Lindquist stepped up to publicize Collier's problems and call for immediate action. In correspondence published in *Indian Truth,* the Indian Rights Association's newsletter, Lindquist attempted to give the lie to Collier's principle of tribal self-government. He accused Collier of having "foisted" the new tribal council on the entire tribe and then, "under cover of darkness," calling a secret meeting with the council to avoid subjecting himself to widespread Navajo hostility. "Why these secret tactics," Lindquist asked, "in a country where 'self-government' and 'home rule' were the watchwords only a few short years ago?" Turning the tables on Collier's self-described sympathies for Indian ways of life, Lindquist criticized government officials for their complete lack of sensitivity to Navajo culture in implementing stock regulations. In short, Collier's propaganda notwithstanding, the Navajos "are still in the throes of regimentation and a superimposed autocratic government."[61]

The following August, IRA secretary Matthew Sniffen took Lindquist's letter, compiled it with his own field observations and the diatribes of Morgan and several other collaborators, and sent the fifteen-page result to President Franklin

D. Roosevelt under the signature of the IRA's president, Jonathan Steere. Before Roosevelt could respond publicly, Sniffen contacted Lindquist, Seymour, and Eastman to have the letter published and commented upon in dozens of newspapers across the country.[62] All things considered, the letter to Roosevelt represented one of the most scathing public indictments of Collier's entire administration. The IRA called Collier's dealings with the Navajos "the single most disgraceful effort at administration ever performed by man." Cataloguing five years of Navajo grievances against Collier, the letter described Navajo affairs as a "costly monument to official stupidity and incompetence," reeking with "bad faith, stupid blundering and misrepresentation of facts."[63]

After many promises and several delays, Collier sponsored a popular election of the Navajo tribal council and, four weeks after the IRA's open letter, J. C. Morgan—Collier's bitter enemy—was elected chairman by a comfortable margin. Taken together, the IRA's letter and Morgan's election helped to defuse the political crisis and relieve the high level of unrest among Navajo tribe members. Collier was forced to adopt a more conciliatory approach toward his Navajo opponents. And in response to Collier's new overtures, Morgan himself began to cooperate with federal officials, leading Superintendent Fryer to call Morgan one of the most "intelligent and responsible" Navajo leaders he ever worked with. Economic problems on the Navajo reservation persisted throughout Collier's administration, but the political deadlock finally began to break in 1938.[64]

In his dealings with the Navajos, then, Collier faced great difficulty reconciling his ideal of tribal self-government with the exigent need for economic rehabilitation and regional land management. Here were the independent and relatively isolated Navajos, an ideal laboratory for testing the full gamut of Collier's initiatives to preserve tribe and land and the traditions that bound the two together. But for several years, the only tribal government in existence was achieved by what one scholar called "administrative fiat."[65] Bogged down in the pressing effort to preserve the Navajos' land base, Collier lost track of some of the ideals that attracted his reform interests to Indian affairs in the first place. Unable, in his own words, "to bring some rationality into the Navajo mind," Collier succumbed to the condescending and prejudiced attitudes he had long attributed to his missionary enemies.[66] As a result, assimilationists like Lindquist took advantage of their opportunity to savor the delicious irony in Collier's apparent disregard for Navajo attitudes, while at the same time demonstrating their ongoing power to capitalize on Indian sentiment and discredit the methods of Collier's administrative machine.

While missionaries and reformers were exploiting Collier's problems in Navajo affairs, they were also watching Collier hang himself on the horns of another dilemma, this time at Taos Pueblo in New Mexico. Like the Navajos, Pueblo tribes in the early twentieth century had avoided economic dependence on the BIA, thus immunizing themselves from some of the more heavy-handed tools of BIA control. Moreover, because tribal ownership of their lands had been recognized by Spanish land grants dating from the colonial period, Pueblo leaders had enjoyed a largely unbroken legal authority to govern their internal affairs with minimal outside interference. They allocated agricultural lands among tribe members, coordinated community labor on irrigation ditches, and punished most criminal offenses within their own tribe.[67] In fact, Collier's vision for tribal self-government was largely based on his observations of the Taos Pueblo's integral unity of religion and politics, land and society. Collier believed that the sovereign powers of the Taos Indians were inherent within all Indian tribes.[68]

For most missionaries and reformers, in contrast, the Pueblos' powers of self-government were cause for considerable anxiety. They believed those powers curtailed the rights of individual Indians. In 1925, for example, the Indian Rights Association accused Pueblo leaders of trampling on the rights of Christian tribe members who refused to participate in the reputedly obscene and secret ceremonies of Pueblo traditionalists. According to the IRA, Christian Pueblos had seen their lands taken from them and been forced to labor on community projects in which they had no economic interest. At the time, Collier regarded the charges as part of a backhanded attempt to destroy traditional Pueblo culture.[69]

In 1936, though, Collier himself ran into conflict with Pueblo traditionalists. Emboldened by the powers of self-government promised in the Wheeler-Howard Act, the Taos tribal council revived its twenty-year effort to stamp out peyote use within its tribe. Local leaders of the Native American Church were imprisoned on the charge of witchcraft, while their subsistence lands were confiscated for redistribution among other tribe members. For a time, Collier tried to work behind the scenes to gain religious liberty for the peyote users. But Mabel Dodge Luhan, the New York exile who had first invited Collier to Taos in 1920, publicized the conflict in a series of charges she brought against Collier at a Senate Indian Committee hearing that August.[70]

Frustrated in his dealings with Taos leaders over the peyote issue and sore from Luhan's betrayal, Collier took action in September. He and Interior Secretary Harold Ickes ordered the Taos Pueblo to restore "liberty of conscience" to the peyotists, return their confiscated lands, and pay reparations for any other losses they had suffered as a result of imprisonment and other abuses. These actions were necessary, Collier wrote, "to serve that old life of Taos which is deep and self-controlled, tolerant and wise, and beautiful as few things of man are beautiful." Blaming the problems on "the temporary aberration of a few tribal officers" who had fallen under "white influences" (a reference to Luhan), he concluded, "The white invasion will become a memory. Taos—the Indian, the human, the mystic—will go on."[71] Despite Collier's attempt to minimize the long-term impact of the conflict, his goal of tribal self-government nevertheless ran into sharp conflict with his deep commitment to religious freedom. He chose to protect the rights of the religious minority within the tribe rather than honor the tribe's own sovereignty in preserving the communal integrity of its religious traditions.[72]

G. E. E. Lindquist and Flora Warren Seymour enjoyed watching Collier squirm. In an unsigned article for *Indian Truth,* Lindquist pointed out how Collier's solicitude for a peyote-using minority stood in sharp contrast to his apathy toward Christian Pueblos in the 1920s, who had suffered many of the same indignities for their religious nonconformity. And Seymour, the lawyer, raised serious questions about the federal government's legal authority to control transfers of land between Pueblo Indians. "It is very strange that an Indian administration which has made such a lot of talk about self-government should be attempting to take away the most important feature of self-government which the Pueblo Indians possess," she wrote.[73] In his response, Collier called the Lindquist article "misleading" and "inaccurate," and he quibbled with two or three of its minor claims.[74] But as Lindquist pointed out in correspondence with the Indian Rights Association, Collier's response was "a manifest evasion of the real issue"—his inconsistency in protecting the rights of a tribal minority. Under the circumstances, there was little Collier could do but mount an empty protest.[75]

After this brief but poignant exchange, the issue of minority rights within Taos Pueblo cooled for several years until another incident in 1939 brought it back up to the boiling point. Matthew Sniffen learned from an informant that John B. Concha, a Taos Indian, had been imprisoned and threatened with expulsion for not participating in traditional ceremonies. Lindquist went to Taos to investigate. He found that Concha had been one of a small group of Pueblos who organized themselves in order to take advantage of the loan provisions of the Wheeler-Howard Act. But the Taos tribal council refused to recognize their group, the Twin Villages Improvement Organization, thereby obstructing their plans for funding. And when the organization bought grain to sell at a profit, the council prohibited the sale, leaving the grain to rot in storage. Moreover, Concha himself was not allowed to use the tribe's collectively held farm implements, even though he had participated in such required community projects as ditch repairs and roadwork. His dissent was religious, and ironically, he defended that dissent before the council on the basis of Collier's promises to grant Indians their religious liberty. But "because the [Taos] Government is intrinsically religious," Lindquist wrote, Concha's religious dissent was treated as political subversion.[76]

At the time of Lindquist's investigation, the situation was relatively quiet. Concha was out of prison, but he still feared that tribal leaders would carry out their expulsion decree and leave him unable to care for his wife, mother-in-law, and three children. Lindquist recommended that if the council made any move toward expulsion, the Indian Rights Association should carry the case to court and break the Taos traditionalists' hold on internal political affairs.[77]

On the whole, Concha's case was tailor-made for Lindquist's purposes. Since Concha was not a practicing Christian, Lindquist was somewhat distanced from the appearance of missionary self-interest; in this case, he was defending a person's freedom *from* religion, not his freedom to practice the Christian religion. Moreover, Concha's overarching goal—and that of the organization he headed—was to take advantage of the reforms Collier had implemented since becoming commissioner.[78] In contrast to his early treatment of J. C. Morgan, Collier could not dismiss Concha as an intolerant religious fanatic or an anti-administration obstructionist. Collier would have to make a choice between protecting the individual conscience of Concha or the collective authority of the Taos Pueblo.

When the IRA's legal representative presented Lindquist's report on the Concha case to Collier, the commissioner—in sharp contrast to his handling of the peyote controversy—defended the Pueblo traditionalists without hesitation or compromise. Lindquist, he said, was "reckless" in his regard for the truth, and "evidently insensitive . . . with respect to the living realities of Taos." Collier feared that intervention on Concha's behalf would "split asunder the orthodox totality" of Taos religion, politics, and economy, because for the Pueblos, "rain, sunshine, plant growth, animal fertility, the whole stability of what we call the physical world, are . . . dependent upon these ceremonies . . . and upon the participation of the whole tribe in them."[79]

Lindquist called Collier's response "a mass of cloudy verbiage" about a rather simple matter—"the complete establishment of religion" at the Taos Pueblo. Collier's defense of Pueblo ceremonies and their strict enforcement was, for Lindquist, wistful nostalgia for a tribal cohesiveness and archaic mysticism that could no longer exist. Lindquist wrote, "Undoubtedly these deep believers ride in automobiles, use telephones, are familiar with the uses of electricity and a thousand other modern inventions and devices. They do not pray for communications;

they take down the receiver. They are not concerned with a possible heavenly message when they hear the familiar drone of an airplane overhead."[80] For Lindquist, the Pueblo Indians could not enjoy the advantages of Western technology without also adopting the individualized conception of religious liberty enshrined in Western civilization.

In 1939, though, American jurisprudence did not pose the Pueblos' choices in such exclusive terms. According to an Interior Department brief prepared at Collier's request, "the governing bodies of a tribe are not bound to grant religious liberty" to dissenting tribe members. The First Amendment applied to the actions of the federal government alone, not to state or tribal governments.[81] Thus, while the precise scope of tribal sovereignty remained highly contested, Collier acted lawfully when he refused to intervene in the Concha affair. But his handling of the peyote controversy at Taos, taken together with the issues raised by Lindquist's report on John Concha, betrayed the conflict he faced between his civil libertarian ideals and the measure of group participation required by communal Indian religions.

Collier's problems with the Navajo and Pueblo Indians, then, illustrated how the competing priorities of economic development and religious freedom could easily undermine his overarching agenda for self-determination. Temporary assertions of federal authority, Collier seemed to believe, would ultimately serve the Indians' larger interests in economic survival and political autonomy. To be sure, many Indians could not help but detect a familiar pattern of federal domination over Indian life and property. But for Lindquist, Collier had taken an existing educational and welfare agency and ballooned it into an unpopular social experiment in primitivist nostalgia. With the "natural" process of the Indians' amalgamation into American society momentarily interrupted by Collier's policies, Lindquist began to believe that the Indians' best prospects for assimilation lay no longer in a system of paternalistic guidance based in Washington, but in the Indians' emancipation from the federal government altogether.

The Whipple Incident

We have seen that, in the years following the passage of the Wheeler-Howard Act, Lindquist used several strategies to preserve missionary access to BIA institutions and renew public pressure for a return to assimilation policies. At the local level, he encouraged religious educators to cooperate with boarding school administrators to maintain a Christian establishment in Indian education. At the national level, he founded a new organization for missionaries and Christian Indians to voice their opposition to Collier's new policies. And he acted in concert with other Protestant reformers to publicize some of Collier's most notable failures. In other words, Lindquist combined cooperation in the field with belligerence at the higher level of federal policy and the national media. For a time, this two-tiered approach succeeded. Missionary involvement in Indian education held its own, while Collier's program for tribal self-government became mired in a host of administrative problems. But the approach was risky, especially for missionaries who worked in federal boarding schools. One of them, Floyd Burnett, had already sacrificed his job on the altar of opposition to Collier in 1934. It seemed only a matter of time, given Lindquist's mixed strategy, before the same thing might happen again.

And, indeed, Collier found his second missionary martyr in 1942. The sacrificial victim in this case was the Rev. Earl R. Whipple, the religious work director at Albuquerque Indian School. As a Home Missions Council employee, Whipple worked under Lindquist's supervision. And, in accordance with Lindquist's two-tiered strategy, he maintained good relations with school administrators, while also collaborating with Lindquist to gather damaging information about Sophie Aberle, the beleaguered superintendent of the United Pueblos Agency. According to Lindquist's version of events, Aberle apparently learned of Whipple's activities and feared that he might try to testify against her at an impending Senate investigation into Pueblo affairs. She then pulled some strings with the United States Marines and the FBI and had Whipple arrested on the preposterous charge of impersonating an officer. In retrospect, Aberle's precise role in Whipple's arrest has been difficult to verify, but at the very least, both Aberle and Collier failed to do what was in their power to exonerate Whipple from a questionable criminal charge.

If Aberle had been a small cog in the BIA's bureaucratic machine, Whipple's fate might have been altogether different. Instead she was a close friend of Collier's—a scholar (Ph.D., Stanford) and physician (M.D., Yale) who had devoted herself to studying Pueblo cultures and improving Indian health. Collier personally recruited her in 1935 to administer one of the most important agencies in the BIA, later telling her that "much of the philosophy and experimental freight of our Indian effort is centered down in your jurisdiction."[82] But from the time of her appointment in 1935, Aberle had been unpopular among a vocal group of Pueblo leaders. And by 1942, she was facing allegations that ranged from tribal election tampering to vindictive personnel changes at Pueblo schools. Several Indian rights organizations were teaming up to call for a Senate investigation into Aberle's affairs, and the Senate was preparing to oblige.[83]

In this highly charged political climate, there can be little doubt that Lindquist and Whipple were involved in an attempt to unseat Superintendent Aberle. Whipple communicated frequently with disgruntled Pueblo leaders, and he also picked up intelligence about Pueblo affairs from students at Albuquerque Indian School. So along with sending Lindquist regular statements about his activities as religious work director, Whipple also sent numerous off-the-record reports about Pueblo grievances, including evidence that Aberle had systematically sacked employees on the slightest suspicion of disloyalty.[84] By May, Lindquist and Whipple had started bringing the NFIW and the Home Missions Council into the chorus of calls for an investigation, and Lindquist was using Whipple's reports and his own connections with Senate Indian Committee chair Elmer Thomas to advance the cause.[85]

Under the circumstances, Whipple's arrest seemed to be something more than a mere coincidence. In a letter to Mark Dawber of the Home Missions Council, Whipple gave an account of what happened. On June 17, 1942, FBI agents entered his home, asked him to name his occupation, and then charged him with representing himself as "the Director of Religious Work and Educational Advisor at the Albuquerque Indian School, United States Indian Service, and wilfully seeking information of value from the United States government." Agents then proceeded to confiscate Whipple's correspondence with Lindquist.[86]

On paper, the charge was downright trivial. Whipple's title, to be sure, could easily mislead outsiders into thinking Whipple was a formal employee of the BIA. But that title (or some close variant) had been in use at Albuquerque and other BIA schools for more than twenty years. And it had been the BIA that had allowed for the confusion by tolerating the title in the first place. Collier made no effort to alter this arrangement when he became commissioner and revised the regulations for religious instruction. The legal foundation for Whipple's arrest, then, rested on an ambiguity that Collier himself had allowed to stand unchanged.

Confounding the charge of impersonating an officer, though, was the allegedly subversive purpose behind Whipple's "impersonation." Two Marine recruiters claimed that Whipple was feigning official status as a federal employee in order to thwart their recruiting efforts on the Albuquerque campus. However, Whipple insisted that he had vigorously supported the war effort and that his role had been limited to helping students consider the pros and cons of enlistment in their individual cases. At the very most, he claimed, the only discouragement to enlistment he had offered was to ask whether one teenage student might wish to finish his high school degree before signing up.[87]

I have been unable to find any direct evidence that Aberle orchestrated

Whipple's arrest, but the strong suspicions of Lindquist, Whipple, and other observers were not without warrant. Major Shannon, one of the Marine recruiters who brought the charge, had served in the BIA under Aberle, and Shannon had reportedly telephoned Aberle several days before Whipple's arrest, at about the time the FBI began its investigation. Moreover, although Aberle attended Whipple's preliminary hearing and wrote a report about it to Collier, she made no attempt to explain to the court the circumstances surrounding his work and job title. Nor were any other school officials allowed to testify in Whipple's behalf.[88] In a hastily scribbled, unofficial letter to Collier, Aberle explained that some of the information found in Whipple's files bore "a striking resemblance" to unpublicized statements made by her strongest Pueblo critics. Whipple was "definitely *unfriendly*" to the administration, she wrote, and "he was collecting facts for some purpose not yet disclosed."[89]

Collier followed Aberle's lead by trying to persuade the Home Missions Council that Whipple's case was hopeless. He advised the council's officers to distance themselves from Whipple immediately, even though Collier wondered privately whether others had somehow "dragged Whipple into trouble."[90] Of course, Collier's own motivations were clearly both personal and political. Collier resented Lindquist's intrusion into Pueblo affairs, and he was determined to protect Aberle's position. Her removal would have dealt a serious blow to his entire administration. So neither Aberle nor Collier was willing to exculpate Whipple even though they had the power to do so.[91]

After six months of legal proceedings, the charges against Whipple were finally dropped. Unfortunately, the exoneration came too late for Whipple. Collier forced the Home Missions Council to remove him from Albuquerque and Indian missions altogether. And in the aftermath of the entire episode, Whipple suffered a breakdown that placed him in a hospital for a large part of the next year.[92] Collier considered using the Whipple incident to remove all religious work directors from BIA campuses, but he never managed to follow through on the idea.[93] Aberle's administration survived for two more years under the vigilant protection of Collier himself. And Lindquist—well, Lindquist tried to organize a lawsuit against Aberle for instigating Whipple's frivolous indictment, but never succeeded in getting the Home Missions Council to back the charges.[94]

Years of hostility between Lindquist and Collier ultimately descended into this unflattering and tragic soap opera of events. Obsessed by their bare-knuckled animosity toward one another, they showed little regard for those who might get caught in the middle. For a time, it seemed that the spiritual ideals that motivated them might end up lost in their rank political struggle for power and influence. Both enemies and evangels, Lindquist and Collier ended 1942 deadlocked in the battle to control the Indians' future.

At the same time, in the wake of the passage of the Wheeler-Howard Act, Lindquist further demonstrated his capacity for leadership in the public realm. He was an institutional man, an organizer who knew how to build new coalitions like the NFIW and how to milk the BIA's system to gain influence for missionaries in Indian schools. He also proved to be an effective muckraker, a gadfly who could find and exploit instances in which Collier violated his own most deeply held ideals. For the most part, Lindquist was politically astute, but on occasion, he could misjudge the risks involved in his political activism, with rather unfortunate results. To round out the portrait of Lindquist, though, we will need to see how he led Protestant missionaries in reviving the assimilationist agenda in a new context. To that topic—Lindquist's crusade for civil rights for the Indians—we now turn.

6 Crusade against Wardship, 1942-1953

If Lindquist had been nothing more than an agitator taking shots at Collier from the outside, he might well have remained a passing figure in Indian affairs. But Lindquist would not be satisfied with the role of the critic. He had been an insider for too long to be comfortable purely as a spoiler with no comprehensive counter-proposal to Collier's reforms.

The problem was that he could not simply return to the programs for gradual assimilation that he had advocated throughout most of his career. The longer Collier survived as commissioner, the more indelible his stamp upon the BIA became. By the 1940s, Lindquist came to doubt whether the Indian bureau could be rescued from Collier's influences. And without the BIA, which had been the centerpiece of his thinking in the past, there was no viable mechanism for a slow and guarded assimilation. But Lindquist could not go back to the approach he had taken in the 1920s for a second reason: his own personal integrity, it seems, would not allow him. He never admitted it, but in Collier's expansion of the BIA and its involvement in tribal cultures and politics, Lindquist seems to have seen something of the same paternalistic transgressions he himself had committed as an insider.

So in the 1940s, Lindquist launched his drive to end Indian wardship. In doing so, he sought to undo Collier's legacy and, more subtly, to redeem himself from the paternalism of his own. He revived the abolitionist arguments of his earliest opponents and demanded the Indians' rapid emancipation from the bureaucratic domination of the BIA. Forsaking his past attachment to the wardship doctrine, Lindquist refashioned his call for assimilation on the egalitarian grounds of the Indians' civil rights as individuals.

This chapter, then, shows how Lindquist used the problem of wardship to recapture the dynamic middle ground of federal Indian policy. It begins by describing how the Second World War created a more favorable climate for Indian integration and the rhetoric of civil rights. It then offers a careful examination of two pivotal essays Lindquist wrote for the Home Missions Council, titled *Handbook on the Study of Indian Wardship* and "Indian Treaty Making." These documents presented an early and influential rationale for the termination policies that Congress instituted in the late forties and fifties, largely in reaction to Collier's New Deal measures.

Besides making a case for Lindquist's importance in this time period, I also seek to show how Lindquist's persistent prejudices against Indian cultures lingered within the shadows of his bright rhetoric of liberty. Lindquist made a strategic recovery of his authority toward the end of his career, but his rejection of the legitimacy of tribal sovereignty ultimately compromised his legacy as an advocate both with and for the Indians.

To support this argument, I conclude with a discussion of how leading Christian Indians like Arthur Parker and Ruth Muskrat Bronson responded to Lindquist's assault on wardship. Many had been part of the loose coalition he formed to oppose Collier's administration, but that coalition began to break down in the late forties as leading Christian Indians asserted their dual claim to both American and tribal citizenship, both civil and treaty rights. Lindquist insisted that treaty rights were a form of race-based discrimination that was incompatible with the racial equality envisioned in civil rights. But the Christian Indians whom Lindquist had promoted as models of assimilation ultimately dissented on this critical issue. Their dissent highlighted the painful irony that, even in seeking to abolish the federal government's domination of Indian lives, Lindquist was ultimately exercising that domination in yet another form.

Changing Climate for Assimilation

Just as Lindquist and the Home Missions Council began to organize for another strong push on Indian assimilation, several factors helped to create a favorable climate for their initiatives. Collier and the BIA were weakened by the large-scale governmental changes brought on by World War II. Significant reductions in bureau personnel and congressional funding exacerbated the difficulties involved in providing basic health and social services on Indian reservations. In 1941, the War Department's need for expanded office space in Washington, D.C., forced the BIA to move its headquarters to Chicago, where Collier was less effective in keeping his administration's budgetary needs before Congress.[1]

Even more, World War II significantly strengthened existing social pressures toward Indian integration. Military recruitment and increased industrial production pressed Indians into the total national involvement in the war effort. Twenty-five thousand Indians served in the military, while more than forty thousand others left the reservations for wage-earning jobs.[2] At the same time, non-Indian populations migrated closer to the reservations, following an economic boom in western states and the Defense Department's expropriation of important natural resources from tribal lands.[3] Meanwhile, popular media portraits of Indian heroism suggested to the American public that Indians were patriotic citizens ready to merge with mainstream society.[4]

The war also created a strong ideological basis for terminating American Indians' special legal status and dissolving the political separatism of tribal governments. How could Indians be expected to fight Nazi racial tyranny overseas, many wondered, only to return to a nation that segregated them in their own rural ghettos?[5] Civil rights, the emerging solution to the racial oppression of the Jim Crow South, seemed to offer answers to problems in Native American communities as well. International politics and the growing electoral power of African Americans in northern cities tilted the scales in favor of civil rights advocates. Ending racial discrimination in domestic politics became, for many politicians, a prerequisite for America's moral authority on the international scene.[6] Indeed, never in Lindquist's career had political conditions been better for achieving the rapid political integration of Native Americans into American society.

Trends within ecumenical Protestantism worked in Lindquist's favor, too. First, some HMC moderates, who had endorsed the Wheeler-Howard Act as a gradual means to assimilation, were beginning to question their earlier attitude. They cited the disillusion of Henry Roe Cloud, once a young darling of the Protestant mission to the Indians. Although Roe Cloud had served as Collier's most active lobbyist for Indian acceptance of the Wheeler-Howard Act in the mid-1930s, by 1940 he privately told his friends in ecumenical leadership that he was "entirely out of sympathy with the Collier program." In his view, it gave "no hope for the individual Indian to advance."[7] These moderates also felt betrayed when Collier failed to defend one of their missionaries, Earl Whipple, against the dubious charge of impersonating an officer while performing his missionary duties.[8]

Second, the National Fellowship of Indian Workers (NFIW) likewise sharpened its posture against the administrative status quo. Lindquist had founded the fellowship in 1935 to give Christian Indians and field missionaries a stronger voice within Indian affairs and the Home Missions Council. At its national conference in 1941, NFIW representatives accused the government of developing "a top-heavy bureaucracy" that "harmed the Indian" through patronage. At the same time, the group faulted the churches for creating a similar pattern of dependency. "Indians have been tacitly encouraged to seek gifts of clothing and other goods rather than helped to provide these things for themselves," they argued. But the brunt of responsibility for the problem they laid at the feet of the government, which they called upon to secure both the privileges and the responsibilities of citizenship for American Indians.[9]

And third, one may speak more broadly, according to historian William M. King, of a "resurgent Protestant activism" in the early 1940s.[10] Theologians Henry P. van Dusen and John Bennett, along with the lay Presbyterian statesman John Foster Dulles and Methodist Bishop G. Bromley Oxnam, sought to lead American Protestantism into a more prophetic role against colonialism and racist nationalism. They called for a world government that would protect the rights of cultural minorities, and they demanded that the United States government and churches rectify past discrimination by appointing more African Americans to high-level positions. Of course, vast segments of American Protestantism made little or no connection between the rhetoric of democracy overseas and the stigma of racial oppression at home. But for thousands of American families, fascist violence against vulnerable minority groups had become the rationale for risking life and limb in war, and some Protestant leaders wanted to capitalize on that commitment to purge American society of its own shortcomings in democracy. As the executive director for the Protestant Home Missions Council said at the onset of World War II, "The United States must face the question as to whether justice is granted here, or it will not have the right to say anything to the rest of the world."[11]

The Problem of Indian Wardship

It was this wave of antiracism that Lindquist and the ecumenical Home Missions Council attempted to ride to good effect in their lobbying against Indian wardship. The Home Missions Council first took up the issue of wardship in 1939 when it sent Joint Indian Committee members Mark Dawber and Katherine Bennett to ask Collier point-blank whether the Indian bureau was "moving definitely" toward releasing Indians from bureau supervision.[12] Collier declined to answer directly, suggesting instead that his office would cooperate if missionary and reform organizations were to create a panel to study the question. Indeed, Collier discerned the accusatory edge in the question, but he could not deny that he himself had cast much of his administration in emancipatory terms. Like assimilationists, Collier, too, could speak of abolishing the BIA as a means to ending the threat of federal domination.[13] From a rhetorical standpoint, the goal of ending "wardship" could only enjoy universal support. Translating that common ground into consensus on a policy agenda, however, proved to be another thing entirely.

Those difficulties became apparent within the very committee that the Home Missions Council convened to consider the issue.[14] Desiring to address the problem with the widest possible support, the HMC invited more than fifty representatives from governmental, welfare, and reform agencies to discuss the wardship question in 1941. They laid the groundwork for the broadly based—and expansively named—Committee on the Study of Wardship and Indian Participation in American Life. Aside from Lindquist and other representatives from the Home Missions Council, committee members included Father J. B. Tennelly, director of the Catholic Bureau of Education for Indians; Joseph C. McCaskill, a high-ranking official in the Bureau of Indian Affairs, later to become the assistant commissioner; Dr. Thomas Jesse Jones of the Phelps-Stokes Fund, a philanthropic organization supporting Negro and Indian education; Dr. Ruth McMurry of Columbia Teacher's College; Ella Deloria, a Yankton Sioux novelist and student of Columbia anthropologist Franz Boas; and two representatives from the Indian Rights Association.[15]

As one of its first acts in 1942, the committee commissioned Lindquist to compose a booklet "written from the angle of facts, unbiased by pronounced special views," and free from commitment to "controversial policies and points of view."[16] They hoped to use his work as a basis for further discussion and, ultimately, as a resource for a curriculum unit for Indian students themselves.[17] The next year Lindquist, in collaboration with Chicago lawyer Flora Warren Seymour, produced a sixty-page technical essay titled *Handbook on Study of Indian Wardship*. A close look at this important document provides critical insight into how Lindquist advocated assimilation in increasingly political and legal terms.

The main body of the essay began with a definition of wardship that placed race, bureaucracy, and the law in the forefront of the discussion. "Wardship," Lindquist wrote, was "the peculiar legal situation of those designated as Indians, whereby they are dealt with by the Federal Government in matters in which the average American citizen is dealt with by State or local governments; or whereby the Federal services given to all citizens are given to them under a special racial designation."[18] In his definition of wardship, Lindquist was calling attention to the anomaly of the BIA itself—the only federal agency that explicitly performed its services for a racially distinct population. All other minority groups cast their lots with other American citizens in receiving services through state and local governments. But vast numbers of Indians attended separate schools, visited separate hospitals and clinics, and received separate welfare and law-and-order services—all under the supervision of the federal government, all administered by the BIA.

Beyond the sheer existence of the BIA, Lindquist also identified wardship with the BIA's preferential hiring practices toward Indians. Except for a brief period during the Hoover administration, American Indians could be employed by the BIA without passing the same civil service requirements that non-Indian applicants faced. Lindquist argued that this form of patronage perversely kept large numbers of influential Indians invested in the very institution that was segregating them in the first place.[19]

Finally, Lindquist attributed the Indians' wardship status to a set of exemptions on Indian lands, whether tribal properties or those held in trust for individual Indians. Trust protections meant that state and local governments could not tax Indian lands. Also, individual Indians could not sell their trust lands or draw revenue from them without the permission of a BIA superintendent. Requests for trust fund disbursements often brought months of paperwork and forced Indians to explain their financial need just to obtain money that already, properly, belonged to them.[20]

In the narrowest terms, then, wardship for Lindquist consisted of a unique legal status for Indians, which placed them in a direct and encompassing relationship with the federal government, rather than having that relationship mediated (as with other citizens) through state and local governments.

But the problem of wardship for Lindquist extended far beyond these legal encumbrances. It also snowballed into a massive set of social problems. First, wardship led directly to exploitation. Without real-life experience managing their own property, Lindquist argued, Indian lands and moneys stayed just one step removed from aggressive financial interests.[21] Second, wardship created dependence on the federal government. That dependence, according to Lindquist, effectively nullified the promise of tribal self-government found in the Wheeler-Howard Act. It exposed Indians all the more to an insulting federal supervision over tribal business.[22] Third, wardship led to discrimination by state and local governments. Lindquist cited the New Mexico state constitution, which denied Indians the vote on the grounds that they were not taxed. Exemptions from taxation also made state agencies unwilling to extend social security benefits, educational services, and police protection to Indians.[23] Fourth, the unique privileges granted to Indian wards caused, in Lindquist's view, the larger part of contemporary white prejudice against the Indians. The federal government acted as a rental agent for the Indians, with the cost borne not by the Indians, but by the federal treasury. Indians enjoyed free medical services while other Americans had to pay for hospital care out of pocket. No wonder, Lindquist suggested, Native Americans felt unwelcome in off-reservation communities. And finally, Lindquist feared that Indian tribes' unique relationship to the federal government perpetuated Indian complaints over past injustices, both "real and fancied." Preoccupied with "a nursed grievance" and an "expectation of future enrichment based on some loss in the distant past," the Indian "is less eager to carve out his own future." Until the Indians found justice in the full rights of American citizenship, Lindquist argued, they would continue to seek compensation "for the buffalo [their] grandfather[s] did not kill."[24]

That last point signaled the menacing irony of wardship for Lindquist. In spite of all its evils—in spite of its tendency to confer a "hopeless, remediless inferiority" upon its victims—wardship still fostered in Indians the hope that they might profit from maintaining their tribal status.[25] Not that Lindquist blamed them for taking advantage, for example, of freedom from tax liabilities: "[The Indian] would be something beyond human if he did not take the exemptions offered him."[26] But it was the proper task of the BIA to treat those exemptions as temporary evils. The BIA under Collier's administration, though, had treated those exemptions as permanent features of America's civic landscape. For Lindquist, Collier's policies assumed that Indians—like criminals, orphaned children, and the mentally insane—could not be trusted to make decisions for themselves. And that assumption, coupled with Indian attachment to special privileges, made wardship into an intractable bind for the government and the Indians.

As a set of "first steps" that could be taken immediately, Lindquist called for making Indians subject to state laws and taxes, placing Indian children in public schools wherever possible, charging Indians for medical services insofar as they were able to pay, charging Indians for land management services, and rendering all social services to the Indians through the states. Land restrictions, he admitted, would have to be worked out on a tribe-by-tribe basis, but those first steps would serve as a pledge toward the definite end of Indian wardship.[27]

Even though Lindquist's essay addressed widely held concerns about the contemporary state of Indian affairs, its publication was marked by blundering and controversy. The Home Missions Council decided unilaterally to publish the booklet before members of the larger committee (that is, the separately constituted Committee on the Study of Wardship and Indian Participation in American Life) had a chance to read and evaluate it. Moreover, the HMC gave the booklet the imprint not of the Home Missions Council, but of the independent committee, and added a foreword listing the names of the thirteen committee members.[28]

Yet when the committee convened again, several members objected so strenuously to the handbook's contents that they succeeded in blocking its distribution. Some took issue with its frank criticisms of the current administration. Others saw some merit in the criticisms but wanted further study before moving so definitely toward political activism, arguing that Lindquist's essay lacked "an impartial and scholarly point of view." And still others went so far as to defend wardship as a temporary expedient, believing that it at least protected Indians from the threat of starvation.[29]

One of the most outspoken opponents of the wardship essay was Lawrence Lindley, the new general secretary of the Indian Rights Association (IRA). His dissent was particularly significant because it revealed a rift between the IRA and the HMC. Throughout Lindquist's career, the two organizations had maintained strong ties. But under Lindley's direction, the IRA adopted a more cooperative attitude toward Collier and a greater sensitivity to the communal traditions of Indian tribes and their group-differentiated rights. Thus Lindley spoke out against the "rugged individualism" of HMC representatives like Lindquist, who believed that all group rights and tribal holdings would have to be individualized before wardship could end. Lindley also questioned whether Indian lands would have to be fully taxed before BIA services could be passed to the states. And he challenged the booklet's view that federal wardship should be ended because it only increased racial hostility from non-Indians. For him, persistent prejudice against the Indians meant that the government's protective functions were that much more necessary.[30]

Privately, Lindley accused Flora Warren Seymour, Lindquist's collaborator and strongest ally in the wardship committee, of being "devoted . . . to the 'melting pot' whether people want to be 'melted' or not."[31] As he saw the situation, Lindquist and Seymour's push for "precipitate change" in the legal status of the Indians should give way to a "more studied and better calculated procedure."[32] Underneath his consensus-style gradualism, though, lurked Lindley's refusal to concede that the Indians' group-differentiated rights inherently patronized the Indians or blocked their incentive for self-help.[33]

In the face of the IRA's dissent, the committee became so divided by October 1943 that chairwoman M. Katherine Bennett moved to disband it and have its remaining funds returned to the HMC's own Sub-Committee on Indian Wardship. To settle any qualms the HMC might have held, Lindquist presented an expert legal opinion saying that since the HMC paid for the pamphlet's printing, it had the right to distribute that pamphlet even though its imprint bore no formal relation to the HMC. In the following months, the remaining wardship pamphlets were in fact distributed (with new covers and the thirteen names omitted), and a second edition was printed and distributed under the imprimatur of the HMC.[34]

John Collier had initially pledged his cooperation with the study of Indian wardship in 1939, but in the intervening years, he and other high-ranking officials, like the IRA, had repositioned themselves on the issue of federal guardianship. They said that as a result of the government's policy of cultural freedom and tribal self-government, Indians were no longer wards. The federal government's relationship to the Indians had evolved into that of trustee to beneficiary, not guardian to ward. Collier and his legal advisor, Felix Cohen, defended trust protections over Indian properties as part of the federal government's fulfillment of its treaty obligations to the Indians. Far from reflecting on the Indians' incompetence to manage their own affairs, a trust relationship honored the Indians' unique status as the aboriginal occupants of the land. Federally protected reservations, one official argued, were not segregating or demeaning institutions; they were "just corporate holdings," consistent with the distinctive history of federal dealings with the Indians.[35]

So when Collier received his copy of Lindquist's essay, he interpreted Lindquist's assault on wardship as a more fundamental challenge to the BIA's trustee relationship with American Indians. Collier's public notice of the second edition of *Indian Wardship* appeared in the BIA publication *Indians at Work*. He called Lindquist's work a "vacuous document," guilty of "racial envy or scorn" and "contempt for the Indians." The booklet's message, in Collier's words, was to "ignore the treaties and violate them . . . destroy all and each of the Indians' protections; put their lands on the local tax-rolls; lift the government trust from all their properties; throw them to the wolves; go back to the Century of Dishonor; finish off the Indians." The driving concern of *Indian Wardship*, he concluded, "runs counter to the long and present record of the Protestant and Catholic congregations alike."[36] That condemnation was Collier's last public statement on church–BIA relations as commissioner. With the HMC's apparent abandonment of support for the BIA's obligations, there no longer existed any basis for cooperation, as far as Collier was concerned.

Continuities and Reversals

But was Collier right, or was this just another case of Collier distorting the views of those who dared to dissent from his own righteous cause? Did Lindquist's arguments, endorsed by the Home Missions Council, mark a reversal in ecumenical Protestant attitudes about federal Indian policy? Did "racial scorn" and "contempt" really motivate Lindquist's assault on Indian wardship? And did Lindquist, in his push against wardship, truly contemplate the violation of historic treaties with the Indians? Dealing with these questions goes once more to the close and contested relationships between race, culture, and bureaucracy that stood at the heart of the conflict between Collier and Lindquist.

With regard to the first main question—whether *Indian Wardship* represented an about-face from previous Protestant approaches—it is important to remember that according to the logic of assimilation, the appeal to abolish the BIA would appear from time to time. Racial integration, full citizenship, and freedom from the invidious aspects of group identity were the ultimate goals of Protestant lobbyists from the start. So when Lindquist attacked the problems of wardship, he was confronting a set of issues that he had expected assimilation eventually to solve. Looked at one way, in terms of desired outcomes, Lindquist's pamphlet marked no radical reversal of the enduring goal of assimilation.

But viewed another way, in terms of the provisional, mediating steps involved in reaching full assimilation, Lindquist's assault on wardship signaled a most remarkable turnaround. For while missionaries had generally promoted the ultimate integration of Indians into American civilization, they had also been among the strongest advocates for making that integration a slow and carefully guarded process. From his earliest involvement in Protestant missions, Lindquist had joined Protestant leaders in defending the BIA against radical critics. He was a temporizer who saw protecting the Indians from exploitation and property loss as a higher priority in the short term than full political equality. He regularly defended BIA programs in health, education, and law and order, because he believed that state and local governments could not be trusted to perform those services without discrimination and prejudice. In the early thirties, Lindquist defended preferential hiring practices for Indians in the BIA because it offered a measured way to prepare Indians for the larger job market, but without forcing them to compete until they were ready. Everything he did drove in the direction of treating Indians as a special case in need of a special federal instrument for Indian welfare and the protection of Indian properties. But by the early forties, Lindquist had flipped sides against the BIA. His war on wardship—along with the support he received from the HMC in waging it—was indeed substantially new, having appeared in just a few years' time.

There are several ways to interpret this shift. One would be to say that since it meant a change merely in the intermediate steps toward achieving assimilation, it was not highly significant. But the material impact of government policies on Indian communities, I would argue, revolves less around ideally and abstractly conceived objectives than the provisional measures that are actually instituted. And in that respect, Lindquist's change of emphasis could have had profound ramifications in Indian access to basic welfare services and in the further erosion of the Indians' land base.

Another way to interpret the change would be to say that since assimilation always operated on a temporal logic, it would be understandable that someone like Lindquist might begin his career as a gradualist and end it with the belief that assimilation had been, in fact, almost completed. As assimilation neared consummation, eventually even the gradualists would begin calling for an end to the BIA's educational and protective functions, just as the radicals always had.

But time alone does not account for Lindquist's reversals. Other factors were controlling. Collier's effort to disestablish missionary prerogatives in BIA institutions no doubt played a large role in weakening traditional missionary support for the BIA. Until Collier, the BIA had given missionaries privileged access to reservation lands and BIA schools. Missionaries, in turn, had seen an advantage in defending the BIA against radical critics. But with the quid pro quo broken, a key factor in missionaries' commitment to the prolonged existence of the BIA had been lost, opening the door for this new departure.

Also, if the progress of time alone were the determining factor in Lindquist's reversal, one might expect to see him give up his gradualism gradually, so to speak. But until Collier became commissioner of Indian Affairs in 1933, Lindquist showed no sign of weakening his gradual approach. And even then, he declared himself in favor of "ninety percent" of the 1934 Wheeler-Howard Act because he saw most of its provisions as possible tools for the Indians' eventual assimilation. Until around 1940, he directed his energies mostly against Collier, not the BIA itself. He seems to have held out the belief that if Collier could be prodded into resigning, gradual assimilation policies would dominate the BIA's agenda once more. But by the early 1940s, Lindquist determined that Collier's program had become so entrenched that it could not be undone without dismantling the very institution that Lindquist had long supported. Lindquist's drive to terminate the unique legal status of Indian tribes thus involved a repudiation of his earlier advocacy of wardship and gradualism. He had finally concluded that Indian exceptionalism should be eliminated, and with as much speed as the complexities of Indian law would allow.

Collier was right. The Home Missions Council's assault on wardship was a new thing for ecumenical Protestantism. Collier and missionaries had frequently disagreed about the merits of Indian religious and cultural practices, but they had nevertheless shared common ground in recognizing the immediate need to protect Indian resources through trust protections, federal services, and tax exemptions. Now even those grounds for alliance were threatened.

But if Collier was right in perceiving a significant shift, he was wrong to suggest that the effort to end Indian wardship meant an abandonment of the Indians and any vision of justice for them. In fact, Lindquist and other Protestant leaders found a compelling rationale for their views in the religious rhetoric of the rising civil rights movement.[37] That rhetoric was based in the ideals of democracy, individualism, and self-reliance, and galvanized by the international specter of totalitarianism on the left and right. Mark Dawber, executive director of the Home Missions Council and a key supporter of Lindquist's wardship booklet, contended that Indian wardship violated America's highest ideals—ideals that were ultimately rooted in a religious vision of humanity. "American democracy," Dawber wrote, "is based upon the sanctity of the individual, therefore it is primarily a spiritual concern."[38] And early in the HMC's deliberations over wardship, Joint Indian Committee members determined that the federal government's encompassing relationship with the Indians had definite "implications . . . for the Christian religion." "Paternalism leads to dependence and prevents the development of leadership qualities within the group," one member stated. Also, wardship smacked of a castelike rigidity in social systems; it seemed to "place people in a certain status and keep them there." The committee concluded, "One principle on which all the church groups are agreed is that segregation is injurious and that people should be brought together, not set apart."[39]

Lindquist's own writings tied his assault on wardship to a Christian imperative to elevate universal human needs over the culturally specific interests of Indians *as* Indians. "The church of Christ," he began to state repeatedly in the late thirties, "owes the Indian more because he is a human being than because he is an Indian."[40] "The Christian goal," he wrote in a book for the Missionary Education Movement in 1944, "is to make all nations of the earth one. Its standards recognize no racial distinctions nor special privileged class or group." Quoting from the New Testament book of Colossians, he continued, "In the new Christian nature 'there is no room for Greek and Jew, circumcised and uncircumcised, barbarian, Scythian, slave or free; Christ is everything and everywhere.'"[41] Of course, Lindquist did not limit this transcendent vision of a united humanity to the institutional church alone. For him, that unity spilled over into Christian attitudes toward the distribution of power, so that all legal rights and obligations should fall along individual rather than group lines. Within the realm of politics as in the church, the most essential aspect of being human for Lindquist was not the bond of culture and kinship, but individual equality and freedom.

It is important to recognize that Lindquist did not limit his activism to the arena of Indian affairs. In the 1940s, he acted to apply his moral vision consistently across all racial and ethnic groups. He joined other ministers from his hometown of Lawrence, Kansas, in opposing internment and other injustices suffered by Japanese-Americans during World War II.[42] Then, in 1946, Lindquist became a founding member and first president of the Lawrence League for the Practice of Democracy, pledging himself with twelve others to oppose racial intolerance and to fight for the civil rights of all persons regardless of race, religion, and class. In 1948, he was selected to serve on the Kansas State Council on Civil Rights.

Through these state and local organizations he helped organize Lawrence's only cooperative, interracial nursery school and solicited financial aid for the children of African American working parents. He worked with the National Association for the Advancement of Colored People and the Congress on Racial Equality to gain equal access for blacks to area theaters, restaurants, professional societies, and labor unions. And he organized interracial seminars to discuss inequalities in health, education, housing, and employment. In Lindquist's view, it would have been inconsistent to dismantle Jim Crow segregation in his hometown without also undoing the laws that kept Indians subject to white resentment and discrimination farther west.[43]

With this civil rights vision in place, Lindquist and the Home Missions Council overcame any qualms they had about taking a strident new stand against the BIA and its protective functions. Not even the dissent of the Indian Rights Association, the Home Missions Council's guide on so many technical policy issues in the past, could prevent the HMC from promoting policies that sacrificed guardianship over the Indian land base in favor of egalitarian ideals. After nearly a decade of accommodating themselves to Collier's policies, the HMC finally gave Lindquist his chance to strike a blow against the Collier legacy.

Implications for Treaty Rights and Tribal Nationalism

Two other questions remain about Lindquist's work on Indian wardship. Did it reflect a kind of "racial scorn," as Collier charged, and did it ultimately advocate the violation of solemn treaties with the Indians? These questions, too, deserve careful responses.

On its face, the accusation of racial scorn was highly ironic, for the central thrust of Lindquist's argument ran against race-based legislation toward Indians, against the economic and political sources of white hatred, and against state limitations on Indian suffrage and welfare benefits. Yet in resisting attitudes of Indian racial inferiority, Lindquist nevertheless reinforced popular stereotypes of the sour, indolent Indian.[44] Wardship, he argued, robbed Indians of their initiative by creating an expectation that the government owes them a living. Indians could not be expected to make progress toward middle-class prosperity so long as they thought they might gain something by insisting on aboriginal claims. "Dwelling upon real or fancy claims," he wrote, "is a drag upon any race. The Indian is no exception to this rule."[45] Clearly, Lindquist attributed the Indians' alleged lack of thrift to environment and circumstance, rather than biological inferiority. That might have fallen short of "racial scorn," but it did reveal something of the cultural prejudices embedded within Lindquist's form of antiracism.

The consequences of those prejudices become even clearer in the light of Lindquist's writings on federal Indian treaties. Soon after Lindquist and Seymour completed the wardship pamphlet, they composed another document for the Committee on the Study of Wardship and Indian Participation in American Life, entitled "Indian Treaty Making."[46] It showed Lindquist wrestling with the most fundamental legal and moral difficulty in his vision for Indian assimilation: how to take Indians across the bridge from the group-differentiated rights of Indian treaties into the undifferentiated individual rights of American citizenship. His response to that problem reveals more clearly than any other work the profound impact of Lindquist's biases against Indian cultures.

Before we examine Lindquist's study of Indian treaties, a word about the federal government's treaty relationship with Indian tribes will be helpful. Unlike other nationalist movements in American history, tribal nationalism enjoyed a well-established legal and constitutional footing. The Constitution gave Congress authority over relations with Indian tribes.[47] Among the ways the government exercised that authority was through treaties—more than 389 of them before 1871, when Congress stopped making formal treaties but affirmed its commitment to abide by past ones.[48] Tribal relations were, for the federal government, modeled upon international diplomacy. Of course, that did not mean Thomas Jefferson dealt with an Oneida chief in the same way he did the king of France. In Chief Justice John Marshall's famous and controversial phrase of 1832, Indian treaties involved "domestic, dependent nations." Domestic, because surrounded by United States territory, and dependent, because unable to defend themselves from outside imperial threats without the United States' help—but nations nevertheless. As a result, even when American Indians were granted citizenship in 1924, many of them remained a distinct people under the law, with their tribal lands and properties held in trust and important services provided by the federal government.[49]

For a good portion of American history, tribal sovereignty meant something not only to Native Americans, but to Protestant missionaries as well. In the 1830s, for example, Congregational missionary Samuel Worcester went to prison in support of Cherokee treaty rights to internal sovereignty. As long as missionaries worked within the geographical boundaries of the Cherokee government, Worcester argued, neither Georgia nor the federal government had the authority to regulate missionary activities.[50] And during the late nineteenth and early twentieth centuries, missionaries and reformers continued to defend Indian treaty rights. But they did so either in support of assimilation (how can we expect the Indians to aspire to American citizenship if the nation does not live up to its promises?) or out of expedience (to protect Indian land holdings as well as the church properties missionaries had developed on those lands). They believed that as Native Americans came to enjoy the full rights and privileges of American citizenship, they would no longer need the protective guarantees of federal Indian treaties and would happily dispose of their tribally based privileges.[51] Lindquist's essay on Indian treaties appeared, though, at a time when Collier had tried to revive tribal governments, and when experts in Indian law were citing treaty rights as the basis for both the BIA's existence and the Indians' enduring group-differentiated rights.[52]

Lindquist's essay, then, sought to take treaty rights out of the legal mix by having the federal government settle all treaty obligations with one-time monetary payments. He wanted to "commute" Indian treaties and thus put an end to treaty-based arguments for Indian exceptionalism. In his mind, he was not so much "ignoring" or "violating" solemn treaties, as Collier had charged, as he was removing the final vestiges of an outdated system of federal-tribal relations.

Broken down into its component parts, Lindquist's argument made two simple moves, one having to do with the contexts in which treaties had been made, and the other having to do with the impact of historical change on treaty agreements. He argued first, and rather preemptively, that the federal government could commute its Indian treaties because in reality, nothing resembling a bona fide treaty had existed in the first place. Treaties, he said, required a certain parity between parties—a parity that he believed did not pertain to Indian tribes and the U.S. government. Without experience in the hairsplitting intricacies of Western legal language, Lindquist argued, Indians probably did not understand the treaties they signed. And even if Indian leaders could have comprehended what they were signing, the tribal political structures they worked within were not sufficiently advanced to ensure compliance by tribe members. Also, Indian tribes were considerably weaker than the United States in military terms, indicating for Lindquist that they never enjoyed enough power to negotiate treaties on their own terms. Anything that the tribes received was, Lindquist implied, a gratuity from a superior power. By his construction, treaties were hardly the emblems of tribal nationalism that Indian activists later made them out to be.[53]

But Lindquist did not stop there. He also argued that Indian treaties must be interpreted as historical rather than timeless documents. Even if tribes once held power on a par with the United States government (a point, again, that Lindquist categorically denied), they might eventually lose their ability to assert persuasive claims of autonomy. Thus Lindquist argued that Indian treaties should have little bearing on the present, since no twentieth-century Indian tribes could claim anything resembling sovereignty over their lands. For him, treaties had become a "mortgage," which Lindquist defined literally as a "dead hand" upon the Indians' future, a set of "inflexible rules" irrelevant to contemporary conditions. Otherwise, Lindquist pointed out, there could be no explanation for the anomaly of New York's Seneca tribe, who independently declared war on Germany and Japan during World War II, but sent their "warriors" to fight under the banner of the American flag. In Lindquist's caustic words, this assertion of Seneca nationalism was little more than a "pretty fiction." Treaties, he argued, had placed Indians in the untenable position of being both wards of the government and pretenders to national autonomy.[54]

In this essay on Indian treaties, then, Lindquist's biases against Indian cultures led him to conclude that Native tribes could never be regarded as nations in any meaningful sense of the word. On the surface, Lindquist's primary arguments against wardship revolved around the law and universal civil rights, but they were based upon cultural judgments about the superiority of Western languages, political structures, and notions of land ownership. For Lindquist, there were tribes and there were nations. But there could never be tribal nations, and certainly not tribal nations coexisting as social, political, and territorial unities within modern nation-states. Tribal nationalism, in his view, was an oxymoron. Of course, in rejecting claims to tribal nationalism, Lindquist did not believe he was denying Indians the respect they deserved for the cultural contributions they might make to American society. But he was nevertheless setting his own conditions for how those contributions might be made.

The ramifications of Lindquist's thesis should be clear. By denying tribes the status of nations, Lindquist allowed for the possibility that the federal government might commute its treaty obligations unilaterally, without Indian consent. If tribal powers were merely delegated by the United States and not inherent to tribes themselves, then the United States could change the terms of its relationship to Indian tribes without entering into new negotiations. Treaty obligations, in his view, could be subordinated to what non-Indians determined to be a higher justice for the Indians—the privilege of American citizenship.[55] Indian tribes, Lindquist seemed to suggest, were the exception to the rule of bilateral negotiation. In his treatise on Indian treaties, Lindquist's glowing rhetoric about the Indians' liberation from wardship ultimately cast its shadow on the Indians' power to shape the future of their tribes for themselves.[56]

Mixed Outcomes

In the 1940s, though, the American public seemed more interested in the rhetoric of freedom than in the shadows it might have cast upon the Indians. For after years of watching Collier's policies eclipse assimilationist goals, Lindquist's career ended in the sunlight of public visibility and influence. In 1947 he beamed that he was living in "the happiest and most fruitful period of my life."[57] As we shall see, his exuberance might well have been tempered by a fuller appreciation for Native Christian resistance to his views, but it is important to note first just how many things were going his way.

For one thing, within the Home Missions Council, Lindquist's spearheading of the wardship study brought him fully back into the fold. For ten years, Lindquist had moved somewhat on the margins, consolidating his power base in the field while the HMC maintained a cooperative posture with Collier. But between 1943 and Lindquist's retirement in 1953, the records of the HMC's Indian Committee show his consistent influence. In 1948, for example, the committee's proposed legislative program made numerous recommendations that continued to grow out of the wardship study. Congress should, according to the proposal, declare "that the Indian is a citizen and not a ward of the government," "eliminate the last vestige of guardianship over the person of the Indian," and "promote the orderly withdrawal of federal responsibility for administration of Indian affairs."[58]

At the same time, Lindquist's arguments were reaching a wider audience than ever before. The liberal journalist Oswald Garrison Villard praised Lindquist's wardship booklet in the bellwether journal, *Christian Century,* which had previously given strong editorial support to Collier.[59] And Lindquist's book *The Indian in American Life,* a less technical presentation of his arguments in *Indian Wardship,* sold more than sixty-five thousand copies within months of its publication in 1944.[60]

Even more important, Lindquist's drive to end Indian wardship helped to stimulate a new push for Indian assimilation in Congress. On May 24, 1943, not long after Lindquist wrote *Indian Wardship,* Senate Indian Committee Chair Elmer Thomas issued a scathing condemnation of Collier's administration and a call for the abolition of the BIA within one to three years. Report No. 310, as it was called, marked a turning point in Congress's renunciation of Collier's policies and an omen of Collier's forced resignation in 1945. Many of Thomas's recommendations echoed Lindquist's list of "first steps" toward ending federal wardship, such as terminating federal law-and-order jurisdiction over the Indians and transferring all education and social services to the states.[61] Collier himself believed there was a "curious" relationship between Thomas's report and Lindquist's booklet, noting the "reciprocal borrowing" between the wardship essay and "current reports" coming out of the Senate Committee on Indian Affairs.[62]

Other congressional and administrative moves fell in line with Lindquist's goals. Senator Hugh Butler of Nebraska, the powerful head of the budget committee, cited Lindquist's arguments to provide moral sanction for legislation to eliminate federal expenditures toward the Indians.[63] Lindquist lobbied successfully for including Indian war veterans in the provisions of the GI Bill—an important foreshadowing, Lindquist hoped, of the Indians' imminent attainment of political equality.[64] In 1946, consistent with Lindquist's call to commute all Indian treaties, Congress established an Indian Claims Commission for settling outstanding grievances.[65]

The next year, responding to pressure, Acting Commissioner William Zimmerman presented to Congress a list that ranked America's Indian tribes according to the speed with which they might be released from federal guardianship. Like Collier, under whom he had served as assistant commissioner, Zimmerman seems to have interpreted federal withdrawal as one possible fulfillment of the Wheeler-Howard Act's promise of tribal self-government, but it was a step he did not want to take until after tribes enjoyed enough economic security and political power to survive as corporate entities.[66] Congress, however, took the list as a blueprint for terminating the Indians' tribal status altogether. There followed a flurry of bills to that effect in the late forties and early fifties, culminating in the landmark passage of House Concurrent Resolution 108 in 1953. Dropping the aims of the Wheeler-Howard Act of 1934, H.C.R. 108 resolved, "as rapidly as possible, to make the Indians within the territorial limits of the United States subject to the same laws and entitled to the same privileges and responsibilities as are applicable to other citizens of the United States, and to end their status as wards of the United States, and to grant them all of the rights and prerogatives pertaining to American citizenship."[67]

Given the role that Lindquist and the Home Missions Council played in pressing for these congressional mandates, it is apparent that the Protestant establishment in Indian affairs did not disintegrate during Collier's administration. Rather, the self-avowed custodians of national Indian affairs adapted their approach. Until the 1940s, Protestant leaders curried favor with BIA officials by espousing the doctrine of Indian wardship, which supported the BIA's institutional interests in self-perpetuation. But after Collier, Protestant leaders directed their sense of custodial authority toward congressional initiatives that sought to abolish the BIA. They threw their weight largely behind the unadorned power of political equality to overcome the problems of isolation, poverty, and racism. If Indian assimilation could not be accomplished through the agencies of the BIA, it could still be stimulated through legislative fiat. Collier prevented Lindquist from assuming any informal, establishmentarian authority within the BIA after 1933, but Lindquist and the Home Missions Council still found other means to assert their moral authority in Indian affairs.

Yet for all these signs of an effective recovery on Lindquist's part, one significant development suggested that the recovery would not be complete: strong dissent to Lindquist's views from leading Protestant Indians. There was no small irony in this development. For one of the ways that Lindquist tried to revive assimilation goals after Collier became commissioner was to amplify the voices of Christian and assimilated Indians. Thus he founded the National Fellowship of Indian Workers (NFIW) and helped to publicize the anti-Collier grievances of Indians like J. C. Morgan, a Reformed missionary and chairman of the Navajo tribal council in the late 1930s. But the enhanced power of Native leadership in Protestant institutions ultimately proved to be a Trojan horse that jeopardized some of Lindquist's most fundamental goals. Although most Christian Indians sought the civil liberties inherent in American citizenship, they stopped short of calling upon the federal government to terminate its special trust relationship with Indian tribes. In other words, prominent Christian Indians in the 1940s and 1950s continued to defend their special rights *as Indians*.[68]

Within the NFIW itself, this dissent from Lindquist's views manifested itself often in small but discernible ways. Annual NFIW resolutions continued to support a broad program of cultural assimilation, but they quietly avoided calling for the commutation of all treaty rights.[69] Prominent speeches at NFIW meetings also veered from Lindquist's view that civil rights should supercede tribal sovereignty. A 1944 presentation by Arthur C. Parker, the Seneca ethnologist, provides one example. Parker and Lindquist had worked together in ecumenical circles as far back as the 1910s, when Parker assisted Lindquist in his research and writing for the massive survey published as *Red Man in the United States*. Parker also helped to organize Protestant reformers so that they could control the agenda of the Committee of 100 in 1923. But in 1944, at a regional meeting of the NFIW, Parker challenged Lindquist's understanding of wardship. While admitting some of the economic and social problems created by the Indians' federal guardianship, he argued that wardship had united Indian communities in common interest, deterred white encroachment, protected treaty rights, and preserved the Indians' land base through exemption from taxation. Above all, wardship had "called attention to the special status of Indians and . . . excited interest on the part of those disposed to see that the greater nation deals fairly with a minority group having prior claims upon the soil." As a result, Parker proposed that the "melting pot" image for American society be replaced with that of a "great clock," in which various tribes and races, like the clock's cogs and wheels, might "intermesh" rather than melting into a single substance. By reenvisioning American society in terms of "interdigitation" instead of "transmutation," Parker sought to defend the distinct national minority rights of America's indigenous peoples.[70]

Lindquist's interactions with Ruth Muskrat Bronson, a Methodist-turned-Presbyterian from northeast Oklahoma, demonstrate a similar pattern of Indian dissent. Her life intersected Lindquist's in many ways. In the 1910s and 1920s, Bronson was a rising star in ecumenical Protestant circles, traveling the Far East on one occasion with John R. Mott and other missionary dignitaries. She ascended to high-profile positions through her education at the University of Oklahoma, the University of Kansas, Mount Holyoke College, and George Washington University. Lindquist and Bronson worked together for a number of years in Lawrence, Kansas, at the Haskell Institute, one of the Bureau of Indian Affair's leading federal boarding school for Indians. And in 1923, Bronson formally presented Lindquist's most important book, *Red Man in the United States,* to President Coolidge on the White House lawn.[71] As late as 1934 Lindquist and his peers regarded her as an ally in their fight against the Wheeler-Howard Act.[72]

While serving as a college guidance officer in Collier's administration, however, Bronson became more vocal in defending the Indians' cultural freedoms and their rights to tribal sovereignty. And she brought those views back into the circles of ecumenical Protestantism in 1944, when she retired from the Indian service and became a member of both the Joint Indian Committee of the Home Missions Council and the board of the Indian Rights Association. At the same time, she refused a lucrative job offer with the IRA to take an unpaid position for the recently founded National Congress of American Indians (NCAI)—the first major pan-tribal organization to form since the Society of American Indians failed in the early 1920s. Bronson's various organizational affiliations, then, positioned her as an important three-way bridge between the Protestant churches that gave her her start in public leadership, the Collier administration's vision of cultural pluralism and tribal self-government, and the diverse Indian constituencies in the NCAI who wanted to protect both their civil and their treaty rights at the same time.[73]

Moving back into the orbit of the Home Missions Council brought Bronson once more into close contact with Lindquist, only this time the relationship was seriously strained. In particular, she balked at Lindquist's efforts to dissolve the federal government's treaty obligations to the Indians. The difference in approach showed up in her 1944 book, *Indians Are People, Too,* a home missions study published for young adults by the ecumenical Missionary Education Movement. Editors gave her the materials on wardship and treaties that Lindquist had prepared for the Committee on Wardship. And she drew heavily from those materials in her critique of white racism and the government paternalism that Lindquist and Bronson both believed impeded Indian self-initiative and restricted Indians to a racial underclass.[74] In fact, she was especially sensitive to the restrictions that trust protections placed on allotted lands, in part because the BIA had consistently denied her father's requests to sell his property to pay for his children's college ambitions.[75] But Bronson never advocated the nullification of treaty rights as a prerequisite for civil rights and racial equality. Even when she borrowed from Lindquist's writings on Indian treaties, she did not follow his arguments to their conclusion. At one point in his materials, Lindquist had spoken of treaties as a "mortgage," or a drag on the kind of forward-looking vision that he believed inspired people to achieve progress and prosperity.[76] Bronson used the "mortgage" idiom, too. But where Lindquist wanted to commute treaties and nullify the treaty relationship, Bronson sought ultimately to resurrect treaty rights, even if that meant that the federal government had to deal with Indian tribes in perpetuity.[77] In supplemental materials published by the Home Missions Council, Bronson criticized more directly those who, like Lindquist, proposed to abolish Indian wardship. While Lindquist regarded wardship as a form of race-based legislation, Bronson viewed it in part as a function of the Indians' aboriginal occupancy of the land. "Involved in the whole institution of wardship," she wrote, "are solemn treaty commitments made to Indian tribes by our National Government, which could not thus easily be repudiated if we, as a nation, respect our own integrity." Bronson moved quickly from treaty commitments to the principle of bilateral negotiations in federal-tribal relations. If the Indians' exceptional legal status were abolished, she asked, "would we not once again, by the enactment of such legislation, be sealing the destinies of helpless people without their consent or the benefit of their opinions?"[78] Without "long and careful" preparation, she argued, ending wardship would bring "utter disaster" to the Indians and expose them to "predatory" interests. Obviously, Bronson did not support Indian wardship if it meant continued federal domination over Indians and their tribes. But she did not want the abolition of wardship to become, of itself, yet another form of that domination. If the wardship status of the Indians were to be altered, in her view, the change should take place gradually and on the Indians' own terms.

In 1952, at what was probably the last meeting that Lindquist and Bronson attended together, their differences flared once more. A broad spectrum of missionary and reform organizations gathered to discuss two congressional bills that proposed to terminate the tribal status of all Indians living in California and Oregon. Bronson strongly opposed the bills because the affected tribes had not given their consent. In fact, Dillon Myer, the commissioner of Indian Affairs and an aggressive assimilationist, had just informed BIA superintendents in California and Oregon that the Indians' cooperation in termination was desirable but not, in the final analysis, necessary.[79] Lindquist, however, placed the Home Missions Council with Myer squarely in favor of the two bills. Congress, he said in response to Bronson, was doing little more than making "slow progress toward desirable ends."[80]

The gathering ultimately adopted a mediating position. Under Bronson's influence, the group decided to oppose the termination bills, but with Lindquist, it stopped short of calling for tribal consent to matters pertaining to termination. This compromise proved an early glimpse of the gradual approach to assimilation that the Home Missions Council would return to after Lindquist's retirement

Epilogue

G. E. E. Lindquist might have lacked something of John Collier's originality, and his name may be far less prominent than Collier's in national memory. But this should not blind us to what may be gained from a study of his life. For within and around Lindquist flowed all of mainline Protestants' conflicting dreams and shifting approaches to federal Indian policy in the first half of the twentieth century. Their internal conflicts about how to incorporate the Indians within the national life—and whether to cooperate with the BIA in doing so—were completely laid bare by Collier's appointment as BIA commissioner. And while many missionary executives took the path of least resistance, Lindquist became Collier's nemesis in the struggle to defend assimilationist goals.

Financed by two ecumenical missionary organizations in Boston and New York, and unfettered by the parochial demands of a church pastorate or school, Lindquist was able to travel across the country largely as he pleased. He used his freedom to rally his missionary and Native Christian base in the field, while also cajoling national power brokers centered in New York and Washington, D.C. In his widely scattered activities, Lindquist linked together many of the institutions and informal networks that challenged Collier's revolutionary designs on the BIA. Much of Lindquist's activism was, to be sure, in the vein of an obstructionist who exploited vulnerabilities in Collier's administration. But if we peer through the battlefield haze, we can see that Lindquist's legacy endured in several important ways.

First, Lindquist effectively undermined Collier's legislative proposals for land reform and tribal self-government. He joined other reformers and Native leaders in forcing Collier to weaken his draft legislation, the Wheeler-Howard Act, before it was passed in 1934. While Lindquist conceded problems in the policy of land allotment, he nevertheless believed that Collier's plan for tribal corporations would increase Indian land holdings only at the high cost of abandoning the ideal of personal property. He also fought against the expansion of powers that the draft legislation would give to the secretary of the interior, particularly in writing tribal constitutions and converting allotted lands into tribal holdings. The Wheeler-Howard Act in its final form remained one of the most important documents in the history of Indian affairs, but Lindquist's lobbying forced Collier to implement many of his reforms without the benefit of enabling legislation.

Second, in the area of Native Christian leadership, Lindquist was important because he founded regional and national institutions that promoted a politically engaged, indigenous Christianity. In the first half of the twentieth century, Christian Indians represented a large minority of the Indian population. And by 1923, the majority of ordained Protestant ministers serving Indian churches—some 260 out of 438—were Indians themselves.[1] Lindquist leveraged their power in many ways, but most especially in 1935 when he formed the National Fellowship of Indian Workers (NFIW) to strengthen grassroots resistance to Collier's reforms. If Collier entered Indian affairs with a narrow vision of Native life, the NFIW served to remind Collier that, by the 1930s, many Indians were deeply invested in Christian traditions and assimilationist goals of citizenship and private property.

Moreover, Lindquist used creative strategies to prevent Collier from disestablishing missionary influence in Indian affairs. This was no small achievement. Collier had the formal authority to limit radically the missionary presence in BIA institutions, and he used that authority to banish at least two of Lindquist's associates from properties owned by the BIA. But by encouraging missionaries to devote themselves to volunteer service in federal boarding schools, Lindquist was able to ensure that they kept their extraordinary privileges among Indian children. Also, he worked around Collier's executive authority in the 1940s by cultivating his contacts with lawmakers who opposed Collier and shared his desire to begin dismantling the BIA. Under Lindquist's leadership, then, the missionary establishment reconfigured itself rather than concede defeat at Collier's hands.

Most important, Lindquist reformulated the assimilation goals of nineteenth-century reformers by grounding them in a mid-twentieth-century, transcendental ethic of democratic individualism. In the context of the rising civil rights movement among African Americans, this reformulation was strong enough to convince mainline Protestant leaders to take a vigorous and unprecedented stand against the BIA. Although ecumenical Protestants had long regarded the BIA as the guardian of the Indians' welfare, under Lindquist's leadership they came to view it more as an obstacle to the goal of full citizenship. This change strengthened the hand of the postwar termination movement within Congress, and it had broad repercussions on Protestant attitudes toward Indian treaty rights and tribal nationalism as well. For at a time when Collier and his legal experts were citing treaty rights as the grounds for the existence of the BIA and tribal governments, Lindquist made the Protestants' case for commuting those same treaty rights through one-time monetary settlements. With an end to federal treaty obligations, Lindquist argued, tribes would finally escape both the paternalism of federal wardship and the pretense of national sovereignty.

Even now, problems of cultural change, poverty, and legal limbo still shape the everyday lives of indigenous peoples in America. These difficulties would surely strike Lindquist with the feel of familiarity. But the political calculus has shifted somewhat since Lindquist's death in 1967. Tribal nationalism, which almost disappeared from public view at the turn of the century, has surged in the face of ethnic renewal and Indian activists' continued assertion of indigenous rights to collective self-determination. That resurgence, in fact, has hit particularly close to Lindquist's adult home in Lawrence, Kansas. Haskell Indian Institute, where Lindquist began his work for the Home Missions Council, bears today the name Haskell Indian Nations University. The "pretty fiction" of tribal sovereignty, as Lindquist once called it, now dominates the mission of the institution he once served.

Yet these later developments, which largely move against Lindquist's life-long crusade for Indian assimilation, should not obscure the more subtle complexities involved in understanding Lindquist's life on its own terms. For in his encounter with John Collier, Lindquist remade himself and, for a time, the ecumenical organizations that deemed themselves custodians of the Indians' best interests. Thus any interpretation of his life runs up against the unstable logic of assimilation and its ambivalence about how best to integrate Native Americans into American society.

One interpretation might run something like this: Lindquist's advocacy of a gradual approach to assimilation grew out of widespread assumptions that the Indians were not yet (or more strongly, not really) competent to handle their own affairs. His support for the wardship doctrine therefore likely reinforced regnant notions of scientific racism, even if his own writings might have avoided any definite claims of biological determinism. But that was the first half of his career. During the second half of his career he redeemed himself by calling for the abrupt end of wardship, organizing and promoting Christian Indian leadership, and advocating legislation to bring about the full political equality of American Indians.

Another assessment might run like this: Lindquist's early defense of Indian wardship helped to provide at least minimal protections against the near-complete loss of the Indian land base. He took seriously the political, cultural, and social obstacles that made assimilation a somewhat distant prospect, and he sought to shelter Indians from the harsh dislocations taking place as a result of white encroachment. His gradualism also took some account of Native resistance to assimilation and tried to remove the entire process from the more heavy-handed forms of government coercion. But that was the first part of his career. He ended his work among the Indians with a call for the rapid, unilateral termination of all Indian tribal rights, without regard for tribal consent or the disruptions and inequalities that might be caused by removing trust protections and placing Indian welfare services in the dubious hands of the various states.

Which is the legacy of the real Lindquist? Of course, both accounts describe different phases of the problems Lindquist dealt with and the solutions he proposed. I have tried to give credit to the moral visions that undergirded both sides of the assimilationist's dilemma. But even the most profound moral visions are shaped by collective and individual self-interests. And that seems especially true in Indian affairs, where, as Indian law expert Felix Cohen once observed, "the line of distinction between protection and oppression is often difficult to draw."[2] At various points in his career, Lindquist sketched that line differently, and almost never at the same place that Collier drew it. But in the face of the Indians' relative lack of political power in American society, both Collier and Lindquist felt a moral necessity in drawing that line for the Indians' sake.

Today, many Christian Indian leaders believe missionaries and reformers played as large a role in creating Native problems as they did in solving them. George Tinker, a Lutheran scholar and minister of Osage and Cherokee descent, has argued that missionaries contributed to a plague of "individual and community dysfunctionalities that eat away" at tribal cohesion. "With far too much assistance and complicity from the missionaries," he continues, "the U.S. government has carefully manipulated our nations into relationships of total dependence that are today best described as co-dependent."[3] Likewise, Marie Therese Archambault, from the Standing Rock Reservation in North Dakota, has suggested that while Native peoples "appreciated the kindness of the missionaries," they soon learned that the missionary "idea of *to help*" really meant *"to do for."* In the parent-child relationship that resulted, she concludes, "the giver easily dominate[d] the receiver."[4]

Lindquist, of course, recognized growing Native hostility to the inequities of paternalism, and he struggled toward the end of his career to eliminate those inequities through the political empowerment of Indians as individuals. He came to believe that both Collier's pluralism and his own past commitment to a protective gradualism exacerbated the Indians' plight. Yet in that very process of attempting to liberate the Indians from political and ecclesiastical controls, he continued to act on the assumption of Western superiority over tribal nations. Paternalistic relationships, it seems, do not simply fade away. They mutate, often into forms that would strive to be their very opposite. In Indian affairs, the woven fabric of missionary benevolence and authority has indeed proved difficult to unravel.

Notes

Abbreviations Used for Manuscript Collections

AIIP   Records of the American Indian Institute, Board of National Missions, Presbyterian Church (U.S.A.), Department of History and Records Management Services, Philadelphia.

BP   Private papers of Helen Lindquist Bonny, Vero Beach, Florida.

CP   Papers of John Collier, Yale University Library, New Haven, Connecticut; Sanford, N.C.: Microfilming Corporation of America, 1980, microfilm.

IRAP   Indian Rights Association Papers, Historical Society of Pennsylvania, Philadelphia; Glen Rock, N.J.: Microfilming Corporation of America, 1975, microfilm.

LP   Papers of G. E. E. Lindquist, Burke Library, Union Theological Seminary, New York.

NA 75   Records of the Bureau of Indian Affairs, Record Group 75, National Archives, Washington, D.C.

NACP   Records of the Bureau of Indian Affairs, Record Group 75, National Archives–Central Plains, Kansas City, Missouri.

NCCA 26   Records of the Home Missions Council, Record Group 26, National Council of Churches Archives, Presbyterian Church (U.S.A.), Department of History and Records Management, Philadelphia, Pennsylvania.

OFC   Records of the Office of the Commissioner of Indian Affairs, Office File of Commissioner John Collier, 1933–1945, Records of the Bureau of Indian Affairs, Record Group 75, National Archives, Washington, D.C.

RBIC   Records of the Board of Indian Commissioners, General Correspondence, 1919–1933, Records of the Bureau of Indian Affairs, Record Group 75, National Archives, Washington, D.C.

RWH   Records of the Indian Organization Division, Records Concerning the Wheeler-Howard Act, 1933–1937, Records of the Bureau of Indian Affairs, Record Group 75, National Archives, Washington, D.C.

Introduction

1. Hinman, *Christian Activities Among American Indians*, 16–17.

2. For prominent examples of the analytical shift to Native American perspectives in missions studies and cultural studies, see Lewis, *Creating Christian Indians*; McNally, *Ojibwe Singers*; Treat, ed., *Native and Christian*; Kidwell, *Choctaws and Missionaries*; Noley, *First White Frost*; Gutiérrez, *When Jesus Came*; Bowden, *American Indians and Christian Missions*. For a similar shift in federal Indian policy studies, see Ellis, *To Change Them Forever*; Hauptman, *The Iroquois and the New Deal*; Philp, *Termination Revisited*.

3. Other scholars have interpreted the 1920s and 1930s as a key period in the structural displacement of Protestant authority in national affairs (Handy, *A Christian America*; Marty, *Noise of Conflict*). And Collier's policy goals provide obvious support for that view. But I have stressed change and reconfiguration as the key themes in Protestant influence, rather than declension. In doing so, I am drawing from William Hutchison's work in defining a religious establishment as a dynamic network of relationships. Hutchison, *Between the Times*, vii–viii, 3–13. See also Warren, *Theologians of a New World Order*; Schenkel, *Rich Man and the Kingdom*; and Tweed, "An Emerging Protestant Establishment." For a critique of the use of the metaphor of a religious establishment, see Orsi, "Beyond the Mainstream."

4. See Kymlicka, *Multicultural Citizenship*; Wilkinson, *American Indians, Time, and the Law*; Fuchs, *American Kaleidoscope*; Shklar, *American Citizenship*; Smith, *Civic Ideals*; and Deloria and Wilkins, *Tribes, Treaties, and Constitutional Tribulations*.

5. Helen Lindquist Bonny (daughter of G. E. E. Lindquist), interview by author, Salina, Kansas, February 8, 1998.

6. McKinley H. Warren to Ethel Geer Lindquist, May 14, 1953, in scrapbook, "Over Forty Years of Selfless Service to the Indians—From His Friends," BP.

7. Lindquist, *Handbook*; Lindquist, *New Trails*.

8. John Collier Jr., foreword, in Kelly, *Assault on Assimilation*, xv (quotation), xvii.

9. See Philp, *Collier's Crusade*, 4–7, which is based on Collier's own account. For an alternative version, see Kelly, *Assault on Assimilation*, n. 3, 386.

10. "John Collier" [1922], reel 59, CP.

11. John Collier Jr., foreword, in Kelly, *Assault on Assimilation*, xiii.

12. Philp, *Collier's Crusade*, 19.

13. Collier, *From Every Zenith*, 267.

14. See, for example, Collier, *From Every Zenith*, 118–20; and Collier's editorial in *Indians at Work* 3 (May 1, 1936):1–4.

15. On the complex maneuvering that landed Collier in the Indian Office, see Kelly, "Choosing the New Deal Indian Commissioner," 269–88.

16. John Collier Jr., foreword, in Kelly, *Assault on Assimilation*, xx.

17. The best historical study of this tradition in American piety is Albanese, *Nature Religion in America*.

18. Collier, untitled, June 24, 1942, reel 32, CP.

19. Collier, untitled, January 16, 1944, reel 32, CP.

20. Collier, Biographical Sketch, n.d., reel 59, CP.

21. Helen L. Bonny, "Episodes from GEEL's Life," n.d., BP.

22. *Destination Lindsborg*, 1997.

23. Sermon notes in the back of Lindquist's New Testament, BP.

24. Their two face-to-face meetings took place at the Advisory Council on Indian Affairs in 1923 (described in chapter 2) and the Plains Indian Congress in Rapid City, South Dakota, in 1934 (described in chapter 4).

25. Lindquist to Mark Dawber, May 2, 1945, Box 15, Folder 351, LP.

26. Telegram, Collier to B. G. Courtright, August 7, 1939, Box 9, Miscellaneous 1939–1941, OFC.

27. Charles Tranter to Lindquist, July 19, 1943, and Lindquist to Tranter, July 26, 1943, Box 31, Folder 695, LP.

28. Personal correspondence, Helen Lindquist Bonny to the author, June 26, 2000.

29. Two scholars describe Lindquist as a Methodist from Minnesota, while another calls him a Lutheran, and yet another, following a mistaken 1934 newspaper report, names him as Dr. C. C. Lindquist. In fact, Lindquist was a Congregationalist from Kansas, and although he did receive an honorary doctorate from Bethany College in Lindsborg, Kansas, that did not take place until 1939. Bernstein, *American Indians and World War II*, 7; LaGrand, "The Changing 'Jesus Road,'" 485; Kelly, *Assault on Assimilation*, 289; Smith, "The Wheeler-Howard Act of 1934," 528.

1 The Making of an Ardent Assimilationist

1. Summary of Activities for the Society for Propagating the Gospel Among the Indians and Others in North America, May 1, 1953, LP, Box 14, Folder 300.

2. G. E. E. Lindquist, untitled manuscript [n.d.], BP.

3. Barton, *A Folk Divided*, 214–37 (quotation).

4. Blanck, *Becoming Swedish-American*, 210–21.

5. Emory Lindquist, *Bethany in Kansas*, 25, 45. Lindquist's nephew and Rhodes scholar, Emory Lindquist, recalls Elmer's having won oratory contests at Bethany in both Swedish and English. Audiocassette of family conversation, March 25, 1989, BP; see also the biographical paragraph on Lindquist in the Bethany College yearbook, *The Daisy*, 30. On the teaching of Swedish language and literature at Swedish-American colleges, see Blanck, *Becoming Swedish-American*, 86–107.

6. In Lindsborg, Swedish was used in Bethany Church services until 1928, Swedish and English until 1941, and then English alone. In the Evangelical Mission Church, Swedish was used for worship services until 1923, Swedish and English until the late 1930s, and then English alone. Emory Lindquist, *Smoky Valley People*, 182.

7. Quoted in Emory Lindquist, *Smoky Valley People*, 185. For a biography of Swensson, see Pearson, *The Americanization of Carl Aaron Swensson*.

8. Barton, *A Folk Divided*, 88. Barton's assessment echoes Lawrence Fuchs's argument that American nationalism allowed for a "voluntary pluralism" among ethnic groups, as long

as they were loyal to America's civic institutions. Fuchs, *The American Kaleidoscope*. See also Blanck, *Becoming Swedish-American*, 221.

9. Quoted in Emory Lindquist, *Smoky Valley People*, 134.

10. For a historian's attempt to break down the sharp dichotomies between assimilation and pluralism, see Gleason, *Speaking of Diversity*. Arthur Mann emphasizes the compatibility of universal citizenship and cultural particularity within America's "common heritage," in *The One and the Many*. The classic sociological work on immigrant assimilation is Gordon, *Assimilation in American Life*. Perhaps the most useful brief summary is David L. Salvaterra, "Becoming American: Assimilation, Pluralism, and Ethnic Identity," in Walch, ed., *Immigrant America*, 29–54.

11. Anderson, "'Strangers Yet Acquainted,'" 210–22; Emory Lindquist, *Vision for a Valley*, 48.

12. G. E. E. Lindquist, "Impressions of Sweden," *The Covenant Companion*, May 1926. For a discussion of the Evangelical Mission Covenant Church and its liberal individualism, see Hawkinson, "An Interpretation of the Background," 3–13.

13. Carl A. Swensson, quoted in Barton, *A Folk Divided*, 102.

14. Helen Lindquist Bonny (daughter of G. E. E. Lindquist), interview by author, Salina, Kansas, February 8, 1998; Hervey B. Peairs to Robert D. Hall, Secretary for Indian Work, YMCA, April 8, 1912, and Hall to Peairs, April 19, 1912, in Haskell Series, Administrative Files, 1896–1960, NACP.

15. Helen Lindquist Bonny, phone interview by author, January 16, 1998; Hy White, "Indian Wishes to Be on Own, Says One of Top Authorities," *Palm Beach Post*, February 15, 1956, clipping in BP. See also Edward Tsyitee to Lindquist, November 5, 1953, BP. Lindquist's grandniece once wrote his wife, "I can remember one time when Uncle Elmer taught us to sing 'Christmas is here again' in Swedish, and to Ma Ma's chagrin we went dancing around singing it over and over," Sarah [Train] to Ethel Lindquist, February 19, 1967, BP.

16. See Lindquist's book *Bland Nordamerikas Indianer, bilder ur indianeras utvecklingshioria intill vara dagar* [Among the North American Indians: Portraits of the Indians' Progress up to the Present Day], 1926.

17. Lindquist, "Impressions of Sweden," *Covenant Companion*, January–May, 1926. Lindquist appears to have translated speeches in French and German, as well as Swedish. Lindquist to Ethel Geer Lindquist, August 25, 1925, BP.

18. Elmer Lindquist to Emily Lindquist, June 14, 1908, BP.

19. Walter Roe (d. 1913) attended Williams College in Massachusetts, where he received the Doctor of Divinity degree, and entered Indian missions at Colony, Oklahoma, in 1897 under the auspices of the Women's Executive Committee of the Reformed Church. "Walter C. Roe," 789–90.

20. Elmer Lindquist to Emily Lindquist, June 14, 1908, BP.

21. Lindquist to George Hinman, January 21, 1930, Box 15, Folder 335, LP.

22. Carey, *William Carey*, 51, 72, 154; Walls, *The Missionary Movement*, 79–80.

23. For example, Elkanah Walker, Cushing Eells, and Asa Brown Smith—pioneer missionaries to the Pacific Northwest—felt called to Africa and the Far East, but the 1837 financial panic forced them to stay closer to home. Miller, *Prophetic Worlds*, 85–86. Likewise, the Riggs "dynasty" among the Sioux would never have existed if Stephen R. Riggs had followed through on his initial plans to go to China. See his autobiographical work, *Mary and I*, 28.

24. McLoughlin, *Cherokees and Missionaries,* 137.

25. See Higham's valuable work on this subject, *Noble, Wretched, and Redeemable,* 103–10; and William R. Hutchison, *Errand to the World,* 68–69. By the twentieth century, a large number of missionaries to the Indians—with Lindquist among them—never learned a native language. For further evidence of the general apathy of American Protestants toward Indian missions—even in the face of the extraordinary privileges President Grant gave them—see Keller, *American Protestantism.*

26. On the colonial nature of U.S.–Indian relations, see Hoxie, *A Final Promise,* 147–88; Craig, "Christianity and Empire," 1–41; Williams, "United States Indian Policy," 810–31.

27. See Walls's essay in *The Missionary Movement,* 221–40; William R. Hutchison, "A Moral Equivalent for Imperialism: Americans and the Promotion of 'Christian Civilization,' 1880–1910," in Torben and Hutchison, eds., *Missionary Ideologies,* 167–78. For one missionary's account of white injustices against the Indians see Kinney, *Frontier Missionary Problems,* 30–58.

28. Walter Roe to Henry Roe Cloud, November 21, 1910, reel 1, AIIP.

29. Roe, "The Mohonk Lodge," 176–79. Compare Randolph Bourne, an early cultural pluralist who, in similar fashion, worried that assimilation was creating ethnic mongrels who had given up the best in their own cultures only to adopt the values of white society's lowest common denominator: "Our cities are filled with these half-breeds who retain their foreign names but have lost the foreign savor. This does not mean that they have actually been changed into New Englanders or Middle Westerners. It does not mean that they have been really Americanized. It means that, letting slip from them whatever native culture they had, they have substituted for it only the most rudimentary American—the American culture of the cheap newspaper, the 'movies,' the popular song, the ubiquitous automobile.... This tame flabbiness is accepted as Americanization." Bourne, "Trans-National America," 86–97.

30. Prucha, *Great Father,* 2:611–30; and Ahern, "Assimilationist Racism," 23–32.

31. See especially Coleman, "Problematic Panacea," 143–59; Coleman, *Presbyterian Missionary Attitudes toward American Indians;* Banker, "Presbyterians and Pueblos," 23–40; Beaver, *Church, State, and the American Indians,* 190–92; and Dippie, *The Vanishing American,* 166–67.

32. Pratt, "The Indian No Problem," 851–56.

33. Ibid. See also Pratt's attempt to initiate newly appointed Commissioner Cato Sells into the world of Indian affairs, warning him that Indian mission interests actually ran counter to assimilation. Pratt to Sells, November 12, 1913, copy in Box 19, Joseph W. Latimer, Record Group 46, Records of the United States Senate, Records of the Committee on Interior and Insular Affairs, Subcommittee on Indian Affairs, Sen. 83A-F9 (70th–82nd), National Archives, Washington, D.C.

34. Dippie, *The Vanishing American,* 183–89.

35. See Hoxie, *A Final Promise,* 162–69; Adams, *Education for Extinction,* 307–33; and Ellis, *To Change Them Forever,* 131–52.

36. Moffett, *The American Indian on the New Trail,* 1–28, 80, 105, 249, 277. See also F. B. Riggs, "In Indian Education," 284–87. Moffett was part of a distinguished family of missionaries, including his brother, Samuel Austin Moffett, who helped establish Presbyterian missions in Korea, and his nephew, Samuel Hugh Moffett, who served in China and later became Princeton Theological Seminary's Henry Winters Luce Professor of Ecumenics and Mission.

37. Roe, "The Mohonk Lodge," 176–79. For more favorable interpretations of the Roes

and gradualist policies, see Holm, "Indians and Progressives," 127–63; Dippie, *The Vanishing American,* 183–85; and Prucha, *Great Father,* 2:760–62. Henry E. Fritz has found a similar shift toward gradualism and an increasing respect for "the communal character of Indian cultures" in the Board of Indian Commissioners during the 1910s, in "The Last Hurrah of Christian Humanitarian Reform," 147–62.

38. Robert D. Hall to Hervey B. Peairs, April 19, 1912, in Haskell Series, Administrative Files, 1896–1960, NACP.

39. Lindquist, "American Indian Students on the New Trail" [n.d.], clipping in BP. Note that Lindquist, like Moffett, used the language of "racial characteristics" to discuss Indian students. This might be interpreted as a sign of the influence of scientific racism on Lindquist's thought. But elsewhere, Lindquist discussed the Indians' traits as the product of environment, not biology (Lindquist, "The American Indian Boy and His Future" [n.d.], clipping in BP).

40. Lindquist, "American Indian Students on the New Trail" [n.d.], clipping in BP. Another early critique of Pratt and the radical assimilationist approach is intimated in Lindquist's speech to a national Conference on Christian Work for the American Indians, October 19, 1914. See the handwritten outline, "Recruiting Leaders for Indian Christian Service," reel 29, IRAP.

41. Lindquist, "The American Indian Boy and His Future" [n.d.], BP.

42. Lindquist, "Sub-committee on Survey: Report on Government Non-Reservation Schools for the Joint Committee on Indian Missions," April 15, 1919, Box 1, Folder 4, LP. See also the address by Robert D. Hall, Lindquist's supervisor in YMCA work, "Moral Training in Indian Schools," 87–88.

43. E. A. Allen to Lindquist, March 1, 1915, Central Classified Files (hereafter CCF), 23818-15-047 Chilocco, NA 75.

44. Lindquist to E. A. Allen, March 3, 1915, CCF, 23818-15-047 Chilocco, NA 75.

45. Crum, "Henry Roe Cloud," 171–84. See also Moffett, "The Red Men and the Gospel," 751.

46. Roe Cloud attended the Presbyterian Santee Mission School in Nebraska and evangelist Dwight L. Moody's academy at Mt. Hermon, Massachusetts. Roe Cloud, "From Wigwam to Pulpit," 328–38.

47. Roe Cloud's attitudes reflect something of what Evelyn Brooks Higginbotham has called the "politics of respectability." Roe Cloud sought to subvert race subordination, but he did so on the basis of such white American values as racial self-help, Victorian cleanliness, and the Puritan work ethic. Higginbotham, *Righteous Discontent,* 185–229.

48. Roe Cloud, "The Future of the Red Men in America," 529–32. See also Crum, "Henry Roe Cloud," 179.

49. Barnard, *From Evangelicalism to Progressivism,* 109–27. Lindquist's most famous survey was published as *The Red Man in the United States* in 1923. Roe Cloud was the only Indian surveyor involved in the famous 1928 Meriam report. Lewis Meriam et al., *The Problem of Indian Administration.* John D. Rockefeller Jr. funded both surveys.

50. Fullerton, *Essays and Sketches,* 168. For Bosworth's influence, see especially Lindquist's most "theological" work, *The Jesus Road and the Red Man,* which makes repeated references to Bosworth's writings.

51. Bosworth, *Studies in the Life of Jesus Christ*, 53, 67, 125; Bosworth, *What It Means to Be a Christian*, 9, 83–84.

52. Bosworth, *What It Means to Be a Christian*, 5–7.

53. See the correspondence between Walter Roe and Henry Roe Cloud, 1908–1913, reel 1, AIIP. Ultimately, Roe Cloud gathered support from the Olcotts (mining), the McCormicks (International Harvester), the Rockefellers (Standard Oil Company), and the Phelps-Stokes family (real estate and banking). Anson Phelps Stokes Jr. (1874–1958), Yale's Secretary and administrator of Yale-in-China, helped put Roe Cloud in touch with the managers of his sisters' endowment, the Phelps-Stokes Fund, for support. Stokes would later play an important role in founding the Institute for Government Research (later the Brookings Institute), which employed Roe Cloud as a consultant in the Meriam Report on Indian affairs (1928).

54. Roe Cloud, "From Wigwam to Pulpit," 339.

55. "Report of the Committee on Indian Missions, 1913," Reel 130, Group 325, IRAP.

56. On discipline problems, see Henry A. Vruwink to Lindquist, April 13, 1917, reel 1, AIIP. Financial struggles persisted until 1927, when the Presbyterian Church (USA) took over the school.

57. Reported in Roe Cloud to E. E. Olcott, April 3, 1922, reel 1, AIIP.

58. Roe Cloud to E. E. Olcott, October 29, 1923 (quotation), and Roe Cloud to E. E. Olcott, April 3, 1922, reel 1, AIIP.

59. Annual Report for the American Indian Institute, 1927, reel 1, AIIP.

60. Crum, "Henry Roe Cloud," 183.

61. Two valuable historical works on the SAI are Hertzberg, *The Search for an American Indian Identity*, and Porter, *To Be Indian*, 91–142.

62. Coolidge, "The Indian American," 20–24; *The Society of American Indians: A National Organization of Americans*, 2d ed. [n.p.]. For an account of Coolidge's controversial marriage to the wealthy daughter of a New York hotel proprietor, see Duncombe, "The Church and the Native American Arapahoes," 363–71.

63. "Statement of Purpose," Society of American Indians, October 16, 1912, reel 137, Group 350, IRAP.

64. Montezuma personally published his address under the title, *Let My People Go*, a copy of which may be found in reel 132, frame 350, IRAP. According to a biography by Peter Iverson, Montezuma was mistakenly known as an Apache Indian, while his true tribal affiliation was Yavapai. Iverson, *Carlos Montezuma*, 4–5, 153–60.

65. Montezuma, *Let My People Go*, reel 132, frame 350, IRAP.

66. Moffett, "The Society of American Indians," 262–65.

67. Minutes, Society of American Indians, November 26, 1918, reel 33, IRAP.

68. Arthur C. Parker to Matthew K. Sniffen, October 18, 1918, reel 33, IRAP.

69. Parker, "Problems of Race Assimilation in America," 301.

70. Charles Eastman to Sniffen, November 16, 1918; Sniffen to Eastman, November 23, 1918 (quotation), reel 33, IRAP. See also Thomas Moffett and Matthew K. Sniffen to Arthur C. Parker, September [illegible], 1918, and Thomas Moffett to Sniffen, January 16, 1919, reel 33, IRAP. My findings conflict significantly with Thomas A. Britten's suggestion that the IRA was a leading advocate for the abolition of the BIA. Britten, *American Indians in World War I*, 178.

71. Sniffen to Rev. D. F. Dole, November 28, 1921, reel 37, IRAP. See also, Brosius to

Sniffen, May 15, 1920, reel 35, IRAP. For the fraud accusations against Thomas L. Sloan (Omaha), a Montezuma supporter, see Lindsey, *Indians at Hampton Institute*, 212–13; Agent, Indian Rights Association, to Secretary of the Interior, March 10, 1913, reel 27, IRAP.

72. Brosius to Thomas Moffett, November 29, 1919, reel 33, IRAP.

73. See, for example, Minutes, Conference of the Friends of the Indian, January 20–21, 1918, reel 33, IRAP.

74. Lindquist, *Red Man in the United States*, 390–91.

2 Indian Dances and the Defense of Federal Guardianship, 1920–1933

1. Transcript, Advisory Council on Indian Affairs, December 12/13, 1923, p. 67, reel 39, IRAP.

2. For a fuller account of the Indian dance controversy, see Daily, "Guardian Rivalries," 61–122. Other discussions of the Indian dance controversy appear in Kelly, *Assault on Assimilation*, 295–348; Philp, *Collier's Crusade*, 55–70; Dorcy, "Friends of the American Indian," 204–52; and Jacobs, "Making Savages of Us All," 178–209. My research has focused on the BIA's involvement in suppressing Indian dances in the Southwest and the Northern Plains. For perspectives on Indian dances on the Southern Plains, see Ellis, "We Don't Want Your Rations," 133–54; and Kracht, "Kiowa Powwows," 321–50.

3. For the Religious Crimes Code, see U.S. Department of the Interior, *Rules Governing the Court of Indian Offenses*.

4. Meritt to W. C. Orton, September 11, 1915, Central Classified Files (hereafter CCF) 96511-15-063, General Services, NA 75.

5. E. D. Mossman to Commissioner Cato Sells, April 13, 1918, and James H. McGregor to Sells, April 13, 1918, CCF 21685-18-061, General Services, NA 75.

6. For some of the variations in enforcement, see the letters found in CCF 20057-13-063, General Services, NA 75; CCF 23600-19-063, General Services, NA 75; and CCF 10429-22-063, General Services, NA 75. The field service's lack of fervor in suppressing Indian dances was apparent, with a few exceptions, in "Extracts from Annual Reports of Superintendents, Year 1920, on Dancing," CCF 86448-20-063, General Services, NA 75.

7. See Memo, Frances Leupp to Father William Ketcham [1909], CCF 44745-09-063, General Services, NA 75.

8. J. Brownlee Vorhees to Leupp, February 26, 1909; Leupp to Vorhees, February 27, 1909; L. C. Barnes to Leupp, June 3, 1909, CCF 16209-09-063, General Services, NA 75.

9. See Hutchison, *Modernist Impulse*, 87–105; Hutchison, *Errand to the World*, 102–11; Grant Wacker, "A Plural World: The Protestant Awakening to World Religions," in Hutchison, ed., *Between the Times*, 253–77; LaGrand, "The Changing 'Jesus Road,'" 479–504. For a critique of this "gentler liberalism," see Tinker, *Missionary Conquest*, 114–15.

10. Minutes, Conference of Friends of the Indian, January 22/23, 1918, p. 37, reel 33, IRAP. See also Hugh Burleson, "The Soul of the Indian," 804–10.

11. Richard H. Pratt to Charles Burke, June 13, 1921, CCF 56256-21-063, General Services, NA 75.

12. See, for example, Matthew Sniffen to Mary P. Lord, April 26, 1921, reel 85, IRAP.

13. Samuel Brosius to Commissioner Cato Sells, October 20, 1920, reel 35, IRAP.

"Investigation into the practices of the Sioux Indians on the Dakota Reservations with particular reference to the Indian dances; conducted by Commissioner Charles Burke," October 24, 1922, p. 43, CCF 10429-22-063, General Services, NA 75.

14. Burris to Sells, June 26, 1920, CCF 36469-20-154, Western Navajo, NA 75; "Complaints Against Missionary Frey," December 1, 1920, CCF 101550-20-816.2, Western Navajo, NA 75.

15. "Complaints Against Missionary Frey," December 1, 1920, CCF 101550-20-816.2, Western Navajo, NA 75; E. M. Sweet Jr., Memorandum on Burris Charges, February 6, 1921, Evander Sweet Collection, Box 4, Folder 16, Holt-Atherton Department of Special Collections, University of the Pacific, Stockton, California. On countersubversionary polemics, see Davis, "Some Themes of Counter-Subversion," 205–44.

16. A full assessment of the veracity of the inspectors' affidavits is impossible to undertake at this point. It should be noted, however, that there was a genuine clash of mores between the Hopis and the Christian missionaries. For example, Hopi clown ceremonies commonly involved sexual innuendo, and, as Margaret Jacobs has pointed out, moral reformers apparently mistook the clowns' performances as "actual representations of everyday Pueblo life," when in fact, the clowns' bawdy acts were meant to help "regulate community behavior by making fun of inappropriate actions" (Jacobs, "Making Savages of Us All," 184, 187, 190–96). When Ramón Gutiérrez recently used the secret dance file to document his portrait of pre-Columbian Pueblo and Hopi cultures, Native writers sharply criticized him for reducing Native cultures to "a litany of sexual orgies" ("Commentaries on *When Jesus Came, the Corn Mothers Went Away: Marriage, Sexuality, and Power in New Mexico, 1500–1846*, by Ramón Gutiérrez," 141–77). Moreover, the conflict between Christian and traditional Hopi Indians had its roots deep within long-standing intratribal factions. See Loftin, *Religion and Hopi Life*, 71–81; Clemmer, *Roads in the Sky*; and Levy, *Orayvi Revisited*. Copies of the Sweet affidavits on Hopi secret dances can be found in the IRAP, reel 36, after the date December 31, 1921 (although the IRA did not actually see the file until two years later). Portions of the file have been printed in Duberman, Eggan, and Clemmer, eds., "Documents in Hopi Indian Sexuality," 99–130.

17. See copy of Circular 1665 (though designated as Circular 1664) signed by Cato Sells and dated March 17, 1921, in CCF 86448-20-063, General Services, NA 75.

18. Nelson, *The Prairie Winnows Out Its Own*, 7; Carlson, *Indians, Bureaucrats, and Land*, 136–41, 145. On the Competency Commissions, see Prucha, *Great Father*, 2:879–85. Thomas A. Britten also argues that the Great War provided some impetus for a renascence of Indian cultures, especially in war songs and victory dances. Britten, *American Indians in World War I*, 150–53.

19. See Hudson and Corrigan, *Religion in America*, 346–49.

20. Walker, *Lakota Belief and Ritual*, 204–5, 238–39; Moore, "How Giveaways and Powwows Redistribute the Means of Subsistence," in Moore, ed., *Political Economy of North American Indians*, 240–69.

21. Minutes, Committee on Indian Missions of the Home Missions Council and Council of Women for Home Missions, March 19, 1920, Box 7, Folder 11, NCCA 26; Home Missions Council, *Thirteenth Annual Meeting of the Home Missions Council*, 1920.

22. See the correspondence in the BIA's file on Lindquist's survey, CCF 103124-21-061, NA 75.

23. "Findings of the Sioux Falls Conference," April 7, 1922, reel 38, IRAP.

24. "Investigation into the practices of the Sioux Indians on the Dakota Reservations with particular reference to the Indian dances; conducted by Commissioner Charles Burke," October 24, 1922, CCF 10429-22-063, General Services, NA 75. On the growing call to end federal wardship and withdraw funding from the BIA, see U.S. Department of the Interior, *Report of the Commissioner of Indian Affairs,* 1920; U.S. Department of the Interior, *Fifty-Second Annual Report of the Board of Indian Commissioners,* 1921; Rusco, *Fateful Time,* 86–92. On the activities of Montezuma and Latimer, see Iverson, *Carlos Montezuma,* 160–73; and the writings of Latimer in Box 19, Joseph W. Latimer, Record Group 46, Records of the United States Senate, Committee on Interior and Insular Affairs, Subcommittee on Indian Affairs, Sen. 83A-F9 (70th–82nd), National Archives (Washington, D.C.).

25. "Investigation into the practices of the Sioux Indians," October 24, 1922, CCF 10429-22-063, General Services, NA 75. The strength of Burleson's opposition to giveaways was extraordinary in light of his previous writings on Indian cultures. As late as 1919, Burleson told the Home Missions Council Annual Meeting, "I hope we are in the way of re-adjusting some of our ideas of society and of economics a little more to the vision of the Indian soul." Burleson, "Soul of the Indian," 810.

26. The Supplement to Circular No. 1665 can be found in CCF 10429022–063 Part I, General Services, NA 75, and in the IRA Papers, reel 38, under February 14, 1923. The "children" quotation appeared in George Foster Peabody to Matthew Sniffen, April 11, 1923, reel 39, IRAP.

27. Kelly, *Assault on Assimilation,* 114–20; Dippie, *Vanishing American,* 284–96.

28. Kelly, *Assault on Assimilation,* 163–254; Philp, *Collier's Crusade,* 26–54.

29. "Burke Gives Indians Year to End Dances," *New York Tribune,* March 22, 1923, p. 9, col. 3; "Robbing the Indians' Faith," editorial, *New York Tribune,* March 22, 1923, p. 12, col. 1; Princess Atalie Unkalunt, Letter to the Editor, *New York Times,* March 27, 1923, p. 18, col. 6; Alida Sims Malkus, "Those Doomed Indians," *New York Times,* April 8, 1923, sec. 5, p. 1, col. 1.

30. The Joint Indian Committee served as an arm of the Home Missions Council and the Federal Council of Churches, representing more than twenty major Protestant denominations. Matthew Sniffen to Samuel Brosius, April 6 and 7, 1923, reel 87; Brosius to Sniffen, April 9, 1923, and Elmer E. Higley to Sniffen, April 23, 1923, reel 39, IRAP.

31. Edith M. Dabb, "Evils of Tribal Dances," *New York Times,* December 2, 1923, p. 8, col. 1.

32. Lindquist, *Red Man,* vi–vii, ix–x.

33. Lindquist, *Red Man,* ix.

34. Margaret D. Jacobs argues that Christian reformers saw Indians and Indian cultures as more dynamic and capable of adaptation than cultural pluralists did. Jacobs, *Engendered Encounters,* 82–105.

35. Advertisement [n.d.], in scrapbook titled "Comments and Reviews on 'Red Man in the U.S.' and 'The Jesus Road and the Red Man,' etc.," BP.

36. Lindquist, *Red Man,* 68–69, 269–70.

37. Lindquist, *Red Man,* 392.

38. Austin, "The American Indian."

39. Phillip, "Red Man Still with Us But Not of Us."

40. Lindquist, "American Indian Students on the New Trail" [n.d.], clipping in BP.

41. See for example Roe, "The Mohonk Lodge," 176–79.

42. Collier, "The Red Slaves of Oklahoma," 96.

43. Advisory Council transcript, p. 63. For the resolution in its original form (as indicated by Moffett's handwriting in the title of the document), see "Indian Dances and Ceremonies" [1923, n.d.], reel 40, IRAP. For the resolution in its final form, see Work, *Indian Policies,* 9–10. John Collier and Elizabeth Shepley Sergeant reported that the original resolution was "bloodthirsty" while the final resolution was "toothless." They overstated the differences between the two, since the only things cut from Moffett's resolution were introductory paragraphs that quoted from Burke's dance circulars. See Collier, "Red Slaves of Oklahoma," 98; Sergeant, "The Red Man's Burden," 201.

44. Advisory Council transcript, p. 70.

45. Advisory Council transcript, pp. 71–72. See also Collier, "Do Indians Have Rights of Conscience?" 346–49.

46. Stanley Went to Matthew Sniffen, December 10, 1923, reel 39, IRAP.

47. A copy of her address appeared in "Miss Muskrat Wins the Prize," 672–74.

48. "Indian Girl Is Guest at the White House," *New York Times,* December 14, 1923, p. 2, col. 8. See also Lindquist's own account in Haskell Institute's *Indian Leader,* "Advisory Council on Indian Affairs Meets at Washington," 27, no. 20 (February 8, 1924):10–14.

49. Collier, "The Red Slaves of Oklahoma," 99–100. See also Elizabeth Shepley Sergeant's comparable account, "The Red Man's Burden," 199–201.

50. Collier to Mr. Hoffman, December 14, 1923, Pearl Chase Papers, Community Development and Conservation Collection, University of California at Santa Barbara Library; quoted in Kelly, *Assault on Assimilation,* 19n, 414. Years later, Lindquist reportedly claimed that Collier tried to stop distribution of the book with threats of a lawsuit for defaming the Indians. Matthew Sniffen to Edward Curtis, February 4, 1935, and February 5, 1935, reel 95, IRAP. The Protestants' view of the book presentation appeared in a letter written the same day from Stanley Went of the Institute for Social and Religious Research to Commissioner Burke: "May I hasten on behalf of the Institute and in my own behalf to express our deep appreciation of the interest you have taken in 'The Red Man in the United States' and in all your splendid cooperation in arranging the highly satisfactory presentation to the President." CCF 74732-23-061 General Services, NA 75.

51. "Indian Girl Is Guest at the White House," *New York Times,* December 14, 1923, sec. 8, p. 2, and December 23, 1923, sec. 6, p. 1; *New York Tribune,* December 15, 1923, p. 5. Lindquist's scrapbook contains articles on the book presentation in dozens of newspapers (BP).

52. Second Supplement to Circular No. 1665, March 5, 1924, Orders, Circulars, and Circular Letters: Circulars, 1904–34, NA 75.

53. Matthew Sniffen to Herbert Welsh, August 13, 1924, reel 41, IRAP. On the course of the dance controversy after the Advisory Council see Kelly, *Assault on Assimilation,* 306–48; Philp, *Collier's Crusade,* 57–70. See also Jacobs, "Making Savages of Us All," 197.

54. Lindquist, *Red Man,* 267–68.

55. Collier, *From Every Zenith,* 136–42; and Collier, *Indians of the Americas,* 255–59.

56. Advisory Council transcript, p. 100.

57. Kelly, *Assault on Assimilation*, 317–20; Platform, Friends of the Indian Conference, January 18–19, 1926, reel 42, IRAP.

58. Prucha, *Great Father*, 2:793–94.

59. Philp, *Collier's Crusade*, 71–91.

60. Lindquist to Matthew K. Sniffen, October 27, 1924, reel 41, IRAP.

61. On scholarship for this period, see Philp, *Collier's Crusade*, 71–112; Darcy, "Friends of the American Indian"; Holm, "Indians and Progressives"; Jones, "'Hope for the Race of Man'"; Robbins, "Herbert Hoover's Indian Reformers Under Attack," 157–70; Prucha, *Great Father*, 2:790–939.

62. Lindquist to Malcolm McDowell, April 7, 1930, General Correspondence, 1919–1933, Decimal 010, RBIC.

63. On background of the SPG (officially named the Society for the Propagation of the Gospel Among the Indians and Others in North America), see Lindquist, "Early Work Among the Indians," 533–38; Lindquist, "An Indian Society's Sesqui-Centennial," *Southern Workman*, 1937, clipping in BP; Weiss, *Society for Propagating the Gospel*. Lindquist's sending agency should not be confused with the similarly named Society for the Propagation of the Gospel in Foreign Parts, founded by the Church of England in 1701.

64. Eliot to Malcolm McDowell, February 15, 1930, and McDowell to Eliot, February 20, 1930, General Correspondence, 1919–1933, Box 1, RBIC.

65. See Milner, "Albert K. Smiley: Friend to Friends of the Indians," in Milner and O'Neil, eds., *Churchmen and the Western Indians*, 143–75; Harmon, "When Is an Indian Not an Indian?" 95–123; Ahern, "Assimilationist Racism,'" 23–32.

66. See U.S. Department of the Interior, *Fifty-Second Annual Report of the Board of Indian Commissioners*, 6–10. *Sixtieth Annual Report of the Board of Indian Commissioners*, 11–13, 25.

67. Prucha, *Great Father*, 2:825 (quotation); Fritz, "The Last Hurrah of Christian Humanitarian Reform," 147–62.

68. Prucha, *Great Father*, 2:932; Philp, *Collier's Crusade*, 93–94.

69. Lindquist to McDowell, April 1, 1930, Box 2, General Correspondence, 1919–1933, Decimal 010, RBIC.

70. Meriam et al., *Problem of Indian Administration*. Like Lindquist's survey of Indian missions, the Meriam Report was generously funded by John D. Rockefeller Jr. For background information and correspondence regarding the Meriam report, see Parman, "Lewis Meriam's Letters." The quotation is from Parman, "Lewis Meriam's Letters," part 1, 256.

71. Lindquist to Samuel A. Eliot, April 7, 1931, and Lindquist to Malcolm McDowell, August 5, 1930, Box 2, General Correspondence, 1919–1933, Decimal 010, RBIC; Eliot to McDowell, March 9, 1931, and May 29, 1931, Box 1, General Correspondence, 1919–1933, RBIC; Lindquist to Earl Henderson, April 28, 1932, and June 2, 1932, Box 2, General Correspondence, 1919–1933, Decimal 010, RBIC. In another incident a well-educated appointee at a school in Nebraska stayed at his post for just two days, having been unprepared for the agricultural and vocational aspects of an Indian school curriculum. When he left he reportedly said, "I didn't think I was sent here to take care of your darned horse barns, cow stables and Jersey hogs." Lindquist to Malcolm McDowell, August 25, 1931, Box 2, General Correspondence, 1919–1933, Decimal 010, RBIC.

72. Lindquist to Samuel Eliot, April 7, 1931, Box 2, General Correspondence, 1919–1933, Decimal 010, RBIC.

73. Ryan, Memorandum, Means that have been taken to safeguard the raising of standards, n.d., Box 18, Folder 388, LP.

74. Lindquist to Ryan, May 25, 1931, Box 2, General Correspondence, 1919–1933, Decimal 010, RBIC.

75. Malcolm McDowell to Lindquist, October 2, 1931, Box 2, General Correspondence, 1919–1933, Decimal 010, RBIC.

76. Lindquist, "Conference Held in Oklahoma City, Oklahoma," October 27, 1931, 213–216, in *Special Reports, 1931–1932*, vol. 10, RBIC.

77. Ryan, Address to the Indian Rights Association Annual Meeting, January 14, 1932, reel 48, IRAP.

78. Lindquist, "Receding Frontiers in Indian Country," *Southern Workman*, March 1931, copy in BP. See also Lindquist, *Handbook for Missionary Workers*, 18.

79. Lindquist, "Report on the Klamath Indians," February 3, 1931, in *Special Reports, 1915–1933*, vol. 9, RBIC. For a revealing analysis of tribal councils during this period, see Carlson, "The Economics and Politics of Irrigation Projects on Indian Reservations, 1900–1940," in Barrington, ed., *Other Side of the Frontier*, 233–58.

80. See *Special Reports, 1915–1933*, vols. 9–10, RBIC.

81. On the complex maneuvering that landed Collier in the Indian Office, see Kelly, "Choosing the New Deal Indian Commissioner," 269–88.

82. Philp, *Collier's Crusade*, 118–20.

3 Collier's New Deal for the Missionaries, 1933–1934

1. Collier's interview for *New York Times Magazine*, July 14, 1935, has been republished in Wax and Buchanan, eds., *Solving "The Indian Problem,"* 48–56.

2. Collier, *From Every Zenith*, 267, 268. See also "A Bird's-eye View of Indian Policy, Historic and Contemporary," October 29, 1935, reel 53, IRAP. On the broader shift toward cultural pluralism in American thought, with special reference to federal immigration policy during the 1930s, see Weiss, "Ethnicity and Reform," 566–85.

3. Collier to Ben Dwight, February 19, 1936, Box 18, Religious Freedom, OFC.

4. John Collier, Circular No. 2970, January 3, 1934. Copy in NCCA 26 Box 7, Folder 11. On Collier's controversial reforms in the area of Indian religions, see Prucha, *Great Father*, 2:951–52; and Philp, *John Collier's Crusade*, 131–33.

5. Rachlin, "Tight Shoe Night," 84–100, quotation on p. 99. At least one scholar has found that after Collier became commissioner, some Indian dances were transformed from a social or carnivalesque orientation to a more solemn expression of respect for deceased elders. Foster, *Being Comanche*, 127. At the Fort Belknap Reservation in Montana, though, Collier's administration coincided with a decline in dance traditions among the Gros Ventres and Assiniboines. Fowler, *Shared Symbols, Contested Meanings*, 156–63. Clearly, Circular 2970 must be interpreted as just one among many factors shaping local practices.

6. This comparison of the two charters is based on Hertzberg, *Search for an American Indian Identity*, 259–84; and G. E. E. Lindquist, "Preliminary Report on Peyote," prepared for

the Home Missions Council and the Council of Women for Home Missions, July 5, 1938, BP. There were also anecdotal reports about the revival of the Sun Dance and other traditions on the northern Plains. "Indians Resume Dancing," *New York Times,* August 12, 1934, p. 4, col. 6.

7. See for example C. L. Lynch to John Collier, January 27, 1934, OFC; Donald H. Biery to commissioner, July 24, 1935, Central Classified Files (hereafter CCF) 41317-35-816 Sherman Institute, NA 75; and the letters from agents to Collier in CCF 14790-35-816 General Services, NA 75.

8. W. O. Roberts to John Collier, January 23, 1934, OFC.

9. William R. King to Matthew K. Sniffen, January 24, 1934, reel 51, IRAP.

10. Mark Dawber, *Composite Annual Administrative and Activity Report* (1934), Methodist Episcopal Church Board of Missions and Church Extension, 42–44, copy in Office File of W. Carson Ryan Jr., Director of Education, 1931–1935, Box 1, NA 75 [hereafter cited as Ryan Office File].

11. G. E. E. Lindquist to Matthew Sniffen, March 26, 1935 (quotation), and Lindquist to Sniffen, June 14, 1935, reel 53, IRAP; see also Mary M. Crawford to John Collier, February 3, 1934, Collier Office File, NA 75; Mary Crawford, circular letter, January 19, 1935, Box 19, Folder 419, LP; Walter Mitchell to John Collier, May 17, 1935, reel 53, IRAP.

12. Statement by Patrick Miguel, August 17, 1935, reel 53, IRAP.

13. Matthew Sniffen to J. M. Steere, August 19, 1935, and Walter Mitchell to John Collier, May 17, 1935, reel 53, IRAP.

14. William Goudberg to Mission Friends, December [n.d.] 1935, reel 53, IRAP.

15. See Matthew Sniffen to J. Denton Simms, May 15, 1933, reel 50, IRAP; "Mexicanizing Indian Education" and other articles on Mexico itself in *Christian Advocate, Pacific Edition,* January 10, 1935; and unsigned letter to the editor, "Opposing Efforts to Christianize the Indians," *Albuquerque Tribune,* April 22, 1934, clipping in Box 5, Part 5-A, RWH.

16. G. E. E. Lindquist to John Collier, November 1, 1933, Box 15, Folder 339, LP.

17. "Dr. Frank Smith's Report of His Interview with Mr. Collier," entered in minutes of Joint Indian Work Committee, November 29, 1933, Box 7, Folder 11, NCCA 26; J. E. Balmer to commissioner, October 12, 1933, CCF 46327-33-816.2 Western Navajo, NA 75; Lawrence E. Lindley to Matthew K. Sniffen, January 28, 1935, reel 52, IRAP; Office Memorandum to Dr. Ryan, May 2, 1934, Ryan Office File, Box 1, NA 75; Minutes, Conference of Friends of the Indian, April 22–23, 1938, enclosure in G. E. E. Lindquist to Matthew K. Sniffen, January 19, 1940, reel 57, IRAP.

18. Hinman, *Christian Activities Among American Indians,* 16–17.

19. Peairs to Bertha C. Mason, August 5, 1907, Haskell Series, Subject Correspondence Files, 1904–1941, Religion, NACP.

20. The General Regulations for Religious Worship and Instruction in Government Schools of 1910 may be found in CCF 14228-10-816, General Services, NA 75, while a 1932 version (with only slight revisions) appeared in G. E. E. Lindquist, *A Handbook for Missionary Workers,* 62–64. On the Protestant-Catholic debates that led to the 1910 regulations, see Prucha, *Churches and the Indian Schools, 1888–1912,* 161–88.

21. John Collier to Asa Ten Fingers, August 7, 1934, CCF 41317-35-816 Sherman Institute, NA 75.

22. Untitled typescript, Box 7, Folder 11, NCCA 26.

23. See J. M. Somerndike to Collier, December 5, 1933, Box 18, OFC (quotation); *Composite Annual Administrative and Activity Report* (1934), Methodist Episcopal Church Board of Missions and Church Extension, 42–44, copy in Ryan Office File, Box 1, NA 75; Transcript, Conference of Friends of the American Indian, April 22–23, 1938, enclosure in Lindquist to Matthew Sniffen, January 19, 1940, reel 57, IRAP.

24. Minutes, Joint Indian Committee, September 9, 1933, Box 7, Folder 11, NCCA 26. A copy of the "Regulations for Religious Worship and Instruction, Amendment No. 2," January 15, 1934, is located in Box 7, Folder 12, NCCA 26. The debates surrounding Collier's new regulations anticipated parallel arguments around "release time" practices in public schools fifteen years later, when the Supreme Court eliminated religious instruction from school campuses in the McCollum Case (1948). See Marty, *Modern American Religion*, vol. 3, *Under God Indivisible, 1941–1960*, 220–30.

25. Minutes, Joint Indian Committee, September 9, 1933, Box 7, Folder 11, NCCA 26. Compare the 1910 statement by a Home Missions Council official who likewise argued, in the context of Catholic-Protestant hostilities, that educated children "are more capable of determining their affiliations than would be their uneducated parents on the Reservations." Sam H. Woodrow to R. A. Ballinger, February 25, 1910, CCF 14728-10-816 General Services, NA 75.

26. Ann Seesholtz and William R. King to Religious Work Directors, May 4, 1934, Box 7, Folder 8, NCCA 26; and Seesholtz to Members of the Joint Indian Committee and Executives of Home Missions Boards, May 9, 1934, Box 7, Folder 12, NCCA 26. Two other Home Missions Council statements of support for Collier's new regulations appeared in "Home Missions Council Annual Report, 1935," pp. 43–44, reel 130, frame 325, IRA Papers; and *Composite Annual Administrative and Activity Report* (1934), Methodist Episcopal Church Board of Missions and Church Extension, 42–44, copy in Ryan Office File, Box 1, NA 75.

27. Two juvenile skits published by the Missionary Education Movement show that as missionaries understood it, Native traditionalists staged dances and ceremonies specifically for Indian students returning from boarding schools. In that way, missionaries believed tribes were attempting to integrate students back into the traditions and norms of community life. Winifred Hulbert, *Hogan Beneath the Sunrise;* and Willcox, *Pueblo Pioneers.*

28. Jace Weaver has argued that First Amendment freedoms historically have eluded Native traditions precisely because those traditions involve altogether different conceptions of the sacred community. Weaver, "Losing My Religion" in Weaver, ed., *Native American Religious Identity,* 217–29.

29. James H. McGregor to John Collier, March 18, 1935, CCF 14790-35-816 General Services, NA 75.

30. Henry Roe Cloud to commissioner, April 17, 1935, CCF 14790-35-816 General Services, NA 75. Later evidence suggests that Collier did in fact tolerate Roe Cloud's interpretation of the regulations. See Collier to Rufus W. Weaver, April 17, 1937, CCF 14790-35-816 General Services, NA 75.

31. F. J. Scott to commissioner, March 19, 1935 (quotation); and L. E. Dial to commissioner, March 19, 1935, CCF 14790-35-816 General Services, NA 75.

32. F. W. Boyd to commissioner, March 26, 1935, CCF 14790-35-816 General Services, NA 75.

33. James T. Ryan to commissioner, March 18, 1935, CCF 14790-35-816 General Services,

NA 75. Yet another construal of the regulations applied the written consent requirement only to those parents whose religious affiliation was not already known to school administrators. T. B. Hall to commissioner, October 19, 1935, CCF 14790-35-816 General Services, NA 75.

34. Donald H. Biery to commissioner, July 24, 1935, CCF 41317-35-816 Sherman Institute, NA 75.

35. Alida C. Bowler to commissioner, September 17, 1934, CCF 50605-34-816 Carson, and John Collier to Rev. Alfred Lockwood, July 2, 1935, CCF 41317-35-816 Sherman Institute, NA 75.

36. Joseph DuBray to John Collier, May 26, 1934, CCF 26148-34-816 General Services, NA 75; E. M. Dabb to Ann Seesholtz, December 17, 1934, reel 52, IRAP; Lawrence E. Lindley to John H. Wood, July 31, 1935, reel 53, IRAP; Office Memorandum to Dr. Ryan, May 2, 1934, Ryan Office File, Box 1, NA 75. School superintendents likewise believed that the new regulations would "practically eliminate the Missionaries from the field." S. F. Stacher to commissioner, March 30, 1935; cf. T. B. Hall to commissioner, October 19, 1935, CCF 14790-35-817 General Services, NA 75.

37. Office Memorandum to Dr. Ryan, May 2, 1934, Ryan Office File, Box 1, NA 75; Philp, *John Collier's Crusade*, 132.

38. Ann Seesholtz and William R. King to Religious Work Directors, May 4, 1934, Box 7, Folder 8, NCCA 26 (quotation); Seesholtz to Members of the Joint Indian Committee and Executives of Home Missions Boards, May 9, 1934, Box 7, Folder 12, NCCA 26; "Home Missions Council Annual Report, 1935," pp. 43–44, reel 130, frame 325, IRAP.

39. Marginalia on Lindquist's copy of Amendment No. 2, Regulations for Religious Instruction and Worship, January 15, 1934, Box 28, Folder 598, LP; cf. Lindquist to Matthew Sniffen, November 24, 1934, reel 52, IRAP. Lindquist was alluding to the Hebrew story in Exodus 32, where the Israelites forged an idolatrous golden calf while they were camped at the base of Mt. Sinai.

40. "Pastor Flays 'Paganism' of Indian Policy," *Daily Oklahoman* (Oklahoma City), October 19, 1934, clipping in Box 18, Religious Freedom, OFC.

41. Findings of the Oklahoma City Conference, November 1, 1934, enclosure in Lindquist to Matthew Sniffen, November 24, 1934, reel 52, IRAP.

42. "Interview Given A[ssociated] P[ress] Representative, November 2, 1934, Collier Office File, Box 18, Religious Freedom, NA 75.

43. Lindquist to Matthew K. Sniffen, November 24, 1934, reel 52, IRAP; Minutes, Board of Directors, December 5, 1934, reel 99, IRAP; Sniffen to Lindquist, December 10, 1934, reel 95, IRAP.

44. Lawrence E. Lindley to John W. Wood, July 31, 1935, reel 53, IRAP. See the two amendments (both numbered as Amendment No. 3) dated February 7, 1935, and October 28, 1936, in CCF 41317-35-816 Sherman Institute and CCF (1940–1956) 00-42-816 General Services, NA 75.

45. F. Ernest Johnson, an officer of the Federal Council of Churches, worried in 1935 that Protestants "no longer were representing the community in its moral aspect," but were becoming instead "mere 'pressure groups'" in a highly factionalized public arena. He was referring primarily to the failure of Prohibition, but his view expresses as well the sense of disfranchisement Protestant missionaries felt with respect to the BIA. Johnson, *Church and Society*, 131.

46. Lindquist, "American Indian Students on the New Trail" [n.d.], clipping in BP.

47. Years later she maintained that, technically speaking, the Board of Indian Commissioners still existed, since Collier did not have the legal authority to abolish it. Seymour to Matthew K. Sniffen, June 26,1935, reel 53, IRAP.

48. See, for example, the discussion of Oklahoma Indian land issues in Minutes, January 11–12, 1933, RBIC. Seymour opposed a bill that would extend federal trusteeship over the moneys for some members of the Five Civilized Tribes, saying it was time for the Indians to assume "the ordinary responsibilities of citizenship." Lindquist and most board members, though, argued that the bill was an important protective measure for Indians "who were on the border line of starvation and for whom the state had accepted no responsibility as to education, medical relief, and economic advancement." See also Minutes, January 14–15, 1931, and May 10–11, 1933, RBIC; and Seymour, "Indian Rights," 101–4.

49. "Flora Warren Seymour," in Block, ed., *Current Biography 1942*, 753–55; Matthew Sniffen to G. E. E. Lindquist, July 9, 1933, reel 51, IRAP (quotation).

50. Seymour, "Federal Favor for Fetishism," 397–400. Seymour's attitudes on Indian affairs apparently had their origins in her connections with one of the most vocal advocates of radical assimilation, New York attorney Joseph W. Latimer. After Richard H. Pratt and Carlos Montezuma died in the early 1920s, Latimer picked up the mantle of their call for the abolition of the BIA. Coincidentally, Latimer was a native of Illinois and was connected with Knox College, where Seymour's husband and his family were major benefactors. See copies of Latimer's newsletter, *The American Indian*, and other paraphernalia on Latimer in Box 19, Joseph W. Latimer, Record Group 46, Records of the United States Senate, Committee on Interior and Insular Affairs, Subcommittee on Indian Affairs, Sen. 83A-F9 (70th–82nd), National Archives (Washington, D.C.) [hereafter cited as Records of the Senate Subcommittee on Indian Affairs, RG 46, NA].

51. Eastman, *Sister to the Sioux;* Eastman, "Our New-Old Indian Policy," 1471–73; Wilson, *Ohiyesa: Charles Eastman, Santee Sioux,* 44–46, 164; Alexander, "Finding Oneself Through a Cause," 1–37.

52. "A New Type of Indian Commissioner," *Christian Century* 50 (April 26, 1933):549; "Shall American Indians Be Deprived of Federal Guardianship?" *Christian Century* 52 (May 8, 1935):597; Paul Hutchinson to Harold Ickes, May 31, 1934, Collier Office File, Box 18, Adverse Propaganda, NA 75.

53. Eastman, "Does Uncle Sam Foster Paganism?" 1016–18.

54. Collier, "A Reply to Mrs. Eastman," 1018–20. For a discussion of the philosophical influences behind Collier's language ("world will") see Stefon, "The Indians' Zarathustra," parts 1 and 2, *Journal of Ethnic Studies* 11, no. 3 (1984):1–29, and 11, no. 4 (1984): 28–45.

55. John Collier to Asa Ten Fingers (Executive Secretary, Pine Ridge Missions Council, Oglala, South Dakota), August 7, 1934, CCF 41317-35-816 Sherman Institute, NA 75.

56. Charles A. Eastman (Ohiyesa), *Soul of the Indian.*

57. Elaine G. Eastman to John Collier, August 15, 1934, Collier Office File, Box 18, Adverse Propaganda, NA 75.

58. Eastman, "Uncle Sam and Paganism," 1073.

59. G. E. E. Lindquist, "Revival of Tribalism," 1118.

60. Eastman to Seymour, October 21, 1934, reel 52, IRAP.

61. Parman, *Navajos and the New Deal,* 55, 172.

62. J. C. Morgan, Letter to the Editor, "A Navajo Dissenter," *Christian Century* 51 (October 31, 1934):1379–80.

63. Collier, Letter to the Editor, *Christian Century* 51 (November 14, 1934):1459.

4 Battle over the Wheeler-Howard Act, 1934

1. R. Scott Appleby, "Missions and the Making of Americans: Religious Competition for Souls and Citizens," in Sarna, ed., *Minority Faiths,* 233.

2. For a late example of the IRA's vigorous defense of a tribe's treaty rights, see the correspondence of Samuel Brosius with regard to Walapai claims in Arizona, especially Brosius to Matthew Sniffen, August 5, 1930, reel 46, IRAP.

3. It is difficult to find an adequate term for the political vision that Collier entertained. Cultural pluralism seems appropriate for describing his approach to Indian cultural and religious traditions, so perhaps *legal* or *civic pluralism* can denote the view that the federal government had a unique and enduring legal obligation to Indians. Although Martin E. Marty has used the term with an altogether different meaning, I will use *civic pluralism* to refer to federal recognition of the unique rights of Native Americans and other national minorities that existed prior to the creation of the American nation-state. Marty, *Modern American Religion,* vol. 2, *Noise of Conflict, 1919–1941,* 5–6. See Will Kymlicka's useful terminology for group-differentiated rights in *Multicultural Citizenship,* especially pp. 12–33.

4. Prucha, *Great Father,* 2:659–86.

5. Prucha, *Great Father,* 2:864–96; Hoxie, *A Final Promise,* 147–87. For a full-scale economic study focusing on land policies during the assimilation period, see McDonnell, *Dispossession of the American Indian, 1887–1934.*

6. Prucha, *Great Father,* 2:864–96; McDonnell, *Dispossession of the American Indian, 1887–1934,* 87–120.

7. See Collier, "The Indians' Master-Problem: Land," 4–7; Collier, "A Lift for the Forgotten Red Man, Too," 10–11; Press Release, John Collier's Address to the Indian Rights Association, January 19, 1934, reel 51, IRAP; U.S. House Committee on Indian Affairs, *Readjustment of Indian Affairs,* 15–29 [hereafter cited as *Committee Hearings on H.R. 7902*].

8. The scholarship on the Wheeler-Howard Act is voluminous. Summaries of the act and the debates that surrounded it appear in Prucha, *Great Father,* 2:954–68; Philp, *John Collier's Crusade,* 135–60; Philp, ed., *Indian Self-Rule,* 1–109; Smith, "The Wheeler-Howard Act of 1934," 521–33; Stefon, "The Indians' Zarathustra," parts 1 and 2; Taylor, *The New Deal and American Indian Tribalism;* Koppes, "From New Deal to Termination," 543–66; Rusco, *Fateful Time;* and Deloria and Lytle, *Nations Within.* Several valuable studies have dealt with the impact of the Wheeler-Howard Act on particular tribes, such as Rosier, "'The Old System Is No Success'"; Philp, "The New Deal and Alaska Natives"; Parman, *Navajos and the New Deal;* Hauptman, *Iroquois and the New Deal;* Hoxie, *Parading Through History,* 325–43.

9. *Committee Hearings on H.R. 7902,* 1–7. On the impact of African colonial administration on Collier's views see Hauptman, "Africa View," 359–74.

10. *Committee Hearings on H.R. 7902,* 7–8.

11. *Committee Hearings on H.R. 7902,* 8–11.

12. *Committee Hearings on H.R. 7902*, 11–14. For an analysis of how tribal courts operated on one reservation, see Hoxie, *Parading Through History*, 308–12. Hoxie found that most Indian judges tended to be older, and that they acted much as traditional elders to shape community social life. In practice, then, Indian courts tended to exercise their authority in mediating rather than penal functions.

13. The devolution of the BIA also had an appeal to legislators, who constantly sought ways to shrink appropriations in Indian affairs, and to civil libertarians, who worried about the expanding powers of the federal government.

14. *Committee Hearings on H.R. 7902*, 63–66.

15. See the Soliticitor's Opinion on the Wheeler-Howard Act, October 25, 1934 (Box 10, Part 12, RWH), which details the sovereign powers that Collier and his legal experts saw invested in tribal self-government. That document was hidden from public view in order to avoid an adverse public reaction. Deloria and Lytle, *Nations Within*, 158–69. Other scholars have suggested that Collier's administration did not in fact mark a significant break with the past. For example, Ward Churchill has argued recently that Congress approved Collier's push for tribal self-government because it determined that important natural resources on tribal lands could be exploited more easily if the lands continued to be held by federally dominated tribes, rather than by individual Indians. Thus, Collier merely perpetuated the colonial relationship between Indian tribes and the federal government. Churchill, "The Crucible of American Indian Identity" in Champagne, ed., *Contemporary Native American Cultural Issues*, 39–67. See also the conclusion of Britten's article, "Hoover and the Indians."

16. Lindquist's article against the original Wheeler-Howard Act appeared as "The Government's New Indian Policy: Proposed Revival of Tribalism, Seen from the Missionary Angle," *Missionary Review of the World* 57 (April 1934):182–84. Lindquist put together his "Fourteen Points" soon after Oklahoma newspapers reported that he had called the bill "socialism and communism in the rankest sense." He repeatedly brushed off the quotation as "absurd." Minutes of the Plains Indian Congress, March 5, 1934, Box 4, Part 2-AA, RWH. Lindquist wanted to make his case against the Wheeler-Howard Act without being associated with the red-baiting that some of Collier's opponents indulged in. Lindquist first presented his "Fourteen Points" as an enclosure in a letter to J. Henry Scattergood, where he also discussed the press's misrepresentation of his views (February 27, 1934, reel 51, IRAP). The false quotation was repeated in numerous instances, most especially in Ray Kirkland, "Commissioner of Indian Affairs Urges Tribesmen to Accept Soviet Type Rule," *New York Herald Tribune*, April 8, 1934, sec. 2, p. 11, col. 1. Collier entered the *New York Herald Tribune* article into the record, along with his own response, in *Committee Hearings on H.R. 7902*, 180–85. It should be noted, though, that Lindquist did not distance himself from at least one of the "red-baiters" in the debate, Flora Warren Seymour. In an article for *New Outlook*, she called the Wheeler-Howard Act "the most extreme gesture yet made by the administration in this country toward a Communistic experiment." Seymour, "Trying It on the Indian," 22–25.

17. Enclosure, Lindquist to J. Henry Scattergood, February 27, 1934, reel 51, IRAP. Lindquist expanded on this point in his oft-delivered speech, "Turning the Clock Back on Poor Lo," saying:

For almost fifty years [the Indians] have been taught the value of property rights while

the sacredness of land titles has been held up to them as basic in law and ordered government. To be suddenly asked to convey title to their individual allotments back to the tribe
and take in return a life interest in the tribal estate seems just a bit shadowy and inse-
cure to them. The more progressive folk, who have held on to their allotments through
thick and thin, very naturally raise this question: "Are we to be penalized for our thrift
while those who have sold or mortgaged their allotments for a song or a drink of hard
liquor are to become 'corporation trustees' and govern us, when they have shown no
capacity to govern themselves?"

Copy of the speech filed under May 8, 1939, reel 56, IRAP. For another missionary's defense of
allotment policy, see Presbyterian missionary to the Nez Perce of Idaho, Mary M. Crawford, to
Julia [illegible], December 26, 1933, and Crawford to John Collier, February 3, 1934, OFC.

18. Enclosure, Lindquist to J. Henry Scattergood, February 27, 1934, reel 51, IRAP.
Lindquist failed to mention whether he supported the provisions in Title II making it easier for
Indians to gain civil service appointments in the BIA. As a member of the Board of Indian
Commissioners, Lindquist had favored preferential hiring practices for the Indians while the
Rhoads administration opposed them. On principle, then, one would expect Lindquist to have
supported Collier's proposal for Indian applicants.

19. *Committee Hearings on H.R. 7902,* 173–75. It should be noted that Collier's administration did not endorse the views of the Rollette County Commissioners. See Harold Ickes to
John A. Stormon (Chairman of the Board of County Commissioners), May 5, 1934, Box 7, Part
6-C, RWH.

20. *Congressional Record,* 73rd Congress, 2nd Session, June 15, 1934, p. 11742. The
Congressional Record also documents support for the Wheeler-Howard bill from William Hughes
of the Catholic Bureau of Indian Missions and Levi M. Rouillard, missionary supervisor of the
Episcopal Church for South Dakota (ibid.; and William Hughes, "Indians on a New Trail,"
reprint from *Catholic World,* July 1934, in Box 27, Wheeler-Howard Bill Circulars, Records of
the Senate Subcommittee on Indian Affairs, RG 46, NA). See also the statement by Methodist
leader Mark Dawber in *Composite Annual Administrative and Activity Report* (1934), Methodist
Episcopal Church Board of Missions and Church Extension, 42, copy in Ryan Office File, Box
1, NA 75. For sporadic support for the bill by Christian Indian leaders, typically on the grounds
of tribal economic development, see Duane F. Porter (Chippewa) to John Collier, April 28,
1934, Box 5, Part 5-A; Thomas J. Rouillard (Sioux) to John Collier, May 3, 1934, Box 5, Part 5-
A; F. P. Frazier (Sioux) to John Collier, May 23, 1934, Box 6, Part 6-A; Rev. Philip Gordon
(Chippewa) to John Collier, May 8, 1934, Box 8, Part 7; Rev. Matthew Simpson to John Collier,
April 9, 1934, Box 7, Part 6-A, RWH. Other non-Native religious figures who supported the bill
included the Right Rev. James Freeman (Bishop of the National Cathedral in Washington), C.
L. Rowe (the Secretary of the YMCA), the Catholic Daughters of America, and the members of
the Friends Social Service Committee (see "Comment on the Wheeler-Howard Bill by Reli-
gious Leaders and Missionaries of Various Denominations" [n.d.] Box 8, Part 7; C. L. Rowe to
John Collier, May 7, 1934, Box 3, Part 2-B, RWH).

21. "Letter Regarding Home Missions Council Meeting," May 1, 1934, Box 19, Folder
417, LP. See also Minutes, Joint Indian Committee, April 20, 1934, Box 7, Folder 12, NCCA 26.

22. Marginalia, "Letter Regarding Home Missions Council Meeting," May 1, 1934, Box

19, Folder 417, LP. See also Minutes, Joint Indian Committee, April 20, 1934, Box 7, Folder 12, NCCA 26. Michael C. Coleman argues that missionaries and their board administrators also differed in their response to the rapid methods of assimilation enjoined in the Dawes Act of 1887. At that time, field-workers feared that allotment in severalty would scatter existing tribal communities and make evangelism more difficult. Also, they expressed doubts that their eastern superiors truly understood Indian problems and worried that reforms wrongly assumed solutions would be quick and easy. In the 1930s, in the context of Collier's assault on assimilation, positions were reversed. Field-workers took a more hard-line approach toward assimilation while mission board administrators called for more caution against disrupting integrated Indian societies. Coleman, "Problematic Panacea," 143–59.

23. Copy of letter entered in the Indian Rights Association Papers, reel 52, under date April 30, 1934, and in *Congressional Record*, 73rd Congress, 2nd Session, June 15, 1934, p. 11738.

24. One exception to this pattern was Arthur C. Parker, the Seneca anthropologist and director of the Rochester (N.Y.) Museum of Arts and Sciences. Parker had been one of Lindquist's coauthors in *Red Man in the United States* (1923), and as moderator of the Council of One Hundred in 1923, he guided its pronouncements toward the assimilation gradualism that Lindquist and he shared. Parker criticized Collier's policies as segregationist and likely to promote further government paternalism. See his quoted remarks in Lindquist's "Fourteen Points," enclosure, Lindquist to J. Henry Scattergood, February 27, 1934, reel 51, IRAP.

25. Lindquist to Edith M. Dabb, March [n.d.] 1934, reel 52, IRAP.

26. In a recent biography of Bronson, Gretchen G. Harvey apparently could find no indication of how she interpreted the Wheeler-Howard Act in 1934. Harvey, "Cherokee and American." It appears that Bronson's sympathies with Protestant assimilationists like Lindquist were still strong in the midthirties, although that would change by the midforties. Flora Warren Seymour reported on a meeting in which Bronson and two other Indian employees in the BIA "opposed essential features of the [Wheeler-Howard] bill without mentioning it by name. . . . Yet it would take a very captious person to say that they were propagandizing against the new policy. Still the effect was there. They themselves are good arguments against segregation, so far as that goes." Seymour to Matthew Sniffen, May 28, 1934, reel 52, IRAP.

27. "Supt. Roe Cloud's Address to the Sioux," *Indian Leader* (Haskell Institute, Lawrence, Kansas) 37, no. 35 (May 4, 1934):1–5; copy Box 19, Folder 426, LP.

28. Roe Cloud, "Indian Opinion of the Wheeler-Howard Bill"; Roe Cloud, "Indian Reactions to the Indian Reorganization Act"; Roe Cloud, "Conditions Among the Indians."

29. Not all of Lindquist's associates responded to Roe Cloud's activities with such resentment. Kate Leah Cotharine, secretary of the assimilationist Massachusetts Indian Association, called Roe Cloud's stand "disappointing," but, she noted, as a BIA employee "he would be influenced financially" if he took any other position. Cotharine to Matthew Sniffen, April 13, 1934, reel 52, IRAP. See also Flora Warren Seymour to Edith M. Dabb, March 16, 1934 [enclosure in Matthew Sniffen to J. Henry Scattergood, March 20, 1934], reel 51, and Seymour to Sniffen, December 3, 1935, reel 53, IRAP. For a good biographical essay on Roe Cloud, see Crum, "Henry Roe Cloud, a Winnebago Indian Reformer," especially 179–82 on Roe Cloud's activities in support of the Wheeler-Howard Act.

30. For Flora Warren Seymour's published attacks on the Wheeler-Howard Act, see "An

Open Letter to the President of the United States," April 23, 1934, reel 52, IRAP; and Seymour, "Trying It on the Indian." For an official response, see "Excerpt from Address by Ward Shepard." For Elaine G. Eastman's views, see Eastman, "Collier Indian Plan Held Backward Step" [letter to the editor], *New York Times,* June 3, 1934, sec. 4, p. 5, col. 7; response by Collier, "Our Indian Policy Has Definite Aims" [letter to the editor], June 10, 1934, sec. 4, p. 5, col. 7; and Eastman's unpublished counterresponse, Letter to the Editor, June 13, 1934 [mistakenly dated as June 13, 1933, and filed under that date], reel 50, IRAP.

31. This description of Lindquist's activities is based upon correspondence in the Indian Rights Association Papers between February and April 1934 and upon copies of various missionary statements that appear in Lindquist, "The Government's New Indian Policy," 184; *Congressional Record,* 73rd Congress, 2nd Session, June 15, 1934, p. 11733; untitled text of resolutions by missionaries at Fort Defiance, Arizona, March 13, 1934, Box 29, Folder 446, LP; "From Rapid City," *Indian Truth* 11, no. 3 (March 1934):4; and excerpt from *Rapid City Journal,* March 5, 1934, in Ryan Office File, Box 1, NA 75. On the claim that Lindquist followed Collier step by step, it is noteworthy that Lindquist made a point to attend those congresses that Collier attended, while merely working with other missionaries by correspondence to organize opposition at those congresses Collier did not attend. See Lindquist to Edith M. Dabb, March [n.d.] 1934, reel 52, IRAP, where Lindquist noted that he would not attend the congresses at Phoenix, Arizona; Chemawa, Oregon; and Riverside, California–the three congresses that Collier missed. Collier complained in House hearings that the same propaganda against the bill kept surfacing at each congress, perhaps referring to Lindquist's "Fourteen Points" or other material based on it. *Committee Hearings on H.R. 7902,* 180–89. On the Congresses, see Prucha, *Great Father,* 2:959–60; Philp, *John Collier's Crusade,* 145–54; and Deloria and Lytle, *Nations Within,* 101–21.

32. Lindquist to J. Henry Scattergood, February 27, 1934, reel 51, IRAP; Minutes, Plains Indian Congress, March 5, 1934, Box 4, Part 2-AA, RWH.

33. "Collier Assails Critics; Says Lindquist Conclusions Untrue," *Muskogee Times–Democratic* (Oklahoma), March 23, 1934, clipping in Box 27, Wheeler-Howard Bill Newspaper Clippings, Records of the Senate Subcommittee on Indian Affairs, RG 46, NA; see also "Selfish Groups Block Indian Aid, Collier Claims; Commissioner Says Missionaries Also Fighting Measures," *Washington Daily News,* April 20, 1934, clipping in Box 27, Wheeler-Howard Bill Newspaper Clippings, Records of the Senate Subcommittee on Indian Affairs, RG 46, NA; James H. McGregor to John Collier, May 4, 1934, Box 3, Part 2-B, RWH.

34. "Missionaries Among Navajos and Hopis Flay Collier Bill," *Albuquerque Tribune,* March 26, 1934, clipping in Box 9, Part 9; "Missionaries Rap New Indian Bill," *Oklahoma City Times,* March 26, 1934, clipping in Box 5, Part 5-A; M. P. Smith to John Collier, March 17, 1934, Box 5, Part 5-A; G. W. Emigh to John Collier, April 5, 1934, Box 7, Part 6-B, RWH.

35. See the Christian Reformed Church petition read (in part) into the *Congressional Record,* 73rd Congress, 2nd Session, June 15, 1934, p. 11732; "Pastor Flays Paganism of Indian Policy," *Daily Oklahoman* (Oklahoma City, Oklahoma), October 19, 1934, clipping in Box 18, Religious Freedom, OFC; John H. Zylstra to Collier, June 27, 1934, with enclosed resolution, Records of the Senate Subcommittee on Indian Affairs, Box 27, Wheeler-Howard Bill–Petitions Against, RG 46, NA; James H. McGregor to John Collier, April 4, 1934, Box 4, Part 2-B, RWH.

Notes to pages 94–96 **177**

36. Matthew Sniffen to Edith M. Dabb, April 4, 1934, reel 97, IRAP; see also Dabb to Sniffen, May 24, 1934, reel 52, IRAP, and James H. McGregor to John Collier, April 4, 1934, Box 4, Part 2-B, RWH. On at least one or two reservations—most notably at Jemez Pueblo—some tribe members were arguing that Christian missions had been freeloading on tribal lands, and that churches should at least pay rent to tribal funds for the right to occupy their missions. So the BIA's land grants to Christian missionary organizations were indeed becoming an area of conflict in some locales. See especially CCF 25321-31-816.2 General Services, and CCF 26346-23-816.2 Southern Pueblo, NA 75.

37. Samuel Brosius to Matthew Sniffen, February 24, 1934, reel 51, IRAP.

38. L. C. Lippert to Commissioner, June 19, 1934, Box 3, Part 2-B, RWH.

39. Philp, ed., *Indian Self-Rule*, 18–19, 58–60; see also *Committee Hearings on H.R. 7902*, which is interspersed with petitions from Indians and tribal groups against the bill, especially 234–37, 388–96, and 489–90; Memorial to the House of Representatives, National Indian Confederacy, March 1, 1934, Box 27, Wheeler-Howard Bill Newspaper Clippings, Records of the Senate Subcommittee on Indian Affairs, RG 46, NA; and the minutes of the various Indian Congresses in Boxes 1 and 2, Parts 1-A and 2-A, RWH.

40. Johnny Wright et al. to the Commissioner of Indian Affairs, March 20, 1934, Box 5, Part 4-B, RWH.

41. Telegram, Keetoowha Society (Cherokee) to John Collier, April 5, 1934, Box 5, Part 4-B, RWH. For a few other samples of Indian opposition based on fears about treaty rights, see the transcripts of the Indian congresses in Boxes 1 and 2, Parts 1-A and 2-A, RWH; J. C. Morgan, letter to the editor, *Farmington Times Hustler* (New Mexico), January 26, 1934, clipping filed under February 5, 1934, reel 51, IRAP; extracts from an article by Clayton Kirk in *Klamath News* (Oregon), March 27, 1934, in reel 52, IRAP; Chester Armstrong to Lawrence E. Lindley, April 17, 1934, reel 52, IRAP.

42. Parman, *Navajos and the New Deal*, 55, 172. See also J. C. Morgan's Letter to the Editor, "A Navajo Dissenter," *Christian Century* 51 (October 31, 1934):1379–80; Collier, Letter to the Editor, *Christian Century* 51 (November 14, 1934):1459.

43. Lindquist to Edith M. Dabb, March [n.d.] 1934, reel 52, IRAP. See also Minutes, Fort Defiance Congress, March 12–13, 1934, Box 2, Part 1-B, RWH; J. C. Morgan, "Navajo Tribal Council Postpones Action on Self-Government Bill, *Farmington Times Hustler* (New Mexico), March 23, 1934, p. 1, clipping in Box 9, Part 9, RWH.

44. Telegram, Collier to Stella Atwood, April 30, 1934, reel 19, CP.

45. For Burnett's claim to be of Indian descent (one-eighth), see Burnett to Elaine G. Eastman, June 18, 1934, Box 18, Folder 399, LP; Burnett to Mrs. Richard Codman, February 6, 1936, Box 1, American Indian Federation, OFC.

46. Floyd O. Burnett, Letter to the Editor, *Press and Enterprise* (Riverside, California), April 30, 1934, in CCF 21110-34-816.2 General Services, NA 75.

47. Donald H. Biery to John Collier, May 1, 1934, CCF 21110-34-816.2 General Services, NA 75. For a newspaper report of Lindquist's church lobbying efforts in Riverside, see "Wheeler-Howard Bill Opposed by Speaker," clipping in Box 9, Part 9, Wheeler-Howard Records, NA 75.

48. Biery to Collier, May 1, 1934, and May 2, 1934, CCF 21110-34-816.2 General Services, NA 75. The correspondence between Lindquist and Burnett has been lost, but Lindquist's prominent role in prompting Burnett's activities can be inferred from Lindquist to Edith M.

Dabb, March [n.d.], 1934, reel 52, IRAP; and the letters of Superintendent Biery to John Collier in CCF 21110-34-816.2 General Services, NA 75. Also, in a curious twist, the initial rumors of Burnett's activities stemmed from F. David Blackhoop, Music Director at Sherman Institute, who was transferred to Sherman in 1931 from Phoenix Indian School after Lindquist, acting for the Board of Indian Commissioners, accused him of sexual improprieties. Blackhoop obviously had an axe to grind against Lindquist, and he used Burnett to get back at him. See Blackhoop to George P. Clement, May 2, 1934, CCF 21110-34-816.2 General Services, NA 75; Gessner, *Massacre*, 126–27; and Trennert, "Corporal Punishment."

49. Biery to Collier, May 1, 1934, CCF 21110-34-816.2 General Services, NA 75.

50. Biery to Collier, May 2, 1934, CCF 21110-34-816.2 General Services, NA 75.

51. The telegraph was quoted in an attachment to Burnett to Collier, May 10, 1934, CCF 21110-34-816.2 General Services, NA 75.

52. Collier to William R. King, May 7, 1934, CCF 21110-34-816.2 General Services, NA 75.

53. Burnett to Collier, May 10, 1934, CCF 21110-34-816.2 General Services, NA 75.

54. Biery to Collier, May 12, 1934, CCF 21110-34-816.2 General Services, NA 75.

55. William R. King to Matthew Sniffen, May 28, 1934, reel 52, IRAP (quotation); and Anne Seesholtz to John Collier, May 23, 1934, CCF 21110-34-816.2 General Services, NA 75.

56. Elaine G. Eastman to Paul Hutchinson, May 26, 1934, Box 18, Folder 399, LP; and Hutchinson to Harold Ickes, May 31, 1934, CCF 21110-34-816.2 General Services, NA 75.

57. Paul Hutchinson to Harold Ickes, May 31, 1934, and Ickes to Hutchinson, June 14, 1934, CCF 21110-34-816.2 General Services, NA 75.

58. Flora Warren Seymour to W. R. King, June 21, 1934, Box 18, Folder 399, LP.

59. Philp, *John Collier's Crusade*, 158–59.

60. Prucha, *Great Father*, 2:963. The Wheeler-Howard Act, in slightly abridged form, appears in Prucha, ed., *Documents of U. S. Indian Policy*, 222–25. For a detailed comparison of the original bill with the bill in its approved form, see Deloria and Lytle, *Nations Within*, 140–53, 266–70.

61. *Congressional Record*, 73rd Congress, 2nd Session, June 15, 1934, p. 11732. For a full account of the revisions made to the Wheeler-Howard Act, see Rusco, *Fateful Time*, 220–81.

62. Sniffen and Lindquist differed, though, in precisely which provisions they opposed. Lindquist opposed the provision that ended the practice of allotment, although he had no problem with the moratorium on allotments that had been in existence since the Meriam report. Sniffen disliked the provision that exempted Indians from civil service requirements–a position that Lindquist had lobbied for as a member of the Board of Indian Commissioners. Matthew K. Sniffen, "Wheeler-Howard Bill Abandoned," May 18, 1934, reel 52, IRAP; Lindquist to Matthew Sniffen, May 30, 1934, reel 52, IRAP; see also Jonathan Steere, "Commissioner Collier's Wheeler-Howard Bill [1934, June?], reel 52, IRAP; Sniffen to Elaine G. Eastman, November 27, 1934, reel 95, IRAP.

63. Flora Warren Seymour to Matthew K. Sniffen, May 23, 1934, reel 52, IRAP.

64. Compare the views of Rudolf Hertz, Congregational missionary to the Santee Sioux in Nebraska, who supported the final version of the Wheeler-Howard bill while simultaneously declaring himself "opposed to anything that even suggests segregation, whatever the grounds for it may be." His position illustrates the assimilationist tendencies that could be seen within the final draft of the act. Rudolf Hertz to Lawrence Lindley, December 11, 1935, reel 53, IRAP.

5 Struggle to Redeem the BIA, 1935–1942

1. G. E. E. Lindquist, Brief Summary of Activities, May 1, 1935, Box 14, Folder 300, LP.

2. This composite portrait of religious education directors' activities is based on monthly reports to Lindquist made by religious work directors under Home Missions Council supervision (Boxes 4 and 5, LP).

3. Monthly Report, A. Willard Jones to G. E. E. Lindquist, November 1941, Box 4, Folder 65, LP.

4. Philip M. Riley to G. E. E. Lindquist, June 16, 1942, Box 5, Folder 84, LP; Minutes, Joint Indian Committee, May 18, 1942, Box 1, Folder 11, LP; A. Willard Jones to Mark Dawber, September 19, 1942, Box 4, Folder 65, LP; Minutes, Executive Committee of the Joint Indian Committee, October 15, 1937, Box 7, Folder 12, NCCA 26.

5. Margery Hibbard, Report for November and December 1943, Box 4, Folder 69, LP.

6. Myrthus W. Evans to Willard Beatty, November 30, 1944, CCF (1940–1956) 45286-44-816 General Services, NA 75.

7. A. Willard Jones to G. E. E. Lindquist, Monthly Report, May 1942, Box 4, Folder 65, LP.

8. Mazie Crawford to Matthew Sniffen, May 13, 1935, reel 53, IRAP.

9. Matthew Sniffen to Anne Seesholtz, December 14, 1934, reel 95; Seesholtz to Sniffen, December 19, 1934, reel 52; and Sniffen to Seesholtz, December 20, 1934, reel 95, IRAP.

10. Lindquist, *Red Man,* 428–29.

11. John Collier to Richard L. Neuberger, August 10, 1937, Box 1, American Indian Federation, OFC; and for reports from BIA agents who attended AIF meetings incognito, see Floyd W. LaRouche, "American Indian Federation Holds an Annual Convention [1936]," and Memorandum, Ben Dwight to A. C. Monahan, August 8, 1938, Box 1, American Indian Federation, OFC. On Collier's predatory use of the FBI against his Indian opponents, see Hauptman, "American Indian Federation"; and Hauptman, *Iroquois and the New Deal.*

12. Flora Warren Seymour reported that Lindquist had "spoken of most of the Bruner followers as men he knew," with the exception of several figures from southern California. Seymour to Matthew Sniffen, October 3, 1934, reel 52, IRAP. Lindquist's correspondence with AIF leaders has apparently been lost.

13. *The American Indian,* published between 1926 and 1931 by Lee F. Harkins (Choctaw-Chickasaw), was a general interest magazine for Indian readers in Oklahoma. Its articles frequently mourned the impending loss of Indian cultures while also supporting assimilation policies toward Indian lands and tribal funds. Many of its articles featured wealthy Oklahoma Indians as models of racial achievement.

14. Here, too, correspondence has apparently been lost. But see A. L. Tandy Jemison to Lindquist, c. May 1953, in folder, "Over Forty Years of Self-Less Service to Indian Americans–From His Friends," BP; and Lindquist to Thomas Moffett, September 14, 1937, reel 55, IRAP.

15. Joseph Bruner, O. K. Chandler, and Alice Lee Jemison to Members of Congress, April 27, 1936, Records of Assistants to the Commissioner, Office File of Fred H. Daiker, 1929–1943, Box 1, AIF, NA 75.

16. Circular Letter, Alice Lee Jemison, March 23, 1938, Box 1, AIF, OFC; Mark Dawber to Matthew Sniffen, March 8, 1938, reel 55, IRAP.

17. Telegram to chairman of Indian Subcommittee of House of Representatives, enclosure with Lindquist to Matthew Sniffen, March 26, 1935, reel 53, IRAP; Mazie Crawford to Matthew Sniffen, May 13, 1935, reel 53, IRAP. See also a statement by the United Session of Nez Perce Indians that used the AIF's evidence for Collier's atheism to back up its sharp criticism of Henry Roe Cloud, a fellow Presbyterian minister who served under Collier and defended his policies. "To the Presbytery of Northern Idaho," May 19, 1935, Box 1, AIF, OFC; "Christian Indians Think Missions," *Missionary Review of the World* 58 (December 1935):567; Lewis, *Creating Christian Indians*, 157–58.

18. Joseph Bruner to Harold Ickes, October 16, 1936, Box 1, AIF, OFC.

19. Lindquist's weak ties to the AIF might have been the basis for Collier's charge that Lindquist belonged to the "Mussolini Silver Shirts" and was actively "stirring up the Indians in favor of Fascism" (Lindquist to Mark Dawber, May 2, 1945, Box 15, Folder 351, LP). Neither Lindquist nor his close associates with the Indian Rights Association or the Home Missions Council endorsed the AIF's tactics or its ties with fascism. Upon hearing of Bruner's mixture of Americanism with segregationist and anti-Semitic attitudes, Matthew Sniffen quoted Samuel Johnson's famous saying, "Patriotism is the last refuge of a scoundrel." Sniffen to Lawrence Lindley, October 31, 1936, reel 54, IRAP. Even those who shared the AIF's militancy against Collier, such as Flora Warren Seymour and Elaine G. Eastman, criticized the AIF for slandering Collier rather than debating the larger principles involved. Seymour to Matthew Sniffen, September 21, 1934, reel 52; Sniffen to Elaine G. Eastman, October 2, 1934, reel 52; Eastman to Sniffen, March 23, 1935, reel 53; Sniffen to Eastman, December 20, 1935, reel 95; Arthur C. Parker to Sniffen, November 9, 1936, reel 54; Seymour to Sniffen, January 12, 1939, reel 56, IRAP. Lindquist's best-documented connection to the group, his friendship with Floyd Burnett, apparently placed him close to one of the moderating influences within the AIF. According to one of Collier's informants, Burnett told delegates to the 1936 AIF convention that rather than simply fight Collier, they should present their grievances to him and "depend upon his broadmindedness" to receive a "fair" hearing. Floyd W. LaRouche, "Extracts from a Report of the American Indian Federation's Annual Convention of 1936, at Salt Lake City," Box 1, AIF, OFC.

20. The AIF has been the subject of considerable debate among historians. Most scholars have accepted Collier's own view that the AIF should be discredited as a result of its association with the Silver Shirts and the German-American Bund. See for example Philp, *Collier's Crusade*, 170–73, 202–4. But Laurence M. Hauptman has argued that only a handful of AIF members established the link with fascist groups. For him, the AIF should be interpreted primarily as part of a long line of radical anti-BIA Indian sentiment running from Carlos Montezuma in the early twentieth century to Indian activists of the 1960s and 1970s. He views the AIF as a grassroots, indigenous organization, and not simply as a product of Christian fundamentalism and right-wing hyperpatriotism. Hauptman, "American Indian Federation." I have adopted a middle position, recognizing that the AIF should be regarded as a deeply rooted indigenous organization, while also showing that its association with right-wing extremism had a direct impact on its value as a lobbying tool for Lindquist and most Euro-American missionaries.

21. Minutes, Subcommittee of the National Fellowship of Indian Workers, Joint Indian Committee, May 15, 1942, Box 1, Folder 11, LP.

22. Brief Summary of Activities from April 30, 1935, to May 1, 1936, Box 14, Folder 300, LP.

23. NFIW, Report of Committee on Continuation, July 11, 1935, Box 18, Religious Freedom, OFC.

24. NFIW *News Letter,* "Supplementary Report of Committee, Madison Conference, 1935," No. 2 (Spring 1936), 2, RG 26, Box 7, Folder 23, NCCA 26 (quotation); Findings of the Oklahoma Regional Conference, 1938, Box 9, Folder 153, LP; Report of Findings Committee, Pacific Northwest Regional Conference, 1940, Box 9, Folder 155, LP; Findings of the National Conference, Farmington, New Mexico, 1941, Box 9, Folder 154, LP.

25. Findings Committee of the Indian Missionary Section, Fifteenth Annual Wisconsin Rural Leadership Summer School and National Fellowship of Workers, July 9, 1936, enclosure with Mark Dawber to Fellow-workers, September 22, 1936, reel 54, IRAP.

26. Findings Committee of the Indian Missionary Section, Fourteenth Annual Wisconsin Rural Leadership Summer School, University of Wisconsin–Madison, July 1–12, 1935, Box 18, Religious Freedom, OFC; NFIW *News Letter,* "Supplementary Report of Committee, Madison Conference, 1935," no. 2 (Spring 1936), 2, Box 7, Folder 23, NCCA 26. Within a single letter sent to "Pastors and Fellow-workers," Burnett made appeals for both the AIF and the NFIW, indicating his view that the two organizations appealed to the same constituency. Burnett to Pastors and Fellow-workers, May 19, 1936, Box 1, AIF, OFC.

27. Proceedings, Madison Conference, 1935, Box 9, Folder 146, LP.

28. See for example Findings Committee of the Indian Missionary Section, Fourteenth Annual Wisconsin Rural Leadership Summer School, University of Wisconsin–Madison, July 1–12, 1935, Box 18, Religious Freedom, OFC; Findings Committee of the Indian Missionary Section, Fifteenth Annual Wisconsin Rural Leadership Summer School and National Fellowship of Workers, July 9, 1936, enclosure with Mark Dawber to Fellow-workers, September 22, 1936, reel 54, IRAP; Findings of Madison Conference, June 1938, Box 9, Folder 149, LP; Lindquist to Lawrence E. Lindley, September 20, 1940, reel 56, IRAP.

29. Minutes, Joint Committee on Indian Work, May 18, 1936, Box 7, Folder 12, NCCA 26.

30. The Joint Indian Committee's relationship with the NFIW apparently underwent several stages before the committee finally gave its full backing. See Minutes, Joint Committee on Indian Work, October 29, 1935, May 18, 1936, and January 12, 1937, Box 7, Folder 12, NCCA 26; Minutes, Joint Indian Committee, October 21, 1940, Box 1, Folder 10, LP.

31. NFIW *News Letter,* no. 5 (April 1937), Box 7, Folder 23, NCCA 26.

32. Over the years, the NFIW attracted prominent BIA officials and congressional leaders to speak at its national and regional conferences. Collier encouraged BIA employees to attend the meetings—in part to keep tabs on the NFIW, but also, it seems, to keep open the missionary-government dialogue that the NFIW sought. See Lindquist to Matthew Sniffen, May 17, 1938, reel 56, IRAP; Mark Dawber to Collier, April 4, 1939, and E. R. Fryer to Collier, June 26, 1939, Box 12, Navajo, OFC; and Collier to A. C. Monahan, May 21, 1940, Haskell Series, Decimal Correspondence, 816.2, Conferences 1940, NACP.

33. Minutes, Subcommittee of the NFIW, Joint Indian Committee, May 15, 1942, Box 1, Folder 11, LP. This development reflected changes throughout the world of Christian missions. In 1938, at the World Missionary Conference at Tambaram, Ceylon, delegates from Africa, Asia, and other missionary areas outnumbered the delegates from Western nations. *World Mission,* 5–6.

34. NFIW *News Letter,* no. 9 (June 1939), copy in Box 7, Folder 23, NCCA 26; Crum, "Henry Roe Cloud," 174.

35. John Webster Grant argues regarding Canadian missions that Christianity has become a thoroughly "Indian" phenomenon, having been a part of Native life now for more than four hundred years. Grant, *Moon of Wintertime,* 264–65.

36. Collier, "Indian Legislation," 4–7.

37. Schwartz, "Red Atlantis Revisited."

38. Biolsi, "Indian Self-government," 23–28.

39. Barsh, "Progressive Era Bureaucrats."

40. Lindquist, "Is the New Deal Turning the Clock Back for Poor Lo?" Address to the Six Nations Association, Rochester, New York, November 16, 1935, Box 10, Folder 206, LP.

41. The original version of the bill appeared in U.S. House Committee on Indian Affairs, *Readjustment of Indian Affairs,* 1–14. On the possibility that the Indian Office might use the bill for manipulative purposes, see Lindquist to Matthew Sniffen, June 13, 1934, reel 52, IRAP. On Indian fears that Collier would only increase bureaucratic domination, see numerous letters and statements in the Records of the Indian Organization Division, RWH; and Boxes 27–29, Record Group 46, Records of the United States Senate, Records of the Committee on Interior and Insular Affairs, Subcommittee on Indian Affairs, Sen. 83A-F9 (70th–82nd), National Archives, Washington, D.C. (hereafter cited as Records of the Senate Subcommittee on Indian Affairs, RG 46, NA). One particularly poignant correspondent was Charlie Victor, who expressed favor for the self-rule features of the Wheeler-Howard Act, but mildly suggested that, for the sake of consistency, tribal government "not be subject to approval of any Federal Agency." Box 5, Part 5-A, RWH.

42. Deloria and Lytle, *Nations Within,* 151. Internal BIA documents reveal that Collier was not completely committed to the voting provision of the Wheeler-Howard Act. A confidential memo dated May 3, 1934, lists nine features of the bill that could be "scrapped" if necessary to allow it to pass, and one of those was the line on Indian referenda. Box 10, Part 11-C, Section 2, RWH.

43. "Futile Voting," 1–3; Lindquist to Sniffen, February 26, 1935, reel 52, IRAP.

44. By the end of 1936, 181 tribes with an aggregate population of 129,750 had voted to accept provisions for tribal organization and self-government, while 77 tribes totaling 86,365 Indians rejected the bill. Prucha, *Great Father,* 2:964–65.

45. Graham Taylor has argued that the Wheeler-Howard Act mistakenly presumed that the tribe, a linguistic-cultural entity, also served as the basic political unit in Indian life. But in fact, many tribes were organized into subtribal units, such as villages. When those tribes attempted to institute tribal self-government, their apparent cultural unity did not translate into political unity. Taylor, *New Deal.*

46. Philp, *Collier's Crusade,* 186. Paul C. Rosier argues that the scholarship on the Indian Reorganization Act has been overly critical, citing the Blackfeet tribe of Montana as a case where Native Americans used the bill to develop substantial control over tribal resources. Rosier, "'The Old System Is No Success.'" His argument provides a valuable corrective, but even his own work reveals Collier's tendency to make unilateral administrative decisions, in spite of earlier promises to the contrary. Rosier, *Rebirth of the Blackfeet Nation,* 105–10.

47. Bailey and Bailey, *History of the Navajos,* 181–84; Iverson, *Navajo Nation,* 3–26.

48. C. C. Brooks to Matthew Sniffen, November 12, 1934, reel 51, IRAP. Parman, *Navajos and the New Deal,* 42–63; Philp, *Collier's Crusade,* 187–93; McPherson, "Navajo Livestock Reduction."

49. Parman, *Navajos and the New Deal,* 69–70.

50. Morgan, "A Navajo Dissenter," 1379–80; John Collier, letter to the editor, *Christian Century* 51 (November 14, 1934):1459.

51. Parman, *Navajos and the New Deal,* 61.

52. Parman, *Navajos and the New Deal,* 66–76. See the comments of Howard Gorman, a Navajo Presbyterian leader, in Meeting of Commissioner Collier with the Navajos at Fort Defiance, June 11, 1935, reel 53, IRAP; Collier to P. B. Duffy, July 18, 1935, Box 1, AIF, OFC.

53. Iverson, *Navajo Nation,* 34; Parman, *Navajos and the New Deal,* 72–77.

54. The text of Collier's address to the tribe was in Collier to C. E. Faris, June 21, 1935, reel 53, IRAP. Over the next several years, it turned out, Collier was able to use administrative measures to acquire almost all the financial and organizational resources that the Wheeler-Howard Act would have provided, making the Navajos' vote less consequential. But the entire campaign, coupled with herd reduction and other initiatives, demonstrated just how difficult it was for Collier to abide by his credo of tribal self-determination. Parman, *Navajos and the New Deal,* 76–80.

55. "Missionary Lands on Navajo," c. August 1935, Box 12, Commissioner Collier's Navajo Documents, OFC; Memo, Beeckmann to John Collier, July 29, 1937, Box 10, "Morgan, Palmer, et al., Activities," OFC. In 1938, CRC opposition to Morgan's political activities, along with other personal animosities between Morgan and his church employers, cost Morgan his position. E. R. Fryer to Collier, October 13, 1937, and Fryer to Collier, December 16, 1937, Box 10, "Morgan, Palmer, et al., Activities," OFC; Morgan to Matthew Sniffen, January 21, 1938, reel 55, IRAP; Parman, *Navajos and the New Deal,* 233.

56. Bailey and Bailey, *History of the Navajos,* 185–93; Aberle, *Peyote Religion among the Navajo,* 2d ed., 52–73.

57. Parman, *Navajos and the New Deal,* 122.

58. Morgan to Matthew Sniffen, May 5, 1937, reel 55, IRAP.

59. Oliver LaFarge, Preliminary Report on the Navajo Situation, August 11, 1937, Box 10, "Morgan, Palmer, et al., Activities," OFC.

60. Morgan to Matthew Sniffen, December 9 and December 19, 1936, reel 54; Morgan to Hon. Dennis Chavez, April 2, 1937, enclosure in Morgan to Matthew Sniffen, April 9, 1937, reel 55, IRAP.

61. Lindquist to Matthew Sniffen, April 7, 1938, reel 55, IRAP; "Navajo Debacle," 1–3.

62. Eastman to Sniffen, August 4, 1938; Lindquist to Sniffen, August 8, 1938; and Seymour to Sniffen, August 9, 1938, reel 56, IRAP.

63. Jonathan Steere to the President, August 27, 1938, reel 56, IRAP.

64. Quoted in Parman, *Navajos and the New Deal,* 236. In exchange for Morgan's support for new grazing regulations, Fryer and Collier allowed Morgan to institute several moral and religious reforms, such as outlawing peyote on the Navajo reservation and tightening up marriage and divorce laws. For a thorough account of Morgan's tenure as chairman of the tribal council, see Parman, 232–63. Moreover, Lindquist's close associate Flora Warren Seymour

continued to publicize Collier's failings with the Navajos in a widely read article, "Thunder Over the Southwest," in the *Saturday Evening Post.*

65. Parman, *Navajos and the New Deal,* 290.

66. Collier to Father Arnold, May 15, 1938, Box 12, Navajo General 1938, OFC.

67. Philp, *Collier's Crusade,* 28–30, 193–97; Ferris, "Sophie D. Aberle," 78–80.

68. See Collier's comments in *Indians at Work* 4, no. 7 (November 15, 1936):3, where he admitted that most of his understanding of Indian "potencies and profundities" was derived from Taos Pueblo.

69. Kelly, *Assault on Assimilation,* 295–348.

70. Ferris, "Sophie D. Aberle," 94–97; Philp, *Collier's Crusade,* 194–96.

71. Collier, *Indians at Work* 4, no. 7 (November 15, 1936):4. For the exchange of letters between Secretary Ickes and the Taos governor, see *Indians at Work* 4, no. 7 (November 15, 1936):9–13; and Box 13, Navajo-Pueblo Boundary Hearings, OFC.

72. Clearly, Collier was in a bind. Internal documents indicate that the solution finally settled upon—executive action by the Interior Department—was thought ultimately to be less threatening to Pueblo sovereignty than the other alternative, which was to allow a federal court to decide the issue. Collier believed a court would decide against Pueblo self-government and establish a far-reaching precedent that would undermine his larger goals. By keeping the matter within the executive branch, Collier believed the intrusion in Pueblo internal affairs could be regarded as an anomaly, with no consequences for the autonomy of the Pueblos in other matters or for the autonomy of all Indian tribes generally. Collier, Memorandum to Secretary Ickes, June 1, 1936, Box 16, Folder Peyote, OFC.

73. Seymour to Lindquist, November 4, 1936, reel 54, IRAP; Seymour to Matthew Sniffen, November 23, 1936 (quotation). For Lindquist's unsigned article, see "Religious Liberty," *Indian Truth* 13, no. 9 (December 1936):2–3.

74. Collier to Editor, *Indian Truth,* December 23, 1936, reel 54, IRAP.

75. Lindquist to Sniffen, January 2, 1937, reel 55, IRAP.

76. Sniffen to Lindquist, February 17, 1939, and Lindquist to Sniffen, "Report on Taos Situation: John D. Concha Case," March 20, 1939 (quotation), reel 55 IRAP.

77. Lindquist to Sniffen, "Report on Taos Situation: John D. Concha Case," March 20, 1939, reel 55, IRAP. According to Kathlene Ferris, Aberle, the superintendent of the United Pueblos Agency, saw problems in Pueblo government as well. Like Lindquist, she wanted to separate religious from civil authority, and she saw the Indian Reorganization Act as a means to accomplish that. Ferris, "Sophie D. Aberle," 80–81.

78. Lindquist to Sniffen, March 22, 1939, and Sniffen to Roger Baldwin, March 31 and April 8, 1939, reel 55, IRAP.

79. Collier to Lawrence E. Lindley, April 19, 1939, reel 55, IRAP, and Box 7, Indian Rights Association, OFC.

80. Lindquist to Sniffen, May 4, 1939, reel 56, IRAP. Portions of this letter were taken from Flora Warren Seymour to Lindquist, May 4, 1939, Box 15, Folder 345, LP.

81. Theodore H. Haas, Memorandum to Collier, December 23, 1941, CCF 1940–1956, 45286-44-816.2 General Services, NA 75.

82. Collier to Sophie Aberle, November 8, 1938, reel 11, CP. Aberle's husband, William Brophy, in fact, was Collier's choice to succeed him as commissioner in 1945.

83. "Pueblos Agency 'Meddles,' Is Charge of Sen. Chavez," *Albuquerque Tribune*, April 13, 1942, p. 1, col. 4; "Suspension of Aberle's Salary Urged in Petition," *Albuquerque Tribune*, April 18, 1942, p. 1, col. 4. For correspondence and other newspaper clippings on disputes at Isleta Pueblo, see Box 22, Navajo and Pueblo, 1941–1943, and Box 87, Isleta Pueblo Delegation, 1942, in Records of the Senate Subcommittee on Indian Affairs, RG 46, NA. For Santa Clara Pueblo agitation against Aberle, see Jose D. D. Narajo to Senator Elmer Thomas, July 4, 1942, reel 58, IRAP. For reform organizations' plans, see Margretta S. Dietrich to Lawrence E. Lindley, February 5, 1942, March 1, 1942, and July 11, 1942; and Lindley to Lindquist, May 26, 1942, reel 58, IRAP. See also Earle F. Dexter to Lindley [n.d., circa July 1942, but filed under 1945 n.d.]; Lindquist to Lindley, July 17, 1942, reel 58, IRAP. The Senate Indian Committee ultimately postponed a trip to New Mexico until 1943. See manuscript notes in Box 16, 1943 Investigation, Records of the Senate Subcommittee on Indian Affairs, RG 46, NA.

84. All of Whipple's reports to Lindquist have been lost (or perhaps expunged) from Lindquist's papers, but several have survived in the papers of the Indian Rights Association. See Whipple to Lindquist, February 28, 1942; confidential addendum, Whipple to Lindquist, April 15, 1942 [misfiled under February 28, 1942]; April 20, 1942; and Lindquist to Lawrence E. Lindley, June 9, 1942, reel 58, IRAP. See also Whipple to Mark Dawber, June 19, 1942; Whipple's statement to his lawyers [June 22, 1942], reel 58, IRAP.

85. Confidential addendum, Earl Whipple to Lindquist, April 15, 1942 [misfiled under February 28, 1942], reel 58, IRAP.

86. Whipple to Mark Dawber, June 19, 1942 (quotation); Whipple's statement to his attorneys [June 22, 1942], reel 58, IRAP; *Albuquerque Tribune*, June 24, 1942, 9, and June 25, 1942, 1.

87. Whipple to Mark Dawber, June 19, 1942; Whipple's statement to his attorneys [June 22, 1942], reel 58, IRAP.

88. Major Shannon had been the Agricultural Supervisor at Albuquerque Indian School until 1941. See Whipple to Mark Dawber, June 19, 1942, reel 58, IRAP. For Aberle's report of the preliminary hearing, see Aberle to Collier, July 3, 1942, Box 27, United Pueblos, OFC.

89. S[ophie Aberle] to John [Collier], n.d., Box 27, United Pueblos, OFC.

90. Collier to Mark Dawber, June 30, 1942; Collier to Aberle, July 6, 1942; and Collier to Aberle, July 7, 1942 (quotation), Box 27, United Pueblos, OFC.

91. Unfortunately, the archival records on this incident are somewhat incomplete, and there remains the possibility that Whipple's arrest had to do not only with intrigue against the BIA, but also with his and Lindquist's reported involvement in New Mexico state politics. At least, that is what Collier told Interior Secretary Ickes in a memorandum about the FBI files on Whipple. Collier claimed that Whipple's file contained no information about "any person employed by the Indian service," but that is impossible to reconcile with the extant records of Whipple's correspondence with Lindquist. Collier, memorandum to Secretary Ickes, September 19, 1942, reel 25, CP.

92. Collier to Mark Dawber, August 18, 1942; and Dawber to Collier, September 2, 1942, Box 27, United Pueblos, OFC; Earle Dexter to Lindquist, April 21, 1943, Box 15, Folder 349, LP; Minutes, Executive Committee of the Indian Work Committee, April 19, 1943, Box 7, Folder 13, NCCA 26.

93. Collier to Aberle, July 7, 1942, Box 27, United Pueblos, OFC.

94. Minutes, Executive Committee of Indian Committee, January 15, 1943, reel 58, IRAP.

6 Crusade against Wardship, 1942–1953

1. Prucha, *Great Father,* 2:1004; Hasse, "Termination and Assimilation," 41.

2. Bernstein, *American Indians and World War II,* 40, 67–71.

3. Burt, *Tribalism in Crisis,* 4–5; Prucha, *Great Father,* 2:1005–9; Bernstein, *American Indians and World War II,* 81–83; Hasse, "Termination and Assimilation," 65, 83.

4. Franco, "Publicity, Persuasion, and Propaganda." Carol Miller has argued that while the dominant narratives of World War II spoke of an "equitably plural, inclusive wartime and postwar society," the Indians' experiences were rather different, since assimilation, she notes, "was never an attainable American dream." Discrimination against Indians meant that the boom economy and wage earnings ended with the war, when non-Indian soldiers returned home and replaced the "temporary" Indian workers. Carol Miller, "Native Sons and the Good War: Retelling the Myth of American Indian Assimilation," in Erenberg and Hirsch, eds., *The War in American Culture,* 217–37 (quotation from 235).

5. Armstrong, "Set the American Indians Free!"

6. Holm, "Fighting a White Man's War," 77; Layton, "The International Context of the United States Civil Rights Movement"; Sitkoff, *New Deal for Blacks,* 84; Sbrega, "The Anticolonial Policies of Franklin D. Roosevelt," 65–84.

7. Matthew Sniffen, Secretary's Report for October 1937, reel 100, IRAP.

8. For a full discussion of this incident, see chapter 5.

9. Findings of the National Conference of the National Fellowship of Indian Workers, June 9–13, 1941, reel 58, IRAP.

10. William McGuire King, "The Reform Establishment and the Ambiguities of Influence," in Hutchison, ed., *Between the Times,* 124.

11. Minutes, Meeting on Indian Wardship, November 24, 1941, Box 1, Folder 11, LP. For secondary literature on this Protestant resurgence and growing attention to race relations, see David W. Wills, "An Enduring Distance: Black Americans and the Establishment," in Hutchison, ed., *Between the Times,* 168–92; William McGuire King, "The Reform Establishment and the Ambiguities of Influence," in Hutchison, ed., *Between the Times,* 124–27; Warren, *Theologians of a New World Order,* 99–108; and Marty, *Modern American Religion,* vol. 3, *Under God, Indivisible, 1941–1960,* 35–53, 65–75.

12. Recommendations, Seminar on the Program of the Government Indian Service, January 5–6, 1939, Minutes, Sub-Committee of Wardship Committee, April 8, 1941 (quotation), and Minutes, Committee on the Study of Wardship and Indian Participation in American Life, June 18, 1943, reel 58, IRAP.

13. Philp, *Termination Revisited,* 3–5.

14. The documentary basis for the discussion that follows is somewhat complex. On the one hand, the papers of the Joint Indian Committee contain partial records for its own Sub-committee on Indian Wardship, which existed from 1941 until 1944. On the other hand, the best records for the more broadly based Committee on Wardship and Indian Participation in American Life, which was created at the initiative of the Home Missions Council but independent

from its control, can be found in the papers of the Indian Rights Association, primarily in reels 57 and 58. Particularly helpful is the lengthy summary of the history of the committee incorporated in the minutes of the June 18, 1943 meeting, reel 58, IRAP. This larger committee existed from 1942 to 1943.

15. Minutes, Meeting on Indian Wardship, November 11, 1941, Box 1, Folder 11, LP.

16. Minutes, Committee on the Study of Wardship and Indian Participation in American Life, June 18, 1943, Exhibit I, reel 58, IRAP.

17. Report, Wardship Committee of the Indian Committee of the Home Missions Council, June 7, 1944, Box 7, Folder 13, NCCA 26.

18. [Lindquist, in collaboration with Seymour], *Handbook on Study of Indian Wardship*, 9. A copy is available in the Records of the Assistants to the Commissioner, Office File of Fred H. Daiker, 1929–1943, Box 1, "Miscellaneous," NA 75. Historically, Lindquist traced wardship to the colonial theory of the Indians' land tenure, which held that Indians possessed the right to use the land, while dominion over the land was held by European nations by virtue of discovery. Chief Justice John Marshall gave the term *wardship* its first official use in 1831 when he declared that tribes were "domestic, dependent nations," whose relationship to the federal government he compared to that of ward to guardian. *Handbook on Indian Wardship*, 8.

19. *Handbook on Indian Wardship*, 24. Lindquist's argument on Indian personnel represents a reversal of his earlier position. See the discussion in chapter 2.

20. *Handbook on Indian Wardship*, 16–19, 27–29. See similar arguments in Fred Daiker to John Collier, Memorandum in re Wardship, Records of the Assistants to the Commissioner, Office File of Fred H. Daiker, 1929–1943, Box 1, "Miscellaneous," NA 75.

21. *Handbook on Indian Wardship*, 12–13.

22. Ibid., 13.

23. Ibid., 23–28.

24. Ibid., 30.

25. Ibid., 31.

26. Ibid., 29.

27. Ibid., 31–32; for the explicit reference to taxing Indian lands, see the second edition of the pamphlet *Indian Wardship* [Lindquist, in collaboration with Seymour], 27, copy in Box 8, Folder 6, NCCA 26.

28. Minutes, Executive Committee of the Joint Indian Committee, January 15, 1943; M. Katherine Bennett to Lawrence E. Lindley, January 29, 1943, reel 58, IRAP.

29. Minutes, Committee on the Study of Wardship and Indian Participation in American Life, June 18, 1943, reel 58, IRAP (quotation); Flora Warren Seymour to Mrs. F. S. [M. Katherine] Bennett, June 12, 1943, Box 1, Folder 11, LP.

30. Lindley to Bennett, June 23, 1942, reel 97, IRAP.

31. Lindley to Bennett, August 20, 1942, reel 98, IRAP. See also the statement on tax exemptions by Charles J. Rhoads, former Indian Commissioner and member of the IRA Board, in Meeting at Haverford College Government House, December 11, 1942, reel 58, IRAP.

32. [Lawrence E. Lindley], Report of Secretary for Oct. 1943, reel 100, IRAP.

33. [Lawrence E. Lindley], Report of Secretary for Sept. 1942, reel 100, IRAP.

34. Minutes, Committee on Indian Work, September 14, 1943; Minutes, Committee on Wardship and Indian Participation in American Life, October 7, 1943; Minutes, Sub-Committee

on Indian Wardship, October 7, 1943; Katherine Bennett to members of Sub-Committee on Indian Wardship, December 3, 1943; Minutes, Sub-Committee on Indian Wardship, February 10, 1944, Box 7, Folder 13, NCCA 26.

35. Report of Joint Meeting of Indian Agencies with Commissioner William Brophy, December 12, 1945, Box 7, Folder 14, NCCA 26 (quotation); McNickle, "We Go On from Here," 14–21; Cohen, *Handbook of Federal Indian Law,* 169–73. For fully evolved discussions of the trustee doctrine, which was just beginning to be worked out in the early forties, see two essays by Felix Cohen, a legal adviser in the Interior Department during Collier's administration and the century's best-known authority on Indian law, "Indian 'Restrictions' Are Privileges," in Beatty, comp., *Education for Cultural Change,* 159–66; and "The Erosion of Indian Rights, 1950–1953," 348–90. David E. Wilkins criticizes the trustee doctrine for not going far enough in recognizing the inherent sovereignty of tribal nations, in *American Indian Sovereignty,* while Clayton Koppes offers a more sympathetic presentation of Collier's views in Koppes, "From New Deal to Termination," 543–66.

36. Collier, *Indians at Work* 12, no. 3 (Sept.–Oct. 1944):3–5.

37. For discussions of ecumenical Protestant engagement in civil rights issues for African Americans before the 1960s, see Sitkoff, *New Deal for Blacks,* 265–66, 283–86; Hulsether, *Building,* 49–55; and Findlay, *Church People in the Struggle,* 11–47.

38. Mark Dawber, "The Place of the American Indian in an On-Going Democracy," NFIW *News Letter,* no. 16 (summer 1941), 6, copy in Box 7, Folder 23, NCCA 26.

39. Minutes, Sub-Committee of Wardship Committee, April 8, 1941, reel 58, IRAP.

40. Lindquist, "The White Man Deals with the American Indian," 27.

41. Lindquist, *The Indian in American Life,* 18.

42. "Twenty Ministers in Statement Regarding Japanese Here," *Lawrence Journal–World,* June 15, 1944, clipping in BP.

43. Pledge of the Lawrence League for the Practice of Democracy, Box 1, Folder 1, Lawrence League for the Practice of Democracy Papers, Kansas Collection, Spencer Research Library, University of Kansas, Lawrence, Kansas. A study of the civil rights movement in Kansas called Lindquist one of the "new reformers" after World War II who "swept the [University of Kansas] campus and Lawrence demanding integration of service businesses as both democratic and moral rights." McCusker, "'The Forgotten Years,'" 9 (quotation), 72–82. See also Monhollon, "Taking the Plunge," 138–59.

44. Although opposing images of the noble and ignoble savage have dominated white notions of the Indian, Robert F. Berkhofer Jr. suggests that there may be a third stable image, which he describes as the degraded, drunken reservation Indian. Lindquist's assault on wardship tends to play on that stereotype. See Berkhofer's *The White Man's Indian,* 29–30.

45. Lindquist, *Indian Wardship,* 30.

46. G. E. E. Lindquist and Flora Warren Seymour, "Indian Treaty Making," April 1943, Box 7, Folder 18, NCCA 26. The essay was published in slightly revised form under Lindquist's name in *Chronicles of Oklahoma* 26 (1949):416–48. Unless explicitly noted, any references to this document will use the published version.

47. Article 1, section 8 of the Constitution reads, "The Congress shall have power . . . to regulate commerce with foreign Nations, and among the several States, and with the Indian Tribes."

48. The count of 389 treaties is based on Lindquist's own total ("Indian Treaty Making," 416), although other authors have derived different numbers.

49. Prucha, *American Indian Treaties*, 1–19.

50. McLoughlin, *Cherokees and Missionaries, 1789–1839*, 239–65.

51. Beaver, *Church, State, and the American Indians*, 193–94; Prucha, *American Indian Treaties*, 367. The extensive papers of the Indian Rights Association document Protestant efforts to defend Indian treaty rights beginning in the 1880s. For a late example, see Samuel Brosius to Matthew Sniffen, August 5, 1930, reel 46, IRAP.

52. See Collier's reference to treaties in his response to the wardship pamphlet, *Indians at Work* 12, no. 3 (Sept.–Oct. 1944):3–5; Cohen, *Handbook of Federal Indian Law*, 9–67.

53. Lindquist, "Indian Treaty Making," 419–23. Judging from the work of other scholars, Lindquist probably underestimated the importance of Indian support in shoring up the security of the United States' borders in its early years. The federal government expended a considerable amount of time and energy in wooing Indians into defensive alliances. Deloria and Wilkins, *Tribes, Treaties, and Constitutional Tribulations*, 6–31. But as Prucha has pointed out, many Indian treaties included provisions that aimed at "civilizing" the Indians and incorporating them into American society. Some even provided for granting citizenship at the end of an interim period. As Lindquist suggests, then, Indian treaties did not necessarily presume to deal with nations that would be permanently separated from the United States. Yet in circumscribing tribal autonomy, treaties also preserved it. Prucha, *American Indian Treaties*, 9–14; Wilkinson, *American Indians, Time and the Law*, 25.

54. Lindquist, "Indian Treaty Making, 423–26, 438–42.

55. For Lindquist's argument for a higher justice that supercedes the letter of treaty obligations, see Lindquist to Ruth F. Kirk, August 21, 1947, Box 16, Folder 353, LP.

56. Lindquist's essay on Indian treaties reached conclusions similar to those of British jurist and social reformer John Westlake. In the early twentieth century, Westlake argued that citizens of "backward" nations deserved the protections of "natural rights" common to all peoples, but that such nations should not be included under international law. Falkowski, *Indian Law/Race Law*, 32–33.

57. Summary of Activities, May 1, 1947, Box 14, Folder 300, LP.

58. Minutes, Coordinating Committee on American Indian Affairs, October 20, 1948, reel 136, IRAP.

59. Villard, "Wardship and the Indian," 397–98.

60. Sales Reports, Annual, 1918–1948, Records of the Missionary Education Movement of the United States and Canada, Record Group 20, Box 6, Folder 15, National Council of Churches Archives, Presbyterian Church (U.S.A.), Department of History and Records Management, Philadelphia; G. E. E. Lindquist, Report of Representative for Indian Work, 1945, Box 7, Folder 18, NCCA 26.

61. U.S. Senate, *Senate Report No. 31;* Prucha, *Great Father,* 2:1000–1001; Bernstein, *American Indians and World War II*, 100–103; Philp, *Termination Revisited*, 2. On the IRA's negative response to Thomas's proposals, see the circular letter "To Our Members and Friends," November 18, 1943, reel 58, IRAP.

62. Collier, *Indians at Work* 12, no. 3 (Sept.–Oct. 1944):5.

63. *Congressional Record,* 81st Congress, 2nd Session, March 30, 1950, 96, Part 14, A2367-A2368; Fixico, *Termination and Relocation,* 55.

64. Lindquist to Helen Brickman, June 2, 1945, Box 16, Folder 354, LP.

65. Philp, *Termination Revisited,* 16–28; Prucha, *American Indian Treaties,* 380–84; Lindquist, "Indian Treaties," 442.

66. Philp, *Termination Revisited,* 71.

67. A copy of H.C.R. 108 appears in reel 114, IRAP.

68. In the discussion that follows, I have focused on the work of Arthur C. Parker (Seneca) and Ruth Muskrat Bronson (Cherokee) in defending Indians' rights as national minorities. But I should note that J. C. Morgan also used both treaty rights and citizenship rights to counter Collier's domination over Navajo tribal affairs. Morgan was a strong cultural assimilationist, but he was not willing to relinquish tribal rights. Morgan, "What Has Become of the Navajo's Treaty with Government?" *Farmington Times Hustler* (New Mexico), January 6, 1934, enclosure in Morgan to Sniffen, February 5, 1934, reel 51, IRAP.

69. See for example the Report of the Findings Committee, Pacific Northwest Regional Conference, 1940, Box 9, Folder 155, LP; Findings of the National Conference, 1941, Box 9, Folder 165, LP; "On to Lake Geneva–1946," Box 9, Folder 166, LP.

70. Arthur C. Parker, "The Six Nations Look at Wardship," in *Eastern Regional Conference of the Fellowship of Indian Workers,* 24–28, copy in Box 9, "Eastern FIW," Record Group 46, Records of the United States Senate, Committee on Interior and Insular Affairs, Subcommittee on Indian Affairs, Sen. 83A-F9 (70th–82nd), National Archives, Washington, D.C.

71. For a full biography, see Harvey, "Cherokee and American."

72. Lindquist to Edith M. Dabb, March [n.d.] 1934, Seymour to Matthew Sniffen, May 28, 1934, reel 52, IRAP.

73. Minutes, Board of Directors, Indian Rights Association, February 2, 1944, reel 99, IRAP. On Bronson's leadership within the National Congress of American Indians (NCAI), and the NCAI's effort to stop forced termination, see Cowger, "'The Crossroads of Destiny,'" 121–44. In referring to Bronson's connection to the Collier legacy, I do not mean to suggest that Bronson was in any way loyal to Collier himself. In fact, she believed that his administration of the Wheeler-Howard Act had been "disappointing" due to a "continued reluctance on the part of government officials to turn the power of self-rule into the hands of the people." Ruth Muskrat Bronson, *The Church in Indian Life* (New York: Home Missions Council of North America, n.d.; copy in reel 130, frame 325, IRAP), 16. See also the review of her book, *Indians Are People, Too,* in the BIA's publication, *Indians at Work* 12, no. 3 (September–October 1944):32–34.

74. Bronson, *Indians Are People, Too,* 25–27, 92, 125, 136, 180–81; Harvey, "Cherokee and American," 18–19.

75. Harvey, "Cherokee and American," 18–19.

76. Lindquist, "Indian Treaty Making," 425.

77. Bronson, *Indians Are People, Too,* 22–28; Harvey, "Cherokee and American," 1–10, 132–33; Philp, *Termination Revisited,* 15.

78. Ruth Muskrat Bronson, *The Church in Indian Life* (New York: Home Missions Council of North America, n.d.; copy in reel 130, frame 325, IRAP), 18.

79. Minutes, Coordinating Committee on Indian Affairs, October 7, 1952, reel 136, IRAP.

By 1952, the Indian Rights Association—Lindquist's partner in the fight against Collier throughout the 1920s and 1930s—fully supported Bronson's point of view. Jonathan Steere, the president of the Indian Rights Association, argued that the BIA's "protective functions" were not "imposed on the Indian people by the Government." Rather, those protections and services were "an obligation assumed by the United States in part payment for value received. The treaties and agreements which we made with the Indians in connection with land purchases are still in force and can be terminated only by agreement of the parties concerned." Jonathan Steere, "Indian Bureau Policy Jeopardizes Indian Rights and Welfare," 1.

80. Minutes, Coordinating Committee on Indian Affairs, October 7, 1952, reel 136, IRAP.

81. A Pronouncement: Indian Affairs, March 3, 1955, Records of the Division of Christian Life and Mission, Record Group 6, Series VII, Box 61, Folder 35, National Council of Churches Archives, Presbyterian Church (U.S.A.), Department of History and Records Management, Philadelphia.

82. George Pierre Castile has argued recently that the shift toward self-determination in the 1960s owed more to moderate Indian activism like that of Bronson than to the militant activism of groups like the American Indian Movement (AIM). Castile, *To Show Heart*, 125–29.

83. Minutes, Coordinating Committee on Indian Affairs, 12-29-53, reel 136, IRAP.

Epilogue

1. Lindquist, *Red Man*, 428–29.

2. Cohen, *Handbook*, 173.

3. Tinker, *Missionary Conquest*, 117.

4. Marie Therese Archambault, "Native Americans and Evangelization," in Treat, ed., *Native and Christian*, 147.

Bibliography

Manuscript Collections

American Indian Institute. Papers. Board of National Missions. Presbyterian Church (U.S.A.),
  Department of History and Records Management Services. Philadelphia.
Bonny, Helen Lindquist. Papers. Private Collection. Vero Beach, Florida.
Collier, John. Papers. Yale University Library. New Haven, Connecticut. Sanford, North Carolina: Microfilming Corporation of America, 1980. Microfilm.
Division of Christian Life and Mission. Records. National Council of Churches Archives. Record
  Group 6. Series VII. Presbyterian Church (U.S.A.), Department of History and Records
  Management Services. Philadelphia.
Home Missions Council of North America. Records. National Council of Churches Archives.
  Record Group 26. Presbyterian Church (U.S.A.), Department of History and Records
  Management Services. Philadelphia.
Indian Rights Association. Papers. Historical Society of Pennsylvania. Philadelphia. Glen Rock,
  N.J.: Microfilming Corporation of America, 1975. Microfilm.
Lawrence League for the Protection of Democracy. Papers. Kansas Historical Collection. Spencer
  Research Library, University of Kansas. Lawrence, Kansas.
Lindquist, G. E. E. Papers. Special Collections. The Burke Library, Union Theological Seminary. New York.
Missionary Education Movement of the United States and Canada. Records. National Council
  of Churches Archives. Record Group 20. Presbyterian Church (U.S.A.), Department of
  History and Records Management Services. Philadelphia.
Senate Committee on Interior and Insular Affairs Records. United States Senate. Record Group
  46. National Archives. Washington, D.C.

Sweet, Evander M. Papers. Holt-Atherton Library, University of the Pacific. Stockton, California.

U.S. Department of the Interior. Board of Indian Commissioners. Records. Bureau of Indian Affairs. Record Group 75. National Archives. Washington, D.C.

————. Bureau of Indian Affairs. Central Classified Files, 1907–1939. Record Group 75. National Archives. Washington, D.C.

————. Bureau of Indian Affairs. Central Classified Files, 1940–1956. Record Group 75. National Archives. Washington, D.C.

————. Collier, John. Office Files. Bureau of Indian Affairs. Record Group 75. National Archives. Washington, D.C.

————. Daiker, Fred H. Office Files. Records of the Assistants to the Commissioner. Bureau of Indian Affairs. Record Group 75. National Archives. Washington, D.C.

————. Haskell Institute. Records. Bureau of Indian Affairs. Record Group 75. National Archives–Central Plains. Kansas City, Missouri.

————. Indian Organization Division. Records Concerning the Wheeler-Howard Act, Bureau of Indian Affairs. Record Group 75. National Archives. Washington, D.C.

————. Orders, Circulars, and Circular Letters. Bureau of Indian Affairs. Record Group 75. National Archives. Washington, D.C.

————. Ryan, W. Carson, Jr. Office File. Bureau of Indian Affairs. Record Group 75. National Archives. Washington, D.C.

Interviews

Bonny, Helen Lindquist. Phone interview by author. January 16, 1998.

Bonny, Helen Lindquist. Interview by author. Salina, Kansas, February 8, 1998.

Newspapers

Albuquerque Tribune, April 13–June 23, 1942.

New York Times, March 27, 1923–August 12, 1934.

New York Tribune, March 22, 1923–April 8, 1934.

Published Works

Aberle, David F. *The Peyote Religion among the Navajo.* 2d ed. Chicago: University of Chicago Press, 1982.

Adams, David Wallace. *Education for Extinction: American Indians and the Boarding School Experience, 1875–1928.* Lawrence: University of Kansas Press, 1995.

Ahern, William H. "Assimilationist Racism: The Case of the Friends of the Indian." *Journal of Ethnic Studies* 4, no. 2 (1976):23–32.

Albanese, Catherine L. *Nature Religion in America: From the Algonkian Indians to the New Age.* Chicago: University of Chicago Press, 1990.

Alexander, Ruth Ann. "Finding Oneself Through a Cause: Elaine Goodale Eastman and Indian Reform in the 1880s." *South Dakota History* 22 (spring 1992):1–37.

Anderson, Philip J. "'Strangers Yet Acquainted': The Personality of Religious Schism in Lindsborg, Kansas." *Swedish-American Historical Quarterly* 49 (July 1998):210–22.

Armstrong, O. K. "Set the American Indians Free!" *Reader's Digest,* August 1945.

Austin, Mary. "The American Indian." *New York Evening Post: The Literary Review* 4 (September 15, 1923):46.

Bailey, Garrick, and Roberta Glenn Bailey. *A History of the Navajos: The Reservation Years.* Santa Fe: School of American Research Press, 1986.

Banker, Mark T. "Presbyterians and Pueblos: A Protestant Response to the Indian Question, 1872–1892." *Journal of Presbyterian History* 60 (1982):23–40.

Barnard, John. *From Evangelicalism to Progressivism at Oberlin College, 1866–1917.* Columbus: Ohio State University Press, 1969.

Barrington, Linda, ed. *The Other Side of the Frontier: Economic Explorations into Native American History.* Boulder, Colo.: Westview Press, 1999.

Barsh, R. L. "Progressive Era Bureaucrats and the Unity of Twentieth-Century Policy." *American Indian Quarterly* 15.1 (1991):1–17.

Barton, H. Arnold. *A Folk Divided: Homeland Swedes and Swedish Americans, 1840–1940.* Carbondale: Southern Illinois University Press, 1994.

Beatty, Willard, comp. *Education for Cultural Change: Selected Articles from Indian Education, 1944–1951.* Washington, D.C.: U.S. Department of the Interior, 1953.

Beaver, R. Pierce. *Church, State, and the American Indians: Two and a Half Centuries of Partnership in Missions Between Churches and Government.* St. Louis: Concordia Publishing House, 1966.

Bennett, M. Katherine. *The Indian in the United States.* New York: Committee on the Study of Wardship and Indian Participation in American Life, 1942.

———. "Let Us Look at the Indian." *Women and Missions,* April 1944, 16–17.

Berkhofer, Robert F., Jr. *The White Man's Indian: Images of the American Indian from Columbus to the Present.* New York: Alfred A. Knopf, 1978.

Bernstein, Alison R. *American Indians and World War II: Toward a New Era in Indian Affairs.* Norman: University of Oklahoma Press, 1991.

Biolsi, Thomas. "Indian Self-Government as a Technique of Domination." *American Indian Quarterly,* 15.1 (1991):23–28.

Blanck, Dag. *Becoming Swedish-American: The Construction of an Ethnic Identity in the Augustana Synod, 1860–1917.* Uppsala: Uppsala University Library, 1997.

Block, Maxine, ed. *Current Biography 1942.* New York: H. W. Wilson Company, 1942.

Bosworth, Edward I. *Studies in the Life of Jesus Christ.* New York: International Committee of Young Men's Christian Associations, 1906.

———. *What It Means to Be a Christian: The Evangelistic Message in Outline.* Boston: The Pilgrim Press, 1922.

Bourne, Randolph. "Trans-National America." *Atlantic Monthly* 118 (July 1916):86–97.

Bowden, Henry Warner. *American Indians and Christian Missions: Studies in Cultural Conflict.* Chicago: University of Chicago Press, 1981.

Britten, Thomas A. *American Indians in World War I: At War and at Home.* Albuquerque: University of New Mexico Press, 1997.

———. "Hoover and the Indians: The Case for Continuity in Federal Indian Policy, 1900–1933." *Historian* 61.3 (1999):518–39.

Bronson, Ruth Muskrat. *The Church in Indian Life.* New York: Home Missions Council of North America, n.d.

———. *Indians Are People, Too.* New York: Friendship Press, 1944.

Burgess, Larry E. "We'll Discuss It at Mohonk." *Quaker History* 60 (1971):14–28.

Burleson, Hugh L. "The Soul of the Indian." *Missionary Review of the World* 42 (September 1920):804–10.

Burt, Larry W. *Tribalism in Crisis: Federal Indian Policy, 1953–61.* Albuquerque: University of New Mexico Press, 1982.

Carey, S. Pearce. *William Carey.* London: Hodder and Stroughton, 1923.

Carlson, Leonard A. *Indians, Bureaucrats, and Land: The Dawes Act and the Decline of Indian Farming.* Westport, Conn.: Greenwood Press, 1981.

Carpenter, Niles, and [G. E. E.] Lindquist. *John Red Hill, Back from the War, Learns about Peyote.* New York: Home Missions Council of North America, 1944.

Castile, George Pierre. *To Show Heart: Native American Self-Determination and Federal Indian Policy, 1960–1975.* Tucson: University of Arizona Press, 1998.

Champagne, Duane, ed. *Contemporary Native American Cultural Issues.* Walnut Creek, Calif.: AltaMira Press, 1999.

"Christian Indians Think Missions." *Missionary Review of the World* 58 (December 1935):567.

Clemmer, Richard O. *Roads in the Sky: The Hopi Indians in a Century of Change.* Boulder, Colo.: Westview Press, 1995.

Cohen, Felix S. "The Erosion of Indian Rights, 1950–1953: A Case Study in Bureaucracy." *Yale Law Journal* 62 (February 1953):348–90.

———. *Handbook of Federal Indian Law.* Washington, D.C.: Government Printing Office, 1942.

Coleman, Michael C. *American Indian Children at School, 1850–1930.* Jackson: University Press of Mississippi, 1993.

———. *Presbyterian Missionary Attitudes toward American Indians, 1837–1893.* Jackson: University Press of Mississippi, 1985.

———. "Problematic Panacea: Presbyterian Missionaries and the Allotment of Indian Lands in the Late Nineteenth Century." *Pacific Historical Review* 54 (1985): 43–59.

Collier, John. "Do Indians Have Rights of Conscience?" *Christian Century* 42 (March 12, 1925):346–49.

———. Editorial. *Indians at Work* 4, no. 7 (November 15, 1936):3.

———. Editorial. *Indians at Work* 4, no. 13 (February 15, 1937):1.

———. Editorial. *Indians at Work* 9, no. 2 (October 1941):1–3.

———. Editorial. *Indians at Work* 12, no. 3 (September–October 1944):3–5.

———. *From Every Zenith: A Memoir and Some Essays on Life.* Denver: Sage Books, 1963.

———. "Indian Legislation: The Bill for Land and Self-Government." *Indians at Work* 1, no. 13 (February 15, 1934):4–7.

———. "The Indians' Master Problem: Land." *Indians at Work* 1, no. 4 (October 1, 1933):4–7.

———. *The Indians of the Americas.* New York: W. W. Norton and Company, 1947.

———. "A Lift for the Forgotten Red Man, Too." *New York Times Magazine,* May 6, 1934, pp. 10–11.

————. "The Red Slaves of Oklahoma." *Sunset* 52 (March 1924):96.

————. "A Reply to Mrs. Eastman." *Christian Century* 51 (August 8, 1934):1018–20.

"Commentaries on *When Jesus Came, the Corn Mothers Went Away: Marriage, Sexuality, and Power in New Mexico, 1500–1846*, by Ramón Gutiérrez." *American Indian Culture and Research Journal* 17 (1993):141–77.

Congressional Record, 1932–1950, Washington, D.C.

Coolidge, Sherman. "The Indian American—His Duty to His Race and to His Country, the United States of America." *Quarterly Journal of the Society of American Indians* 1 (January–April, 1913):20–24.

Cowger, Thomas W. "'The Crossroads of Destiny': The NCAI's Landmark Struggle to Thwart Coercive Termination." *American Indian Culture and Research Journal* 20, no. 4 (1996):121–44.

Cracknell, Kenneth. *Justice, Courtesy, and Love: Theologians and Missionaries Encountering World Religions, 1846–1914.* London: Epworth Press, 1995.

Craig, Robert. "Christianity and Empire: A Case Study of American Protestant Colonialism and Native Americans." *American Indian Culture and Research Journal* 21.2 (1997):1–41.

Crane, Leo. *Indians of the Enchanted Desert.* Boston: Little, Brown, 1926.

Crum, Steven J. "Henry Roe Cloud, a Winnebago Indian Reformer: His Quest for American Indian Higher Education." *Kansas History* 11 (1988):171–84.

Curtis, Susan. *A Consuming Faith: The Social Gospel and Modern American Culture.* Baltimore: Johns Hopkins University Press, 1991.

"A Cycle on the American Indian: A Symposium." *Forum* 72, no. 11 (November 1924): 710–14.

Daily, David W. "Guardian Rivalries: G. E. E. Lindquist, John Collier, and the Moral Landscape of Federal Indian Policy, 1910–1950." Ph.D. dissertation, Duke University, 2000.

The Daisy. Salina, Kans.: Central Kansas Publishing Company, 1909.

Darlington, Ann Charlotte. *Where the Trails Cross: A One-Act Play of Navajo Life.* New York: Missionary Education Movement of the United States and Canada, 1928.

Davis, David Brion. "Some Themes of Counter-Subversion: An Analysis of Anti-Masonic, Anti-Catholic, and Anti-Mormon Literature." *Mississippi Historical Review* 47 (1960):205–44.

Deloria, Ella C. *Speaking of Indians.* New York: Friendship Press, 1944.

Deloria, Vine, Jr., and Clifford M. Lytle. *The Nations Within: The Past and Future of American Indian Sovereignty.* New York: Pantheon Books, 1984.

Deloria, Vine, Jr., and David E. Wilkins. *Tribes, Treaties, and Constitutional Tribulations.* Austin: University of Texas Press, 1999.

Destination Lindsborg. Lindsborg, Kans.: Lindsborg News–Record, 1997.

Dippie, Clifford. *The Vanishing American: White Attitudes and U.S. Indian Policy.* Middleton, Conn.: Wesleyan University Press, 1982.

Dorcy, Michael Morgan. "Friends of the American Indian, 1922–1934: Patterns of Patronage and Philanthropy." Ph.D. dissertation, University of Pennsylvania, 1978.

Duberman, Martin Bauml, Fred Eggan, and Richard Clemmer, eds. "Documents in Hopi Indian Sexuality: Imperialism, Culture, and Resistance." *Radical History Review* 20 (spring/summer 1979):99–130.

Duncombe, Edward S. "The Church and the Native American Arapahoes, Part II: Toward Assimilation." *Anglican and Episcopal History* 66 (July 1997):363–71.

Eastern Regional Conference of the Fellowship of Indian Workers. Lawrence, Kans.: National Fellowship of Indian Workers, 1944.

Eastman, Charles A. (Ohiyesa). *The Soul of the Indian: An Interpretation.* Boston: Houghton Mifflin, 1911. Reprint, Lincoln: University of Nebraska Press, 1980.

Eastman, Elaine Goodale. "Does Uncle Sam Foster Paganism?" *Christian Century* 51 (August 8, 1934):1016–18.

———. "Our New-Old Indian Policy." *Christian Century* 46 (November 27, 1929):1471–73.

———. *Sister to the Sioux: The Memoirs of Elaine Goodale Eastman, 1885–1891.* Ed. Kay Graber. Lincoln: University of Nebraska Press, 1978.

———. "Uncle Sam and Paganism." *Christian Century* 51 (August 22, 1934):1073.

Ellis, Clyde. *To Change Them Forever: Indian Education at the Rainy Mountain Boarding School, 1893–1920.* Norman: University of Oklahoma Press, 1996.

———. "'We Don't Want Your Rations, We Want This Dance': The Changing Use of Song and Dance on Southern Plains." *Western Historical Quarterly* 30 (summer 1999):133–54.

Erenberg, Lewis A., and Susan E. Hirsch. *The War in American Culture: Society and Consciousness During World War II.* Chicago: University of Chicago Press, 1996.

"Excerpt from Address by Ward Shepard, Indian Office Land Policy Specialist, to the Conference on Minorities of the Women's International League for Peace and Freedom, Chicago, May 28." *Indians at Work* 1, no. 21 (June 15, 1934):7–9.

Falkowski, James E. *Indian Law/Race Law: A Five-Hundred-Year History.* New York: Praeger, 1992.

Ferris, Kathlene Faulstick. "Sophie D. Aberle and the United Pueblos Agency, 1935–1944." Master's thesis, University of New Mexico, 1997.

Findlay, James F., Jr. *Church People in the Struggle: The National Council of Churches and the Black Freedom Movement, 1950–1970.* New York: Oxford University Press, 1993.

Fischer, William C., David A Gerber, Jorge M. Guitart, and Maxine S. Seller, eds. *Identity, Community, and Pluralism in American Life.* New York: Oxford University Press, 1997.

Fixico, Donald L. *Termination and Relocation: Federal Indian Policy, 1945–1960.* Albuquerque: University of New Mexico Press, 1986.

Foster, Morris W. *Being Comanche: A Social History of an American Indian Community.* Tucson: University of Arizona Press, 1991.

Fowler, Loretta. *Shared Symbols, Contested Meanings: Gros Ventre Culture and History, 1778–1984.* Ithaca: Cornell University Press, 1987.

Franco, Jeré. "Publicity, Persuasion, and Propaganda: Stereotyping the Native American in World War II." *Military History of the Southwest* 22, no. 2 (fall 1992):173–87.

Fritz, Henry E. "The Last Hurrah of Christian Humanitarian Reform: The Board of Indian Commissioners, 1909–1918." *Western Historical Quarterly* 16 (1985):147–62.

"From Rapid City." *Indian Truth* 11, no. 3 (March 1934):4.

Fuchs, Lawrence. *The American Kaleidoscope: Race, Ethnicity, and the Civic Culture.* Hanover, N.H.: University of New England Press, 1990.

Fullerton, Kemper. *Essays and Sketches: Oberlin, 1904–1934.* New Haven: Yale University Press, 1938.

"Futile Voting." *Indian Truth* 11, no. 9 (December 7, 1934):1–3.

Gessner, Robert. *Massacre: A Survey of Today's American Indian.* New York: Jonathan Cape and Harrison Smith, 1931.

Gleason, Philip. *Speaking of Diversity: Language and Ethnicity in Twentieth-Century America.* Baltimore: Johns Hopkins University Press, 1992.

Gordon, Milton. *Assimilation in American Life.* New York: Oxford University Press, 1964.

Grant, John Webster. *Moon of Wintertime: Missionaries and the Indians of Canada in Encounter since 1534.* Toronto: Toronto University Press, 1989.

Gutiérrez, Ramón A. *When Jesus Came, the Corn Mothers Went Away: Marriage, Sexuality, and Power in New Mexico, 1500–1846.* Stanford, Calif.: Stanford University Press, 1991.

Hall, Robert D. "Moral Training in Indian Schools." *American Indian Magazine* 4 (spring 1918):87–88.

Handy, Robert T. *A Christian America: Protestant Hopes and Historical Realities.* Oxford: Oxford University Press, 1971.

———. "Mary Katherine Jones Bennett." In *Notable American Women,* vol. 1. Cambridge: Harvard University Press, 1971.

———. *Undermined Establishment: Church-State Relations in America, 1880–1920.* Princeton: Princeton University Press, 1991.

Harmon, Alexandra. "When Is an Indian Not an Indian? The 'Friends of the Indian' and the Problems of Indian Identity." *Journal of Ethnic Studies* 18 (summer 1991):5–123.

Harvey, Gretchen. "Cherokee and American: Ruth Muskrat Bronson, 1897–1982." Ph.D. dissertation, Arizona State University, 1996.

Haskell Institute, U.S.A., 1884–1959. Lawrence: Haskell Institute, 1959.

Hasse, Larry J. "Termination and Assimilation: Federal Indian Policy, 1943–1961." Ph.D. dissertation, Washington State University, 1974.

Hauptman, Laurence M. "Africa View: John Collier, the British Colonial Service, and American Indian Policy, 1933–1945." *The Historian* 48, no. 3 (1986):359–74.

———. "The American Indian Federation and the Indian New Deal: A Reinterpretation." *Pacific Historical Review* 52 (1983):378–402.

———. *The Iroquois and the New Deal.* Syracuse: Syracuse University Press, 1981.

Hawkinson, Zenos. "An Interpretation of the Background of the Evangelical Mission Covenant Church of America." *Swedish Pioneer Historical Quarterly* 2 (summer 1951):3–11.

Hertzberg, Hazel. *The Search for an American Indian Identity: Modern Pan-Indian Movements.* Syracuse: Syracuse University Press, 1971.

Higginbotham, Evelyn Brooks. *Righteous Discontent: The Women's Movement in the Black Baptist Church, 1880–1920.* Cambridge: Harvard University Press, 1993.

Higham, C. L. *Noble, Wretched, and Redeemable: Protestant Missionaries to the Indians in Canada and the United States, 1820–1900.* Albuquerque: University of New Mexico Press, 2000.

Higham, John. *Strangers in the Land: Patterns of American Nativism, 1860–1925.* New Brunswick, N.J.: Rutgers University Press, 1988.

Hill, Patricia. "The Missionary Enterprise." In *Encyclopedia of the American Religious Experience,* vol. 3. Eds. Charles H. Lippy and Peter W. Williams. New York: Scribners, 1988.

Hinman, George W. *The American Indian and Christian Missions.* New York: Fleming H. Revell, 1933.

———. *Christian Activities Among American Indians.* Boston: Society for Propagating the Gospel Among the Indians and Others in North America, 1932.

Holm, Thomas M. "Fighting a White Man's War: The Extent and Legacy of American Indian Participation in World War II." *Journal of Ethnic Studies* 9, no. 2 (1981):69–81.

———. "Indians and Progressives: From Vanishing Policy to the Indian New Deal." Ph.D. dissertation, University of Oklahoma, 1978.

Hoxie, Frederick E. *A Final Promise: The Campaign to Assimilate the Indians, 1880–1920.* Lincoln: University of Nebraska Press, 1984. Reprint, Cambridge University Press, 1989.

———. *Parading Through History: The Making of the Crow Nation, 1805–1935.* Cambridge: Cambridge University Press, 1995.

Hudson, Winthrop, and John Corrigan. *Religion in America: An Historical Account of the Development of American Religious Life.* 5th ed. New York: Macmillan, 1992.

Hulbert, Winifred. *The Hogan Beneath the Sunrise: A Dramatic Sketch of Navajo Life Today.* New York: Missionary Education Movement of the United States and Canada, 1932.

Hulsether, Mark. *Building a Protestant Left: Christianity and Crisis Magazine, 1941–1993.* Knoxville: University of Tennessee Press, 1999.

Hutchison, William R. *Errand to the World: American Protestant Thought and Foreign Missions.* Chicago: University of Chicago Press, 1987.

———. *The Modernist Impulse in American Protestantism.* 2d ed. Durham: Duke University Press, 1992.

Hutchison, William R., ed. *Between the Times: The Travail of the Protestant Establishment in America, 1900–1960.* New York: Cambridge University Press, 1989.

International Missionary Conference. *The World Mission of the Church: Findings and Recommendations of the International Missionary Conference.* London: International Missionary Conference, 1939.

Iverson, Peter. *Carlos Montezuma and the Changing World of American Indians.* Albuquerque: University of New Mexico Press, 1982.

———. *The Navajo Nation.* Westport, Conn.: Greenwood Press, 1981.

Jacobs, Margaret D. *Engendered Encounters: Feminism and Pueblo Cultures, 1879–1934.* Lincoln: University of Nebraska Press, 1999.

———. "Making Savages of Us All: White Women, Pueblo Indians, and the Controversy over Indian Dances in the 1920s." *Frontiers* 17, no. 3 (1996):178–209.

James, Harry C. *Pages from Hopi History.* Tucson: University of Arizona Press, 1974.

Jensen, Katherine. "Teachers and Progressives: The Navajo Day-School Experiment, 1935–1945." *Arizona and the West* 25 (1983):49–62.

Johnson, F. Ernest. *The Church and Society.* New York: Abingdon, 1935.

Jones, Carter. "'Hope for the Race of Man': Indians, Intellectuals, and the Regeneration of Modern America, 1917–1934." Ph.D. dissertation, Brown University, 1991.

Keller, Robert. *American Protestantism and the United States Indian Policy, 1869–1882.* Lincoln: University of Nebraska, 1983.

Kelly, Lawrence C. *The Assault on Assimilation: John Collier and the Origins of Indian Policy Reform.* Albuquerque: University of New Mexico Press, 1983.

———. "Choosing the New Deal Indian Commissioner: Ickes vs. Collier." *New Mexico Historical Review* 49 (1974):269–88.

Kidwell, Clara Sue. *Choctaws and Missionaries in Mississippi, 1818–1918.* Norman: University of Oklahoma Press, 1995.

Kinney, Bruce. *Frontier Missionary Problems: Their Character and Solution.* New York: Fleming H. Revell, 1917.

Koppes, Clayton R. "From New Deal to Termination: Liberalism and Indian Policy, 1933–1953." *Pacific Historical Review* 46 (November 1977):543–66.

Kracht, Benjamin R. "Kiowa Powwows: Continuity in Ritual Practice," *American Indian Quarterly* 18, no. 3 (1994): 321–50.

Kymlicka, Will. *Multicultural Citizenship: A Liberal Theory of Minority Rights.* New York: Oxford University Press, 1995.

LaGrand, James B. "The Changing 'Jesus Road': Protestants Reappraise American Indian Missions in the 1920s and 1930s." *Western Historical Quarterly* 27 (Winter 1996):479–504.

Layton, Azza Salama. "The International Context of the United States Civil Rights Movement: The Dynamics Between Racial Policies and International Politics, 1941–1960." Ph.D. dissertation, University of Texas at Austin, 1995.

Levy, Jerold E. *Orayvi Revisited: Social Stratification in an Egalitarian Society.* Santa Fe: School of American Research Press, 1992.

Lewis, Bonnie Sue. *Creating Christian Indians: Native Clergy in the Presbyterian Church.* Norman: University of Oklahoma Press, 2003.

Lindquist, Emory. *Bethany in Kansas: The History of a College.* Lindsborg, Kans.: Bethany College, 1975.

———. *Smoky Valley People: A History of Lindsborg, Kansas.* Lindsborg, Kans.: Bethany College, 1953.

———. *Vision for a Valley: Olof Olsson and the Early History of Lindsborg.* Rock Island, Ill.: Augustana Historical Society, 1970.

Lindquist, G. E. E. "Advisory Council on Indian Affairs Meets at Washington." *Indian Leader* 27, no. 20 (February 3, 1934):10–14.

———. *Bland Nordamerikas Indianer, bilder ur indianeras utvecklingshioria intill vara dagar* [Among the North American Indians: Portraits of the Indians' Progress up to the Present Day]. Uppsala, Sweden: J. A. Lindblad, 1926.

———. "Christian Work Among Indians, Including Problems of Religious Life." *Journal of Religious Thought* 7 (1950):128–35.

———. "Early Work Among the Indians: One Hundred and Fifty Years of Service Among Native Americans." *Missionary Review of the World* 60 (November 1937):533–38.

———. "The Government's New Indian Policy: Proposed Revival of Tribalism, Seen from the Missionary Angle." *Missionary Review of the World* 57 (April 1934):182–84.

———. *A Handbook for Missionary Workers Among the American Indians.* New York: Home Missions Council, 1932.

———. "Impressions of Sweden and the World Conference of Churches." *The Covenant Companion.* January–May 1926.

———. *Indians in Transition: A Study of Protestant Missions to Indians in the United States.* New York: Division of Home Missions, National Council of Churches of Christ, 1951.

———. *Indians in Urban Centers: A Manual for City Pastors, Religious Education Directors, Church Social Workers, and Directors of Social Agencies.* Lawrence, Kans.: Home Missions Council of North America, 1948.

————. *Indians of Minnesota: A Survey of Social and Religious Conditions Among Tribes in Transition.* New York: Division of Home Missions, National Council of Churches, 1952.

————. "Indian Treaty-Making." *Chronicles of Oklahoma* 26 (winter 1949):416–48.

————. *The Jesus Road and the Red Man.* New York: Fleming H. Revell, 1929.

————. "The Legend of the Smoky River." *Bethany Messenger,* February 1906, 5–13.

————. *The Lost Colony of Roanoke Today.* Reprint from *Southern Workman.* November 1928.

————. *New Trails for Old: A Handbook for Missionary Workers Among the Indians.* New York: National Council of the Churches of Christ in the U.S.A., Division of Home Missions, 1951.

————. "The Outlook for the American Indian." *Missionary Review of the World* 62 (November 1939):501–7.

————. "The Pueblo Indian Religion." *Missionary Review of the World* 62 (December 1939):553–54.

————. *Receding Frontiers in the Indian Country.* Reprint from *Southern Workman.* March 1931.

————. "Revival of Tribalism." *Christian Century* 51 (September 5, 1934):1118.

————. "Urgent Needs of American Indians: Unreached American Indians, as Reported at the Wallace Lodge Conference." *Missionary Review of the World* 43 (November 1920):989–94.

————. "The White Man Deals with the American Indian." *World Outlook* 28, no. 3 (March 1938):106, 115, 130.

[Lindquist, G. E. E.] "Religious Liberty." *Indian Truth* 13, no. 9 (December 1936):2–3.

Lindquist, G. E. E., comp. *Red Man in the United States: An Intimate Study of the Social, Economic, and Religious Life of the American Indian.* New York: George H. Doran, 1923; Clifton, N.J.: A. M. Kelley, 1973.

Lindquist, G. E. E., with Erna Gunther, John H. Holst, and Flora Warren Seymour. *The Indian in American Life.* New York: Friendship Press, 1944.

[Lindquist, G. E. E., in collaboration with Flora Warren Seymour]. *Handbook on Study of Indian Wardship.* New York: Committee on Wardship and Indian Participation in American Life, 1942.

————. *Indian Wardship.* Rev. ed. New York: Home Missions Council of North America, 1944.

Lindquist, G. E. E., and Edith M. Dabb. *Guides Along New Indian Trails.* New York: Joint Committee on Indian Missions of the Home Missions Council and Council of Women for Home Missions, 1921.

Lindsey, Donal F. *Indians at Hampton Institute, 1877–1923.* Urbana: University of Illinois Press, 1995.

Lippy, Charles H., and Peter W. Williams, eds. *Encyclopedia of the American Religious Experience.* 3 vols. New York: Scribners, 1988.

Ljungmark, Lars. *Swedish Exodus.* Trans. Kermit B. Westerberg. Carbondale, Ill.: Southern Illinois University Press, 1979.

Loftin, John D. *Religion and Hopi Life in the Twentieth Century.* Bloomington: Indiana University Press, 1991.

Mann, Arthur. *The One and the Many: Reflections on the American Identity.* Chicago: University of Chicago Press, 1979.

Marty, Martin E. *Modern American Religion.* Vol. 2, *The Noise of Conflict, 1919–41.* Chicago: University of Chicago Press, 1991.

————. *Modern American Religion*. Vol. 3, *Under God, Indivisible, 1941–1960*. Chicago: University of Chicago Press, 1996.

————. *Righteous Empire: The Protestant Experience in America*. New York: Dial Press, 1970.

McCusker, Kristine. "'The Forgotten Years' of America's Civil Rights Movement: The University of Kansas, 1939–1961." Master's thesis, University of Kansas, 1987.

McDonnell, Janet. *The Dispossession of the American Indian, 1887–1934*. Bloomington: Indiana University Press, 1991.

McLoughlin, William G. *Cherokees and Missionaries, 1789–1839*. New Haven: Yale University Press, 1984.

McNally, Michael D. *Ojibwe Singers: Hymns, Grief, and a Culture in Motion*. New York: Oxford University Press, 2000.

McNickle, Darcy. "We Go on from Here." *Indians at Work* 11, no. 4 (November–December 1943):14–21.

McPherson, Robert S. "Navajo Livestock Reduction in Southeastern Utah, 1933–1946: History Repeats Itself." *American Indian Quarterly* 22.1 (1998):1–18.

Meriam, Lewis, et al. *The Problem of Indian Administration*. Baltimore: Johns Hopkins University Press, 1928.

Miller, Christopher. *Prophetic Worlds: Indians and Whites on the Columbia Plateau*. New Brunswick, N.J.: Rutgers University Press, 1985.

Milner, Clyde A., II, and Floyd A. O'Neil, eds. *Churchmen and the Western Indians, 1880–1920*. Norman: University of Oklahoma Press, 1985.

Mills, Kenneth. "The Limits of Religious Coercion in Mid-Colonial Peru." *Past and Present*, 145 (November 1994):4–121.

"Miss Muskrat Wins the Prize." *Missionary Review of the World* 49 (September 1926):672–74.

Moffett, Thomas C. *The American Indian on the New Trail: The Red Man of the United States and the Christian Gospel*. New York: Methodist Book Concern and the Missionary Education Movement, 1914.

————. "The Red Men and the Gospel: The Indians of the United States, Christian and Non-Christian." *Missionary Review of the World* 39 (October 1915):751.

————. "The Society of American Indians Is a Success." *American Indian Magazine* 4 (July–September, 1916):262–65.

Monhollon, Rusty L. "Taking the Plunge: Race, Rights, and the Politics of Desegregation in Lawrence, Kansas, 1960." *Kansas History* 20, no. 3 (autumn 1997):138–59.

Moore, John H., ed. *The Political Economy of North American Indians*. Norman: University of Oklahoma Press, 1993.

Morgan, J. C. "A Navajo Dissenter." *Christian Century* 51 (October 31, 1934):1379–80.

Moses, L. G. *Wild West Shows and the Images of American Indians, 1833–1933*. Albuquerque: University of New Mexico Press, 1996.

"Navajo Debacle." *Indian Truth* 15, no. 5 (May 1938):1–3.

Nelson, Paula M. *The Prairie Winnows Out Its Own: The West River Country of South Dakota in the Years of the Depression and Dust*. Iowa City: University of Iowa Press, 1996.

"A New Type of Indian Commissioner." *Christian Century* 50 (April 26, 1933):549.

Noley, Homer. *First White Frost: Native Americans and United Methodism*. Nashville: Abingdon Press, 1991.

Noll, Mark, ed. *Religion and American Politics: From the Colonial Period to the 1980s.* New York: Oxford University Press, 1990.

Orsi, Robert A. "Beyond the Mainstream in the Study of American Religious History." *Journal of Ecclesiastical History* 43.2 (April 1992):287–92.

Parker, Arthur C. "Problems of Race Assimilation in America, with Special Reference to the American Indian." *American Indian Magazine* 4 (October–December 1916):285–304.

Parker, Arthur C., and G. E. E. Lindquist. *The Indians of New York State.* New York: Home Missions Council, n.d.

Parman, Donald L. "Lewis Meriam's Letters During the Survey of Indian Affairs, 1926–1927." Parts 1 and 2. *Arizona and the West* 24, no. 3 (1982):253–80; 24, no. 4 (1982):341–70.

———. *The Navajos and the New Deal.* New Haven: Yale University Press, 1976.

Pearson, Daniel M. *The Americanization of Carl Aaron Swensson.* Rock Island, Ill.: Augustana Historical Society, 1977.

Phillip, Peter. "Red Man Still with Us But Not of Us." *New York Times Book Reviews,* June 24, 1923.

Philp, Kenneth R. *John Collier's Crusade for Indian Reform, 1920–1954.* Tucson: University of Arizona Press, 1977.

———. "The New Deal and Alaska Natives, 1936–1945." *Pacific Historical Review* 50 (1981):309–27.

———. *Termination Revisited: American Indians on the Trail to Self-Determination, 1933–1953.* Lincoln: University of Nebraska Press, 1999.

Philp, Kenneth R., ed. *Indian Self-Rule: First-Hand Accounts of Indian-White Relations from Roosevelt to Reagan.* Salt Lake City: Institute of the American West, 1986.

Porter, Joy. *To Be Indian: The Life of Iroquois-Seneca Arthur Caswell Parker.* Norman: University of Oklahoma Press, 2001.

Pratt, R. H. "The Indian No Problem." *Missionary Review of the World* 33 (November 1910):851–56.

Prucha, Francis Paul. *American Indian Treaties: The History of a Political Anomaly.* Berkeley: University of California Press, 1994.

———. *The Churches and the Indian Schools, 1888–1912.* Lincoln: University of Nebraska Press, 1979.

———. *The Great Father: The United States Government and the American Indians,* 2 vols. Lincoln: University of Nebraska Press, 1984.

Prucha, Francis Paul, ed. *Documents of United States Indian Policy.* Lincoln: University of Nebraska Press, 1975.

Rachlin, Carol K. "Tight Shoe Night." *Midcontinent American Studies Journal* 6 (spring 1965):84–100.

Review of *Indians Are People, Too,* by Ruth Muskrat Bronson. *Indians at Work,* 12, no. 3 (September–October 1944):32–34.

Riggs, F. B. "In Indian Education What Might Have Been and What Still May Be." *Missionary Review of the World* 53 (April 1930):284–87.

Riggs, Stephen R. *Mary and I: Forty Years with the Sioux.* Boston: Congregational Sunday School and Publishing Society, 1880.

Riney, Scott. "'I Like the School So I Want to Come Back': The Enrollment of American Indian Students at the Rapid City Indian School." *American Indian Culture and Research Journal*

22.2 (1998):171–92.

Robbins, William G. "Herbert Hoover's Indian Reformers Under Attack: The Failures of Administrative Reform." *Mid-America* 63 (1981):157–70.

Roe, Walter C. "The Mohonk Lodge: An Experiment in Indian Work." *Outlook* 68 (May 18, 1901):176–79.

Roe Cloud, Henry. "Conditions Among the Indians." *Women and Missions* 12 (April 1935):7–9.

———. "From Wigwam to Pulpit." *Missionary Review of the World* 38 (May 1915):328–38.

———. "The Future of the Red Men in America." *Missionary Review of the World* 47 (July 1924):529–32.

———. "Indian Opinion of the Wheeler-Howard Bill." *Indians at Work* 1, no. 17 (April 15, 1934):19.

———. "Indian Reactions to the Indian Reorganization Act." *Indians at Work* 3, no. 22 (July 1, 1936):324.

Rosier, Paul C. "'The Old System Is No Success': The Blackfeet Nation's Decision to Adopt the Indian Reorganization Act of 1934." *American Indian Culture and Research Journal* 23.1 (1999):1–37.

———. *Rebirth of the Blackfeet Nation, 1912–1954.* Lincoln: University of Nebraska Press, 2001.

Rusco, Elmer R. *A Fateful Time: The Background and Legislative History of the Indian Reorganization Act.* Reno: University of Nevada Press, 2000.

Sarna, Jonathan D., ed. *Minority Faiths and the American Protestant Mainstream.* Urbana: University of Illinois Press, 1998.

Sbrega, John J. "The Anticolonial Policies of Franklin D. Roosevelt: A Reappraisal." *Political Science Quarterly* 101, no. 1 (1986):65–84.

Schenkel, Albert F. *The Rich Man and the Kingdom: John D. Rockefeller, Jr., and the Protestant Establishment.* Minneapolis: Fortress Press, 1995.

Schwartz, E. A. "Red Atlantis Revisited: Community and Culture in the Writings of John Collier." *American Indian Quarterly* 18.4 (1994):507–30.

Sergeant, Elizabeth Shepley. "The Red Man's Burden." *New Republic* 37 (January 16, 1924):201.

Seymour, Flora Warren. "Federal Favor for Fetishism: The American Government and the American Indian." *Missionary Review of the World* 58 (1935):397–400.

———. "Indian Rights." *Adult Bible Class Magazine* 27, no. 4 (January 1933):101–4.

———. "Trying It on the Indian." *New Outlook* 163 (May 1934):22–25.

———. "Thunder over the Southwest." *Saturday Evening Post* 211 (April 1939).

"Shall American Indians Be Deprived of Federal Guardianship?" *Christian Century* 52 (May 8, 1935):597.

Shklar, Judith N. *American Citizenship: The Quest for Inclusion.* Cambridge, Mass.: Harvard University Press, 1991.

Sitkoff, Harvard. *A New Deal for Blacks: The Emergence of Civil Rights as a National Issue.* Volume 1, *The Depression Decade.* New York: Oxford University Press, 1978.

Smith, Michael T. "The Wheeler-Howard Act of 1934: The Indian New Deal." *Journal of the West* 10 (1971):521–33.

Smith, Rogers M. *Civic Ideals: Conflicting Views of Citizenship in United States History.* New Haven: Yale University Press, 1997.

The Society of American Indians: A National Organization of Americans. 2d ed. [n.p.], March 1914. Pamphlets in American History. Glen Rock, N.J.: Microfilming Corporation of America, 1978. Microfiche.

Stanley, Sam, ed. *American Indian Economic Development.* The Hague: Mouton Publishers, 1978.

Steere, Jonathan. "Indian Bureau Policy Jeopardizes Indian Rights and Welfare." *Indian Truth* 29, no. 4 (autumn 1952):1–2.

Stefon, Frederick J. "The Indians' Zarathustra: An Investigation into the Philosophical Roots of John Collier's Indian New Deal Educational and Administrative Policies." Parts 1 and 2. *Journal of Ethnic Studies* 11, no. 3 (1984):1–29; 11, no. 4 (1984):28–45.

"Superintendent Roe Cloud's Address to the Sioux." *Indian Leader* 37, no. 35 (May 4, 1934):1–5.

Szasz, Margaret. *Education and the American Indian: The Road to Self-Determination Since 1928.* 2d ed. Albuquerque: University of New Mexico Press, 1977.

Taylor, Graham D. *The New Deal and American Indian Tribalism: The Administration of the Indian Reorganization Act, 1934–45.* Lincoln: University of Nebraska Press, 1980.

Tinker, George E. *Missionary Conquest: The Gospel and Native American Cultural Genocide.* Minneapolis: Fortress Press, 1993.

Torben, Christensen, and William R. Hutchison, eds. *Missionary Ideologies in the Imperialist Era: 1880–1920.* Copenhagen: Aros, 1982.

Treat, James, ed. *Native and Christian: Religious Identity in the United States and Canada.* New York: Routledge, 1998.

Trennert, Robert A. "Corporal Punishment and the Politics of Indian Reform." *History of Education Quarterly* 29 (1989):595–617.

Tweed, Thomas A. "An Emerging Protestant Establishment: Religious Affiliation and Public Power on the Urban Frontier in Miami, 1896–1904." *Church History* 64 (September 1995):412–37.

U.S. Department of the Interior. *Course of Study for the Indian Schools of the United States.* Washington, D.C.: Government Printing Office, 1901.

———. *Fifty-Second Annual Report of the Board of Indian Commissioners.* Washington, D.C.: Government Printing Office, 1921.

———. *Report of the Commissioner of Indian Affairs.* Washington, D.C.: Government Printing Office, 1920.

———. *Reports of the Department of the Interior.* Vol. 2. Washington, D.C.: Government Printing Office, 1918.

———. *Rules Governing the Court of Indian Offenses.* Washington, D.C.: Government Printing Office, 1883. Washington, D.C.: Congressional Informational Services Microform, 1970–. Microfiche.

———. *Sixtieth Annual Report of the Board of Indian Commissioners* Washington, D.C.: Government Printing Office, 1929.

U.S. House. Committee on Indian Affairs. *Readjustment of Indian Affairs: Hearings Before the Committee on Indian Affairs House of Representatives, Seventy-third Congress, Second Session, on H.R. 7902, A Bill to Grant to Indians Living Under Federal Tutelage the Freedom to Organize for Purposes of Local Self-Government.* Washington, D.C.: Government Printing Office, 1934.

U.S. Senate. *Senate Report No. 31: Survey of Conditions Among the Indians of the United States.* In *Senate Miscellaneous Reports.* Vol. 2, 78th Congress, 1st Session. Washington, D.C.: Government Printing Office, 1943.

Villard, Oswald Garrison. "Wardship and the Indian." *Christian Century* 61 (March 29, 1944):397–98.

Walch, Timothy, ed. *Immigrant America: European Ethnicity in the United States.* New York: Garland, 1994.

Walker, James R. *Lakota Belief and Ritual.* Eds. Raymond J. Demallie and Elaine A. Jahner. Lincoln: University of Nebraska Press, 1980.

Walls, Andrew. *The Missionary Movement: Studies in the Transmission of Faith.* Maryknoll, N.Y.: Orbis Books, 1996.

"Walter C. Roe: A Friend of the Indian." *Outlook* 103 (April 13, 1913):789–90.

Warren, Heather A. *Theologians of a New World Order: Reinhold Niebuhr and the Christian Realists, 1920–1948.* New York: Oxford University Press, 1997.

Wax, Murray L., and Robert W. Buchanan, eds. *Solving "The Indian Problem": The White Man's Burdensome Business.* New York: New York Times, 1975.

Weaver, Jace, ed. *Native American Religious Identity: Unforgotten Gods.* Maryknoll, N.Y.: Orbis Books, 1998.

Weiss, Frederick Lewis. *The Society for Propagating the Gospel to the Indians and Others in North America.* Dublin, N.H., 1953.

Weiss, Richard. "Ethnicity and Reform: Minorities and the Ambience of the Depression Years." *Journal of American History* 66 (December 1979):566–85.

What About Peyote? New York: Home Missions Council, 1941.

Wilkins, David E. *American Indian Sovereignty and the U.S. Supreme Court.* Austin: University of Texas Press, 1997.

Wilkinson, Charles F. *American Indians, Time, and the Law: Native Societies in a Modern Constitutional Democracy.* New Haven: Yale University Press, 1987.

Willcox, Helen L. *Pueblo Pioneers: A One-Act Play of Indian Life in the Southwest.* New York: Missionary Education Movement of the United States and Canada, 1932.

Williams, Walter L. "United States Indian Policy and the Debate over Philippine Annexation: Implications for the Origins of American Imperialism." *Journal of American History* 66 (March 1980):810–31.

Wilson, Raymond. *Ohiyesa: Charles Eastman, Santee Sioux.* Urbana: University of Illinois Press, 1983.

Work, Hubert. *Indian Policies: Comments on the Resolutions of the Advisory Council on Indian Affairs.* Washington, D.C.: Government Printing Office, 1924.

The World Mission of the Church: Findings and Recommendations of the International Missionary Conference. London: International Missionary Conference, 1939.

Index

About the Author

A native of Arkadelphia, Arkansas, David W. Daily earned a bachelor of arts degree at Ouachita Baptist University in 1986 and a master of divinity degree at Yale University Divinity School in 1991, where he was a Sullivan Scholar and a research assistant to literary critic Harold Bloom. He earned his Ph.D. in the graduate program in religion at Duke University, specializing in American religious history. While a student at Duke, he received funding for his dissertation research from the Yale-Pew Program in Religion and American History. Since 2000, he has served as assistant professor of religion at the University of the Ozarks in Clarksville, Arkansas.